W9-AGT-218

Clearly Invisible

Clearly Invisible

Racial Passing and the Color
of Cultural Identity

Marcia Alesan Dawkins

BAYLOR UNIVERSITY PRESS

Cover Design by *the*BookDesigners

Ellen Craft image courtesy of the Mary Evans Picture Library.
Frances E. W. Harper image courtesy of the Library of Congress.
Human Stain images courtesy of Photofest.
Leo Felton image courtesy of the Associated Press.

Library of Congress Cataloging-in-Publication Data

Dawkins, Marcia Alesan.
Clearly invisible : racial passing and the color of cultural identity
/ Marcia Alesan Dawkins.
285 p. cm.
Includes bibliographical references and index.
ISBN 978-1-60258-312-2 (hbk. : acid-free paper)
1. Passing (Identity)--United States. 2. Passing (Identity)--United
States--Case studies. 3. Racially mixed people--Race identity
--United States. 4. United States--Race relations. 5. Rhetoric--
Social aspects--United States. 6. Rhetoric--Political aspects--
United States. I. Title.
E184.A1D2844 2012
305.800973--dc23

2011051774

BAYLOR ®
UNIVERSITY

Printed in the United States of America on acid-free paper with a
minimum of 30% recycled content.

For all who dare to be themselves . . .
. . . and for the daring ones I've known best,
Rafael, Olga, and José Matos.

American culture, even in its most rigidly segregated precincts, is patently and irrevocably composite. It is, regardless of all the hysterical protestations of those who would have it otherwise, incontestably mulatto. Indeed, for all their traditional antagonisms, and obvious differences, the so-called black and the so-called white people of the United States resemble nobody else in the world so much as they resemble each other.

—Albert Murray, *The Omni-Americans*

Table of Contents

List of Illustrations

Preface

Passing is a strange thing. It has a large circumference. It is a way for us to see and not see, a way for us to be seen and not be seen. It looks at us and turns away from us at the same time. Passing shifts our social positions amidst social limitations. Constant movement is what makes passing so easy for us to wonder about and so difficult to understand. Translation: passing demands that we think hard about issues of identity and rhetoric, of the public and the private, in ways that most of us are privileged enough to ignore if we so choose. But if we pay attention, passing can reveal our collective blind spots as well as our individual similarities and differences. Passing forces us to think and rethink what exactly makes a person black, white, or "other," and why we care. It helps us create worlds we can actually live in. And it makes us think about the ties and binds of pleasure, language, and action. It makes us consider the hazards of silence and the hope of communication. Passing is profound.

Clearly Invisible is about devising a specific set of descriptions of its key term: *passing* as a series of rhetorical intersections where tropes and identifications meet texts, personalities, social situations, categories, and hierarchies. Such descriptions, which I call *passwords*, mix a traditional meaning of passing (the phenomenon in which a person gains acceptance as a member of social groups other than his or her own, usually in terms of race, ethnicity, class, gender, sexuality, religion, citizenship, or disability status) with traditional meanings of rhetoric (as ornamental speech and as purposeful, persuasive discourse that constitutes identities). Throughout the book I emphasize these meanings of passing and rhetoric to show how each informs the other. In this way I further define and describe what passing means, creating a critical vocabulary that shows how passing produces the particular social, political, and discursive effects we experience today.

Clearly Invisible is also about how people figure out who they are and relate to one another. Topics you have heard about before—but not quite like this. At least not if the individuals you will read about in the pages that follow have anything to say about it. Thus, the book explores the contemporary expressions and historical experiences of individuals called passers: philosophers, sophists, multiracials, multiethnics, the enslaved, hacktivists, cross-dressers, the disabled, college professors, racists. In the process these passers become Plato, Socrates, Gorgias, Protagoras, Ellen, William, Homer, Iola, Harry, Coleman, and Leo. They become people. People with stories. People whose stories sound familiar but take subtle turns to reveal racial and other tensions lurking just beneath the surface. People whose stories are intriguing, desperate, and mesmerizing, filled to the brim with trepidation over not knowing how they will be perceived. People who confront their worlds boldly and pay little regard to what others consider foreign or familiar, sacred or profane. People who, it would seem, often reveal as much about you and me as they conceal about themselves.

As a whole, *Clearly Invisible* is much more than the sum of critical vocabulary and individual stories. It is a journey that starts and stops, takes us to uncomfortable places, and hopes to yield some greater understanding of what makes us who we say we are. And it reminds us of all the acts of passing that were never revealed. Along the way *Clearly Invisible* uncovers a series of secrets. First, the book reveals that passing has been occurring for millennia, since intercultural and interracial contact began in places like ancient Greece and North America, and that as a result competing narratives and generational conflicts are inevitable. Second, it acknowledges that a fascination with passing is a sign that multiple forms of oppression persist in spite of increasing diversity and political correctness. Third, it confirms that individual identities are never fully self-determined. And finally, the book accepts that everyone passes, even if only for a moment. Not just racial minorities, women, the disabled, the diseased, undocumented immigrants, religious minorities, people with disabilities, gay, lesbian, bisexual, and transgendered people. Everyone passes. Those who enjoy a privileged status in society struggle to identify themselves and relate to the larger world even as they are understood historically as obstacles, as those who thwart others' attempts to assert themselves as whole human beings by any means necessary.

Such acknowledgments require me to explore a host of ambiguities, projections, connections, and estrangements throughout the diverse situations covered in the book. As a result, *Clearly Invisible* presents a fresh look at passing that privileges different points of view at different points in time. Sometimes what passers say is most relevant, and sometimes it is not. Sometimes what passers' friends and families have to say is more revealing. Sometimes what courts and critics say takes precedence. And sometimes what goes without saying says more than everything else.

For these reasons *Clearly Invisible* can be read in several ways. It can be read as a whole or in parts. It can be read as a rejoinder to western paradigms that marginalized the practice and impact of rhetoric. Or it can be read as an updated take on the history of passing as a viable form of identity work. Or it can be read as a practical account of passing's effects on the discourse of multiracial identities. Or it can be read as a theoretical argument about the uniqueness and relativity of every rhetorical perspective and the productive uncertainties that ensue when they are compared and critiqued. In the pages that follow I offer you my take on passing, multiracial identities and rhetorical relativity, a chance to see what I have seen, maybe even a chance to see farther and sharper, and an opportunity to shift between the perspectives (re)presented herein and your own.

Acknowledgments

No book is written alone. This book would be unwritten without the encouragement, insights, and contributions of the following people: Teresa A. Nance, Kermit Moore, Lawrence Little, Ed Goff, Randall A. Lake, Larry Gross, Tom Goodnight, George A. Sanchez, Stacy L. Smith, Colleen Keough, Robin D. G. Kelley, Robert Scheer, Diane Winston, Sandy Green, Adam Liepzig, Ebony A. Utley, Ulli K. Ryder, Steven Mallioux, Leticia T. Suarez, Stella Ting-Toomey, Annette Bow, Chris Bugbee, David Hino, Evelyn Hu-DeHart, Emma Lapsansky-Werner, Jon Paulson, Kate Ransohoff, Sandra Simpson, Sadiqua Hamdan, Dan Sharfstein, Bonnie J. Dow, Craig Carroll, Emily Corrigan, Shinina Butler-Nance, Kasia Anderson, Kate Pieper, Jeffrey A. Hall, Amber Watts-Hall, Deborah Hanan, Gina Ogilvie, Eli Steele, Jason S. Woodson, Ivette Lora, Zainah Alfi, M. Sara Owen, Janielle Z. Matthews, Amanda Lobley, and Jay Grossman DDS and Associates. I am grateful for the honor of knowing individuals of such strength and complication. I hope these words adequately express my admiration and thanks for their time, energy, and integrity, and the ways they shared their diverse knowledge and experiences with me. A special "shout out" to Ebony, whose comments, suggestions, and corrections transformed the process of writing this book from mere tedium into an exciting and unforgettable journey. "Shout outs" to Kasia and Sadiqua for helping me find and express my voice. And, no "shout out" is loud enough to acknowledge my academic family, Terry, Randy, Ulli, and Jeff, who each inspired me to fly with my own wings.

Of course I was also inspired and nourished by the intelligent conversations, observations, and unconditional love of my actual family. I thank Harry Guillermo Mendoza for his love and laughter, for the gift of time, and for being my best friend. My heartfelt appreciation goes to my sister, Lindsay, for being there always and without questions. I offer my eternal gratitude to every member of my extended family for his and her support and willingness to hear me out, especially my cousin Kate Breen and grandmother Jeri Wilson, whose insights into how different generations think about race and passing made me believe in the possibility of positive change.

I thank my parents, Olga E. Matos-Dawkins and John M. Dawkins III, for giving me life and enriching it with a sense of curiosity and a desire for education. They, more than anyone else, have taught me that my only real possessions are integrity, identity, patience and the ability to learn with and from outstanding young thinkers—like Alex Agloro, Marlene Vigil, Ryan Houston, Brad Silnutzer, Elizabeth Hoberman, Omar Baghat, Stephanie Bee, Elyse Peterson, Deven Cooper, and Tiffani Smith. These brilliant individuals encouraged me to tell the story that makes the most difference and not worry about whether it gets the most "likes," "retweets," or "+1s."

And finally, to my editor, Carey C. Newman, who believed in this project from its inception and guided me through the process of writing this book with elegance, exactitude, and excellence, I extend my utmost appreciation. It has truly been an honor.

Passing as Passé?

On rare occasions I find an expression that is sassy, succinct, and thus sexy enough to make its veracity inconsequential. Such is the case with a phrase coined by historians decades ago: "Passing is passé."[1] Passing, usually understood as an abbreviation for "racial passing," describes the "fact of being accepted, or representing oneself successfully as, a member of a different" group.[2] Generally speaking, passing refers to the means by which nonwhite people represent themselves as white. This kind of passing—though not the only type taken up in this project—has been a popular area of literary interest in the United States since the colonial period, slavery, and Reconstruction.[3] The topic also enjoyed attention from Hollywood in melodramatic "issue" films from the 1930s through the 1950s.[4] Then came the 1960s and 1970s and with them a cultural shift through which many nationalist ideologies belittled passing and its narratives, hoping to make them a relic of the past and less a part of mainstream racial narratives. According to the critics of the 1960s and 1970s, passing was an antiquated practice that flew in the face of burgeoning racial and ethnic pride as well as institutional and attitudinal change.[5] In addition, the taboo of heterosexual interracial romantic relationships[6] is said to have eased somewhat with the Supreme Court's

1

1967 *Loving v. Virginia* decision.[7] America and Americans were growing more acquainted with diversity, and, for a while, passing became decidedly "passé" in U.S. literary and political cultures.

This book is evidence that passing is neither a historical artifact nor a simple habit that expresses a superior-subordinate social relationship. It is for this reason that a new "passing renaissance" has emerged. Revived in the 1990s, narratives of passing and politics of multiracial identities resurfaced when updated models of racial identification offered alternatives to past models that hypothesized a "marginal" existence for passers as multiracial individuals.[8] Though described as a precursor to these "new and positive models" of biracial identity development, passing took center stage.[9] As such, there has been much scholarly discourse around passing and its influences on the construction of identities in a variety of cultural, legal, and political contexts.[10] Most notably, the *New York Times* Best-Seller List has been flooded with multiracial autobiographies and stories about passing.[11] Mainstream media outlets also participate in the discussion with reports on 2010 Census results, stating that when it comes to identifying racially today more young Americans choose not to pass and instead choose all racial categories that apply.[12] One explanation for the current multiracial generation's choice not to pass is interpersonal family interaction.[13] Many interracial and multiracial families advocate against passing as a viable form of identity work.[14]

Because of the popularity of rendering passing passé in literature and media, its persistence is often explained as evidence of poor mental health due to confusion stemming from multiracial individuals' struggles with the decision of how to identify racially.[15] Hence, the call for measuring multiracial and monoracial groups by unique standards to explode the myth that multiracials are confused freaks of nature.[16] But research reveals that multiracials do not appear to be any more or less deficient, deviant, or confused than their monoracial counterparts.[17] The many contrary scenarios presented in media can be explained by a general confusion about racial passing and about how to identify racially that seem to be creeping into mainstream consciousness, as many people from many walks of life are becoming increasingly protective of their rights to racial privacy.[18] Increasing discomfort with racial identification suggests that some declarations of multiracial identities could really be the latest incarnations of passing. What is more, growing color-blindness and "color-mute"-ness could indicate a growing hostility toward any use of racial identification.[19]

As a late entry into the discourse of passing and its renaissance, this book explores the old limits and new possibilities of passing for the twenty-first century. For one, the analysis is not restricted to traditional notions of bypassing racial boundaries. Rather, the case studies include Sophists passing as rhetors, women passing as men, able-bodied persons passing as disabled, enslaved persons passing as free, sinners passing as saints, "octoroons" passing and then outing themselves as insurgents, siblings who are passing unknowingly as white and then as black, black classics professors passing as Jewish, and white supremacists passing as white.

These untraditional acts of passing are about much more than mere disguise. Untraditional acts of passing are about rhetoric—the symbolic social construction and reconstruction of identity within particular situational constraints and social networks. And rhetoric includes verbal and nonverbal symbols such as speech, clothing, skin color, tattoos, performances, Facebook posts, physical and social mobility, and many other symbolic exchanges that influence thought and behavior in the interests of identification and social action.[20] My rhetorical focus suggests an updated technology of passing that allows it to move beyond bipolar racial terms of black and white to address issues of gender, religion, class, ability, health, crime, and punishment. We will see that in some ways this updated technology of passing is like being airbrushed in Photoshop. Passing is an artistic technology that creates a smooth gradation of color used to cover so-called imperfections. When we airbrush others (i.e., say someone is one thing when they say something else), we are creating a safety net for ourselves so that we know how to communicate with and around that person. We airbrush ourselves (i.e., say we are one thing instead of another or instead of however else we would otherwise identify) to be more accepted interpersonally and socially and to ensure that our goals can be achieved. To take the analogy of passing and airbrushing a step further, we can say that passing is all about who has the airbrush and who has the latest version of Photoshop.

The need to explore the updated technology of passing and its contributions to an ongoing conversation about rhetoric is why my focus is on acts of successful passing that have been sustained either part-time or full-time, and on those that broke the cycle of silence to argue for social and institutional change and/or for the privilege of self-determination.[21] I also intend to show how acts of successful passing operate rhetorically. I strive to analyze passing from a rhetorical perspective that pays attention to what people say and do in order to understand some of the dilemmas of identification and representation in our present historical and cultural moment. Thus, I will explore whether passing can be a rhetoric of empowerment even though it suggests secrecy, how passing complicates a politics of visibility, if passing is one of the first expressions of multiracial identity in the United States, and whether passing has been appropriated to serve the interests of white supremacy in the twenty-first century.

My focus on passing considers perspectives of past generations and applies them to present and future generations, who yearn for the possibility of liberation from the burden of older racial narratives.[22] Because passing capitalizes on the absence of reliable evidence of difference, it begs the question of whether we know anything about race now that differs substantially from what we have known about it historically.[23] Thus, passing has not passed on. Despite today's newer and better theories about racial formation, racial prejudice, and multiracial identification and marketing, some individuals still benefit from passing. To say that passing is passé is to presuppose that the concepts of race and racism that beget passing are also passé. The wishful thinking that declares race and racism dead will not be supported in this book.

With the above in mind, I want to make clear that, especially because this is a book firmly grounded in the discipline of rhetoric, words matter. With the constructivist turn in critical race and rhetorical studies, many scholars have abandoned the idea that race is biological and instead have endeavored to explain that it is conjectural, a symbolic social construct.[24] To note this epistemological shift and to argue against the historical concept of race as organic and inherent, some scholars have taken to inserting the term "race" in quotation marks.[25] Issues of how to express these ideas become more complex when dealing with jargon for multiracial identities and passing.[26] Several ethnic studies scholars argue that terminology like hybrid, mestiz@, interracial, and mixed race does not challenge historical definitions of race at all and even promotes an antiblack agenda.[27] Mainly, these labels are imprecise and uncritical, for how persons identify as multiracial

depends largely upon how they define race in general and whiteness and blackness in particular. While I agree with the argument
that many monoracial people can claim multiracial ancestry and
choose not to, I am more interested in those who choose to do so
and how they have communicated those choices in passing and in
particular rhetorical situations.

In light of these critiques, I have chosen to use the following
terms when discussing the narratives and characters who are the
subjects of this analysis: *multiracial*, referring to "people who are
of two or more racial heritages"[28] and somehow identify themselves as such regardless of how they are identified by law or social
network or whether they are considered first generation or of multigenerational multiracial ancestry; and *biracial*, referring to the
act of passing itself as a comment on instabilities. First, *biracial
passing* underscores epistemological instabilities of thinking about
racial passing (from black to white) as the principal form of passing
or as the most meaningful or authentic type of passing.[29] Second,
biracial passing accentuates the social and historical instabilities
of monoracial identities and the black-white historical contexts
presented herein.[30] To be clear, in using these terms I am not arguing that such groups or phenomena exist due to biological makeup
or socialization. Nor am I making a historically revisionist assertion to belittle the effects of racism and domination by referring to
everyone as multiracial or by referring to every multiracial person
as black and/or white.[31] Rather, I am seeking to provide a rhetorically driven account of the ways in which such distinctions have
been drawn and challenged and can be overcome.

To that end, the analysis unfolds in six chapters. The first,
"Passing as Persuasion," situates passing in historical and rhetorical terms, develops a new critical vocabulary for its analysis,
and is summarized by five "passwords." Chapter 2, "Passing as
Power," uses the vocabulary developed in the first chapter to treat
Ellen and William Craft's passing as an act of powerful rhetoric
that transforms identities by teaching audiences to engage critically with the world and abandon the notion that passing is simply
someone else's racial problem. Chapter 3, "Passing as Property,"
builds on the preceding chapters and considers whether the passing of Homer A. Plessy, the plaintiff in the infamous *Plessy v.
Ferguson* case, was the first recorded case of what we now call
identity theft. Chapter 4, "Passing as Principle" maps the logic

of Plessy's passing onto Frances E. W. Harper's passing narrative *Iola Leroy, or, Shadows Uplifted,* frames passing as a problem of ethical difference, and reveals a newly discovered rationale for passing as black. Chapter 5, "Passing as Pastime," focuses on the film and novel *The Human Stain* and assesses why passers must fail in order for passing to entertain. The final chapter, "Passing as Paradox," explores the case of Leo Felton, the black-white white supremacist, as an example of how today's increasing fascination with multiracial identities and passing can express a racism that is, paradoxically, supported by a contemporary craving for multi-racial identities to represent a beautiful post-racial society.[32] The conclusion, "Passing as Progress?," moves beyond the black-white racial binary and extends the vocabulary of passing developed throughout the chapters, in which passers come out of the closet to assert their rightful places in the fields of rhetoric and critical (mixed) race studies, and offers insight into how passing continues to shape racial discourse and multiracial identities today.[33]

CHAPTER ONE

Passing as Persuasion

It was one o'clock in the morning when I made a startling discovery. Insomnia led me to my iPad in search of new applications to pass the time. While scrolling through the iTunes App Store I came across a game called Guess My Race. Guess My Race consists of a ten-question "quiz" that presents striking portraits of real people's faces.[1] The user is asked to guess how these otherwise anonymous people answered the question, What race are you?[2] After selecting from among six options, the user discovers how the person actually identifies him- or herself, or how he or she is identified by family and friends. Each answer is accompanied by a quote from the person in the photograph regarding his or her identity or experiences with race. For reasons you will soon see, Guess My Race piqued my interest immediately, so I downloaded it and began to play.

My first score was "1 out of 10 questions correct." Disappointed, I played again: "1 out of 10 questions correct." I wondered if there was something wrong with me or with the game. My next attempt yielded "3 of 10 questions correct." Frustrated with myself and with the game, I put it down and endeavored to get a few hours' sleep. It was a useless attempt. I had been too intrigued by the game, and my mind was flooded with explanations for my poor scores. The more I thought about it, the more I realized that each picture and set of answers in the game creates a momentary crisis of meaning. I did not consider categories like "Haitian," "Catholic," "Hick," and "Undocumented" as racial, so I did not know what answer to select. But by forcing me to consider the possibility that others may think of these categories as racial, the game made me aware of just how inarticulate all racial signifiers can be. My every guess forced me to question what I really know about race. I saw no right way to guess what answers were correct. I wondered if this was what it was like for others during the countless real-life guess-my-race encounters for which I served as subject. Most people did not ask. They just stared in a way that expressed that they were interested by difference. When close friends asked me this question directly, I told them about my ancestry and family history, although I must admit that I used to guard this information from people at large, sometimes disclosed it selectively, and on occasion said nothing or followed Jean Toomer's example and said "the first nonsense that entered my mind."[3] For me the difficulty was not so much in looking like one race or another, whatever that means, but in the unpredictability concerning how the next person I encountered would view or communicate with me.

Guess My Race turned the tables. Not only was I now the bearer of the awkward "what are you" question, but the answers I received confounded me completely. Most of the people I guessed as "white" did not refer to themselves as such. Instead, they referred to themselves as "multiracial" or in ethnic terms such as Jewish, Italian, Arab, Armenian, Hispanic, and so on. Conversely, the majority of people I guessed were "multiracial" referred to themselves as either "white" or "black," even when they acknowledged their multiracial and multiethnic ancestries. Eventually it dawned on me that my problem was not one of knowing the right answer across all ten questions. My problem was of knowing what answer was right in each distinct question. The more I thought of it, the more valid my hypothesis appeared. Guess My Race was not just a lesson in racial identification practices and diversity. It was a lesson in rhetoric and passing.

Rhetoric is all about identity, symbolic expression, and how our identities and expressions can change when we encounter new situations and social networks. Passing—the phenomenon in

which a person of one social group identifies and represents herself as a member of another or others—is about using rhetoric to
grapple with crises of meaning produced when images, identities,
and categories diverge.[4] Rhetoric and passing struggle with the
insecurities of our knowledge, categories, vocabularies, and identities. I take up these insecurities here, exploring what rhetoric says
about passing and what passing says about rhetoric.

To that end, I engage the classical debate between Plato and
the Sophists to explain the relationship between passing and rhetoric, which provides a theoretical and contextual underpinning.
Then I review contemporary rhetorical scholarship concerning
the mechanical dimensions of passing, which provides an account
for how passing continues to be enacted and embodied. Finally, I
introduce several rhetorical tropes to show what is missing from
previous models and analyses and provide a more complete theoretical account. Along the way I introduce a new critical vocabulary for analyzing passing, using the term "passwords." My
passwords acknowledge that passing is fraught with complexities
and complications and reveal that it can be mined to shed additional light on the ongoing rhetorical processes of identification in
a multiracial millennium.

RHETORIC AS PASSING

The history of our rhetorical tradition reveals that characteriza-
tions of rhetoric were hotly contested in fifth-century Greece.[5] And
whose side we take today—Plato's or the Sophists'— remains vital
to how we understand the sociopolitical nature of rhetoric and
the rhetorical significance of passing.[6] A rhetorical view of passing
stresses the importance of knowledge, categories, vocabularies,
and identities as matters of concern for Plato and the Sophists in
very different ways.[7] Sophists considered knowledge relative and
context-based, therefore changing and questionable. They saw
themselves as cultural workers who were largely unconcerned with
"proper" and "improper" categorizations or uses of language.
Instead, Sophists sought to use language tactically. Rhetoric for
them depended on time and timing, on being keenly aware of
opportunities to prevail, and on an ability to create new opportunities for new kinds of communication and identification.[8] But
for Plato, sophistic rhetoric could not have been a more troubling
or inaccurate way to engage the world. Plato saw communication

and identification as the results of precise standards of judgment. These standards of judgment were the outcomes of true knowledge, which he argued was objective, precise, and infallible.[9] Plato taught that humans acquired the ability know, or recall what we have already known, through dialectic.[10] Rhetoric was empty speech that, at its best, could recount mere opinion, but could never communicate fact or true knowledge.

If we take Plato's side, we can conceptualize rhetoric as a form of passing, because it is a matter of deception rather than an act of assertion.[11] In *Phaedrus* Socrates claims that rhetoricians have no respect for true knowledge because they only care about convincing their audiences that what they say is true.[12] And in *Gorgias* Plato relegates rhetoric to the sidelines because its sole concern is duping ignorant audiences by appealing to their cultural common sense (or *doxa*).[13] Plato characterizes Socrates as someone who knows the truth and decides whether to reveal it, and Sophists as passers who deceive audiences. Plato argues that rhetoric cannot stand apart from true knowledge as its own way of knowing. Rather, rhetoric must always be topical, and it is the topic that is most important.[14] Plato enables us to conceptualize rhetoric as a form of passing and deception.[15]

If we take the Sophists' side, then rhetoric can also be considered a form of passing, but for very different reasons. For a Sophist, neither rhetoric nor passing would be attributed traditionally to the needs of the privileged (like Plato).[16] Instead, both are subaltern ways of adjusting to structural inequities.[17] A Platonic view fails to acknowledge that sophistic rhetoric commands a complex relationship between passer and audience and creates a context for moral behavior as that which earns acceptance from subaltern communities apart from any acceptance earned from dominant communities.[18] Like sophistic rhetoric, passing makes effective persuasion dependent on creative identification and behavior, not on following a set of transcendental laws or rules.[19] Taking a sophistic perspective allows us to see rhetoric as highly configurable and accessible, an environment within which truth is conditional and contestable.[20] As a result, the goals are neither objectivity nor certainty but probability and possibility.[21]

Probability and possibility free rhetoric from Plato's quests for absolute truth and true knowledge. Instead, knowledge and truth (or what is right to do or say) emerge from interacting personae as well as openness to alternative points of view.[22] As opposed to Plato's assumption that knowledge belongs to the privileged few who can access it through dialectic, sophistic rhetoric enables a self-enhancing diversity of producing truths, communication styles, and interactive communities. This more democratic approach is confirmed by the sophist Gorgias, who, in the *Encomium of Helen*, shows that human beings are capable of seeing things differently as a result of experiences created by effective uses of language.[23] Gorgias explains that rhetoric is an active truth-making force even though it is not a mirror image of some *episteme* that exists outside of language.[24] Sophists teach us that a willingness to embrace probability and possibility is the cornerstone of rhetorical power.[25] The Sophists' problem, then, is not framed entirely accurately by Plato as one of passing and deception, failing to do or say the right thing based on objective knowledge. Their problem is of passing and persuasion, doing or saying the right thing in a given setting and knowing that the right thing in one setting might be the wrong thing in another.

A sophistic conception of rhetoric also clarifies the effects of passing: that challenging a model of truth based on objective knowledge threatens the identities such knowledge privileges. Plato's *Sophist* addresses this directly in its discussion of how to distinguish one kind of person from another, specifically distinguishing the Sophist from the Statesman and Philosopher. Plato argues that all who engage in rhetoric will turn out to be passers or "*eironikoi mimetai*—literally, 'dissembling imitators.'"[26] In defining the Sophist as an imitator or passer, and by consequence his rhetoric as passing, Plato's Visitor succumbs to labeling passing as appropriation, or taking a social status to which no claim to ownership can be made.[27] The Sophist is a passer who takes the position of a Statesman or Philosopher knowing that he knows nothing the Philosopher knows. He uses language that makes a particular audience think he is a philosopher. But a different audience or a *real* and authentic philosopher would know and tell others that the Sophist is passing as a philosopher. Identity, for Plato, is defined by the possession and presence of a quality, particularly knowledge. Individuals are identifiable and authentic when they demonstrate that they possess this particular quality. When they fail to do so, they are charlatans and passers—ghosts, representations without substance. In today's world we might liken passers to identity thieves who make claims to ownership that cannot be verified.[28]

A sophistic perspective, however, reveals Plato's conception of identity as authentic possession to be hierarchical and exclusionary. Those who do not demonstrate knowledge are excluded automatically—women, non-Greek "barbarians," the enslaved, and all those who are otherwise culturally marginalized.[29] When members of these groups speak convincingly, they subvert Plato's objective knowledge and authentic identifications.[30] Rhetoric from the margins suggests that Plato may be a passer himself because he claims to have access to absolute knowledge but fails to acknowledge the possibility of varied ways of knowing based on differing cultural situations, experiences, and rhetorical traditions.[31] Plato's vision of objective knowledge, *episteme*, can be considered a form of passing much more debilitating than common sense or opinion, *doxa*, because it forces stability on categories that are fundamentally unstable and hides the operations through which the appearance of stability is created.[32]

The debate over just exactly who is the passer is addressed further in *Protagoras*, when Socrates questions the nature and existence of sophistic wisdom and defines sophistic rhetoric as an offensive ancient art of masking.[33] Though Protagoras defends himself by redefining rhetoric as the secret to success in a stratified and hierarchical society, Socrates again defines Sophistic rhetoric as passing, a form of deception and appropriation—an eloquent yet empty performance that leaves audiences duped rather than educated and informed as to the identity of the speaker and the truth of his topic.[34] Throughout the dialogues we see Socrates attempt to win the debate over identifying the passer by taking on the role of someone who tells the duped audience that Sophists are passers. This outing persona is reanimated in the Allegory of the Cave in *Republic* book VII, when Socrates asks Glaucon to recall his fellow prisoners and what was called wisdom in the cave. Those notorious "shadows passing" that Glaucon remembers are understood to have somehow presented themselves as a truth in the cave.[35] These shadows and copies are critical elements in Plato's larger narrative about the universality and necessity of Truth and ideal forms and the risky rhetoric that passes by referencing inauthentic images.[36]

A finely tuned sophistic perspective, however, reveals the possibility that Plato's shadows passing are false copies of the world above because the sun controls and sheds light upon everything in the visible world. The Sophists' assumption here is that if an origin story for the shadows exists, then an origin story for the sun must also exist. If this is true, then what is visible is relative, always subject to change and to changing relationships among audiences. Therefore, in order for limited vision like Plato's to generate stable categorical meanings (like black and white as bipolar racial categories), society must undergo a process of forgetting the violence and awkwardness of how they came to be. The dialogues bring about this kind of historical amnesia, and Plato's Sophists turn out to be passers who are tragic villains, tricksters, and imitators instead of eloquent communicators who can see, hear, and communicate across cultural and temporal contexts.[37] It can be argued that Plato's move to center his worldview (and equate rhetoric with a deceptive definition of passing) mirrors the way in which the present-day racial identity of whiteness operates strategically by making itself an "invisible center."[38]

By insisting in *Theaetetus* on the "truth" of a fixed center, and marginalizing those who deviate from that center, Plato marginalizes the sophist Protagoras's "man-measure" principle. Protagoras argues that human beings are prospective, that we can see beyond ourselves as we are and see who we can become, and that our experiences are fluid, elusive, and malleable.[39] In *Protagoras* Plato is concerned with unmasking Sophists in order to reveal that they have no true knowledge. Plato then refutes the idea that individuals are capable of making valid decisions for and by themselves based on common sense, intuition, and everyday experience (*doxa*). The dialogues suggest that when we make decisions for ourselves based on *doxa*, we are duped and can only be saved when the outing party (i.e., the Philosopher) speaks the truth. A sophistic conception of rhetoric suggests an alternative reading which challenges the normalizing position of the center (as dialectic) and its occupant, the Philosopher: that people can be persuaded by rhetoric precisely because it occupies gray areas that emphasize possibility and probability.[40] Rhetoric can be interpreted and judged appropriate by the audience's own situation and experience (*doxa*) rather than by objective knowledge (*episteme*).[41]

A sophistic conception of rhetoric allows us to entertain the possibility that alternative modes of identification exist. One of these modes is an extension of *doxa* called *aletheia*. *Aletheia* allows rhetoric to reveal what is valued or valuable by concealing one's position in social hierarchy, either higher or lower, created in discourse. Specifically, *aletheia* explains that in order to recognize who people are, we must be willing to look beyond appearance and understand a person's entire social performance, including that person's social location and political interests.[42] Only when we understand *aletheia* can we understand why particular interests might be revealed and particular identities might be concealed in a given situation.

Specifically, rhetorical sincerity (*aletheia*) and its anthropological counterpart "racial sincerity" (an alternative to authenticity) explain that identity is linked to experience and to one's position in relation to a social hierarchy (i.e., philosopher, Sophist, slave).[43] Once we understand a person's social location and political interests we are equipped to identify who a person is and understand why those interests might be revealed or concealed in a given situation. The concepts of rhetorical and racial sincerity make clear that identity is linked to experience and one's position in relation to social hierarchy (i.e., gender, race, class).[44] The Sophists remind us that neither racial sincerity nor rhetorical sincerity (*aletheia*) constitutes objective knowledge (not *episteme*), but that they are forms of cultural awareness that privilege important aspects of rhetoric. But *aletheia* does not constitute common sense (*doxa*) either. *Aletheia*, literally hidden and unhidden truth, calls for dynamic human relationships in which objectivity and subjectivity are not static. Instead, objectivity and subjectivity collide and allow audiences to participate actively in understanding why and how certain identities are projected. *Aletheia* promotes the rhetor's motive and persuasiveness over her appearance or audiences' labels, allowing new possibilities to emerge.[45]

Aletheia suggests that rhetoric, and by extension passing, create neither wholly true nor wholly false expressions. Rhetoric and passing reveal some things while they hide others, can make the weaker argument appear the stronger, do not allow jumps from correlation to causation, and can subvert a visual model of identification. The optimistic interpretation taken up in this book envisions passing as a form of rhetoric that is racially sincere, compatible with reasoned deliberative discourse, and expresses what fits rightly when people do not fit rightly with the world around them.[46] To summarize, our discussion of rhetoric as passing distinguishes rhetoric from the classical Platonic framework of imposture and passing from the traditional descriptive framework of deception.[47] And our discussion explains that rhetoric does not merely appeal to *doxa*, it asks audiences to examine their own social locations, question their motives for identifying people in particular ways, and understand why passers identify in some ways and not others.

Three implications follow. First, the rhetorical tradition entails generative principles for a study of passing. Our critique reveals that it was important for Plato to define and disgrace rhetoric as passing because it causes the audience to see language as instrumental and to see things as impure, commingled, continuous, and consubstantial, and perhaps even as equivalent or whole.[48] He dismisses sophistic rhetoric precisely because it accommodates an identity that neither configures itself to neat categories nor stops to define its terms. Instead, rhetoric constitutes identity continually and contextually.[49] Second, our analysis sets the stage for considering rhetoric and passing as enabling forces that express agency in the face of structural constraint. Passers emphasize the ability to persuade, attempt to balance personal integrity with community welfare, and demonstrate that a refusal to stay within proscribed boundaries can be simultaneously threatening and empowering. Finally, our discussion of rhetoric as passing contributes to the first of several axioms or *passwords*, each of which presents a relationship between passing and at least one other concept within rhetoric's critical vocabulary.

Password One

Passing engages the classical debate between Plato and the Sophists and challenges the binary of episteme *(objective Truth) versus* doxa *(common sense) through* aletheia *(rhetorical and racial sincerity).*

Password One shows that rhetoric itself is an encounter with passing in which the information passers ascertain through experience connects with the epistemological presumptions and prejudices of audiences to reveal a deeper meaning.

One deeper meaning is that passing carries with it the ability to challenge the nature of knowledge. This deeper meaning is an important implication of *Password One* that marks a shift from traditional definitions and descriptions of passing as deception. Plato values *episteme* (or definition, truth, knowing, logic, and representational clarity, which often lead to binaries), while Sophists value *doxa* (or ambiguities, opacities, contradictions, and indeterminacies, which often collapse binaries). *Password One* suggests that *episteme* is a form of taken-for-granted *doxa* as well as the possibility that *doxa* can be considered a form of *episteme*. This *episteme-doxa* reversal suggests that rhetoric meets passing somewhere between Plato's and Sophists' opposing worldviews, in a slippery middle ground upon which *aletheia* thrives.[50] In attempting to satisfy both Plato and the Sophists, passers become sincere rhetors who demonstrate an incredible knowledge and depth of experience. Passers ultimately challenge the *episteme-doxa* binary because verification of identity is no longer based on authenticity or common sense but on the passer's motivation and commitment to personal, social, and political exigencies.[51] Passers' motives and commitments are expressions of *aletheia* that constitute a purposeful unveiling of identity expressed as reasons or justifications for committing to particular social interests.[52]

Password One (passing challenges *episteme-doxa* through *aletheia*) also suggests that passers can exercise self-determination, establishing a template for experience that helps audiences make sense of possible outcomes for their own lives. Passers can manipulate symbolic space, augment or diminish emotions, refuse fixed identities, rouse action, and celebrate social and personal values in the personae they project. *Password One* allows us to acknowledge the identity work racial passers do in light of the flaws and inconsistencies of the black-white racial paradigm as a function of the *episteme-doxa* paradigm. If it is argued that race consists of knowable, definite, and distinct categories, then passing invalidates the argument. If, on the other hand, it is argued that race is not composed of definite and distinct categories, then all racial categorization is immediately questionable as being arbitrary and capricious, for, as Plato maintains, without distinction social assignment is meaningless. In either case, the stability of race is impossible to maintain. At the epistemological level, passing is inherently critical, exploding the myth of biological racial categorization as well as any institutions this myth upholds. But on a doxastic level, the level of lived experience and application, passing is constrained by the limits of rhetorical personae and empowered by the symbolism of rhetorical performance. Passing emphasizes collisions of perception, situation, truth, true knowledge, and identifications. The remainder of this chapter takes up the project of understanding passing on both of these levels and as a sincere rhetorical expression of identity.

PASSING AS RHETORIC

By emphasizing *aletheia* and perspective over authenticity or common sense, *Password One* dovetails with a contemporary theoretical model of passing that explains its rhetorical dimensions. The triangulated dramatic theatrical model shows how every instance of passing (or every pass) includes three participants and perspectives—"the passer, the dupe, and a representative of the in-group," a "clairvoyant."[53] Each participant plays a role, without which any pass would fail. The passer begins with a racial identity (a self-understanding as multiracial, white, or black, say) and creates a racial identification. The racial identification (how others understand and categorize the passer) is seen one way by the in-group clairvoyant, who knows the passer's "real" identity (as either multiracial, white, or black) and keeps the secret.[54] The dupe identifies the passer according to the racial identity projected by the passer in passing (as either white or black). These identifications are relative to passers', dupes', and clairvoyants' own frames of reference.

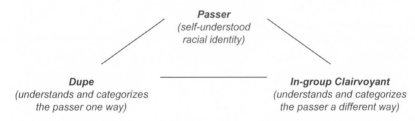

Passer
(self-understood racial identity)

Dupe
(understands and categorizes the passer one way)

In-group Clairvoyant
(understands and categorizes the passer a different way)

FIGURE 1.1
Robinson's Triangulated Dramatic Theatrical Model of Passing

Let us consider a simple hypothetical example of three people whom we will call Abby, Dan, and Cindy. Abby and Cindy have a black parent and a white parent. Abby is so phenotypically ambiguous that others cannot pinpoint her race and regularly ask her "What race are you?" or try to guess her race for clarification. Abby understands her own multiracial ancestry and has developed a racial identity as black and white. Cindy is Abby's first cousin and best friend, who is perceived and also identifies as black. Cindy knows that Abby is black and white, but, because of hypodescent, identifies Cindy as black. Dan is Abby's wealthy love interest, a white man whose close-knit family has expressly forbidden him to date anyone who is not white. Abby knows this about Dan and refuses to introduce nonwhite aspects of her racial identity into conversation, and so conceals information that would invalidate Dan's normative assumption that she is white.[55]

Abby moved from her childhood home in Philadelphia to New York City for work just before meeting Dan. Having gone over a year without seeing Abby, Cindy decides to pay her a visit. Abby goes to pick her up at Grand Central Station and unexpectedly encounters Dan at the exact moment of Cindy's arrival. Cindy, knowing what is going on because she spoke with Abby about it and has seen Dan's picture on Facebook, walks right by Abby and sends her a text message saying, "i c u. ;) meet me @ SBUX across st in 10."[56] What is happening here? Abby, a biracial passer with a racial identity as black and white, is caught between two competing racial identifications. Dan (the dupe) identifies Abby as a white woman. Cindy (the in-group clairvoyant) identifies Abby as a black woman. The triangle produced when their paths cross forces us to ask ourselves how to determine Abby's racial identity. As in the Guess My Race iPad application, the racial guessing game begins. Is Abby really black, or is she really white? The answer depends on the nature of her encounters.[57] Dan knows she is white because he encountered Abby as such and has discovered nothing to the contrary. Cindy knows Abby is black and white, which is often equated racially with being black, because she knows Abby's prepassing racial identity. But there is another possibility. Cindy and Abby also know that if Abby associates with people who look black like Cindy, then Abby becomes black by association.[58]

How, then, do we determine if Abby's pass is ultimately successful? The triangulated dramatic theater suggests that it all depends on Cindy. Cindy is the one who sees, hence her text to Abby saying, "i c u ;)." Because she sees Abby, and knows that Abby is passing, Cindy is the one with the power to tell or show Dan, or anyone else, for that matter, that her cousin is not who Dan believes she is. Only Cindy's collaborative silence will continue to constitute Dan as the dupe. Therefore, the triangulated dramatic theater tells us that passing is persuasive only insofar as the passer creates racial identifications to suit the interests and needs of her audiences, making persuasion an effect of identification.[59] Abby creates a white racial identification for Dan because she knows he will not accept her otherwise. Abby creates a black identification for her cousin Cindy, and also lets her know that she is happy with Dan, so Cindy keeps the secret. And in-group clairvoyants like Cindy often keep the secret because they take pleasure in watching a passer gain access to forbidden territory.[60] As a result, Abby's racial identification is exposed as a matter of racial privacy, and Cindy is the key to maintaining Abby's privacy.

This theatrical model of passing meets rhetoric when the "subversive enthymeme" is added to the triangle.[61] A subversive enthymeme is hidden information that prompts dupes to take the passer at face value. In our example, the subversive enthymeme creates a context of privacy by hiding the assumption that racial identity is necessarily visible and unchanging. The subversive enthymeme then convinces Dan of Abby's white racial identification and convinces Cindy to keep the secret that Abby is not (only) white. The subversive enthymeme works because it allows Dan and Cindy to provide the apparent proof of the correctness of their interpretations. But the story of passing does not conclude with the subversive enthymeme. In order to point out the missing elements in the processes of identification reflected in the triangulated dramatic theatrical model of passing, we must also include issues of rhetorical personae. The passer (Abby) uses silence and concealment tactically to convince the dupe (Dan) of her "acceptable persona."[62] The in-group clairvoyant (Cindy) is the " 'fourth persona,' or collusive audience constituted by the textual wink."[63] As an in-group member, this audience bears witness to a different identification which requires her involvement in the drama (as in Cindy's text to Abby saying, "i c u ;)"). This audience ultimately validates the pass because it knows the secret and can out the passer at any time or protect the passer's privacy.[64]

The existence of the fourth persona makes clear that passers address two counterposed audiences at once. The fourth persona/

in-group clairvoyant can help us make this determination because it is not just a participant in any pass but a spectator who watches, listens, and provides an account.[65] In doing so, the fourth persona/in-group clairvoyant acts as a sleuth who interrogates the claims passing makes about rhetoric and explores what rhetorical tactics are used in passing. We can consider the fourth persona/in-group clairvoyant as a party that implicates passing in the processes of self-expression and performance before multiple audiences and therefore allows us to build a more complete theoretical account of passing that accounts for the privacy required to sustain a successful pass. Based on the fourth persona/in-group clairvoyant, I can present

Password Two

Passing is the invention and interaction of rhetorical personae—the passer's acceptable persona, the dupe, and the in-group clairvoyant or fourth persona.

Password Two explains what I call the mechanics of passing, the movement and interaction of personae in a racialized frame of reference. It also shows that identities are formed by how we see ourselves, but also by how the world sees us. The same passer can be multiracial, biracial, white, or black—and therefore have access to different opportunities and life outcomes—depending on who is interpreting the situation and whether that person chooses to speak or remain silent. Every racial description of a passer is based on the specification of the personae with which that passer coincides. If, for instance, Abby is passing as white, then we can verify that persona by addressing Abby (passer/acceptable persona), Dan (dupe), and Cindy (fourth persona/in-group clairvoyant). The dupe's confirmation, coupled with the fourth persona's/in-group clairvoyant's silent collusion and the passer's own conception of racial identity, supplies us with a more complete sense of how passing works and how identities can change over time.

In conjunction with a perspective that sees rhetoric as passing, *Password Two* accounts for passers' agency, competing audience interpretations, and traditional conceptions of racial passing as passing as white and passing as black.[66] Understanding that people pass as black and as white requires an understanding of passing as inherently rhetorical and as an attempt to articulate multiracial identity in monoracial terms. For whether people pass as white or as black, they pass as monoracial because of the social and political benefits of belonging to either of these recognized communities. As passers, multiracial individuals use rhetoric to engage in identity work that sheds light on their own relationships to whites and blacks and to so-called objective means of racial identification. Therefore, passing in this book is not synonymous with racial passing but with biracial passing.

Password Three

Biracial passing begins as a dynamic, rhetorical process of expression in which passers identify as monoracial (as either black or white) and not as multiracial (as black and white).

Biracial passing distinguishes between opposing and unequal racial realities of either white or black and provides the dramatic possibility of understanding multiracial identification practices in the absence of legal, social, and civil recognition. Biracial passing also signals the challenges passing poses to white-black and *episteme-doxa* cultural intersections—exposing the insecurity of any racial identity or category and the faulty Platonic reasoning upon which racial identities and categories are based.[67] Specifically, biracial passing unlinks race from appearance and biology and argues that race is a symbolic social construction.[68] Passers are not white or black because of traceable amounts of blood, because of skin color, or because of the social stations into which they are born. Instead, they are white or black because they use rhetoric sincerely to say they are white or black and because dupes and fourth personae/in-group clairvoyants either do not discover or divulge any contrary perceptions. Biracial passing thus allows us to take a deeper look at the underexplored phenomenon of passing as black and its relationships with racial and rhetorical sincerity as well as other expressions of identity (i.e., class, gender, religion, ability, mental health). Moreover, as will be demonstrated, biracial passing allows us to explore how passing becomes more sophisticated as multiracials gain recognition as a bona fide social group. For once multiracials are considered a racial group distinct from blacks and whites, it becomes possible to pass as multiracial. This updated take on passing as biracial, multidirectional, increasingly knotty and inherently rhetorical, raises the question of what other tactics are engaged in the process.

Passwords One, Two, and *Three* allow us to see how passing functions on its most basic level as a "representative anecdote," or as contemporary rhetorical scholars define it, a "representation" that governs and impels the vocabulary it encompasses.[69] A representative anecdote is an abridgment, representative yet reductive.[70] A representative anecdote must be both general and specific. It must be able to apply to many contexts but specific enough to apply to a particular context or topic.[71] It includes fundamental discursive characteristics and sociopolitical values. Passing can be considered a representative anecdote as it engages the varied perspectives of personae and the identifications passers construct. Racially speaking, this means that in passing we can see that the "truth" of racial identity is founded exclusively on rather incomplete experience. Rhetorically speaking this means that in passing we can see how personae and tropes (figures of speech involving the figurative use of language) play out categories of inclusion and exclusion. We shall now consider the extent of these tropological relationships as they relate to passers and their acceptable personae, dupes, and the fourth persona/in-group clairvoyant.

RHETORICAL TROPES OF PASSING

If we start with the acceptable persona of the passer, and with events that occur with reference to that persona, then we must also start with synecdoche,[72] which takes the part for the whole, as when Edward Bulwer-Lytton wrote of the pen (writing) as being mightier than the sword (bloodshed).[73] Synecdoche is named as one of rhetoric's "master," or most powerful, tropes because it influences perception and summarizes and defines a situation succinctly.[74] Thus, it provides us a sense of order[75] as well as senses of engagement, simultaneity, and duality.[76] Passers engage synecdoche when they project a racial identity as either white or black. This synecdochic move takes the part for the whole, and objectifies the passer's acceptable racial persona as a "thing" to be perceived by dupes and fourth personae/in-group clairvoyants who engage in subjective interpretations.[77] These acts of perception (as either white or black) by dupes and fourth personae/in-group clairvoyants are recognized as social status and traded upon by the passer as a rhetorical commodity, circulated in exchange for the realization of his or her goals in private and public settings.

Taking the part for whole is the primary understanding and expression of synecdoche. However, it is also in effect when we take the whole for the part, as in metonymy.[78] That is, dupes and in-group clairvoyants alike take the passer's persona as a whole even though they are only identifying with a part. If a passer's racial identity is black and white, then the dupe may identify her as white and the fourth persona/in-group clairvoyant may identify her as black. In either case this is a metonymic interpretation. In rhetorical theory, metonymy is a unique and reductive product of synecdoche because it only identifies a passer in one way that is mutually exclusive (i.e., either black or white but not both).[79] Therefore, a metonymic perspective of racial identification is implicit in any reading of passing that includes synecdoche. The basic strategy of metonymy, as it pertains to passing, is to convey racial identity in terms of partial ancestry or hypodescent (also known as the one-drop rule).[80] Specifically, metonymy makes multiracial people black by finding one drop of black blood that overpowers and spoils white blood and makes people white by finding no drops of black blood. Metonymy comes to full force when it meets synecdoche in passing, as passers use parts of their racial identities to represent the whole. Synecdoche helps us find the right parts of a passer's identity in their right relationship as they mark out the larger whole. So, just like the passer who passes as either white or black, synecdoche is and is not what it represents.

Another aspect of synecdoche pertinent to this discussion is a "relationship of convertibility" between the whole and the part, in which each represents the other.[81] Parts and wholes are not just convertible, they can also present images of and "cover" one another.[82] Acts of passing demonstrate all of the above by introducing and including parts and wholes and allowing for their convertibility and reversal. Thus, passing carries unique freedoms and constraints as an agent of change and as the basis for understanding a more contemporary discourse of multiracial identities.[83]

To return to the hypothetical trio to illustrate this relationship of convertability: when Abby presents herself as white (using synecdoche, or projecting her white part for the whole of her racial identity), she is duping Dan (metonymy, because this audience believes Abby is white and fails to ask if she is anything else). At the same time, Cindy, the fourth persona/in-group clairvoyant, is aware of the other parts of Abby's racial identity as multiracial and black due to the one-drop rule (metonymy, because even if this audience sees the white part of Abby's identity it takes the black part as the "real" part).[84] If Cindy decides to tell Dan that Abby is not (just) white, then we can say that Abby is white before Cindy speaks and she is black after Cindy speaks. Yet each of these identifications remains incomplete. Therefore, it is necessary to acknowledge that synecdoche and metonymy are convertible and reversible in passing and how these representations play out in the passer's encounters with various audiences.

Based on definitions of synecdoche, a substitution of a part for the whole, and metonymy, a substitution of the whole for a part, I can advance

Password Four

Biracial passing begins where synecdoche meets metonymy. Passers use synecdoche to project acceptable personae as either black or white. Dupes and fourth personae interpret passers' representations as metonymy.

Password Four means that synecdoche and metonymy work together to produce racial identifications, but are not without their limitations. The fact that synecdochic representations of black or white manifest in passing as contextually dependent and "convertible" means that passing is the product of a racial system with discrete and unavoidable boundaries. The nature of this closed racial system suggests that synecdoche can only focus on movement between racial endpoints and cannot on its own account for movement beyond, above, or out of them. Synecdoche's, and therefore metonymy's, limited mobility is why passing is often described in ambivalent terms as one part resistant and one part submissive.[85] Theories of passing that adhere only to the domain of synecdochic representation fail to account for the racial and rhetorical movements passers make that can lead to a fuller understanding of passing's subversive potential and contributions to contemporary discourse of multiracial identities.

A fuller understanding of passing demands that a synecdochic description of racial representation be coupled with an ironic approach to racial identification. Irony is a key feature because it is fundamentally critical, allowing us to maintain a critical distance.[86] Irony stretches a concept as far as it can go; it provides the opportunity to gain critical perspective by capturing and prolonging the moment in which convertible representations are poised in mutually informing, yet unresolved symbolic tension.[87] Irony also provides a space to seek out conceptual and practical ways for understanding how racial parts and wholes (expressed as synecdoches and metonymies) belong together so that they can indeed belong. Returning to our hypothetical trio: irony is the lens through which Cindy sees Abby and Dan. Irony allows Cindy (as in-group clairvoyant/fourth persona) to keep enough distance from Dan to keep Abby's secret. And irony also allows Cindy to get close enough to Abby to inform her that she knows what is going on. Irony also allows other representatives of the fourth persona (you and me) to receive Cindy's "textual wink," know that Abby is passing, and decide whether it is appropriate to conceal or reveal it. Critical ironic distance is used to highlight Cindy's, Abby's, and Dan's perspectives and accounts for simultaneous and contrary symbolic representations of racial identities. Multiple perspectives and representations more fully explain the mechanics of passing (*Password Two*) by offering a space for synecdochic-metonymic representations as well as the labels for passing that they produce (i.e., imitation, appropriation, concealment, revelation). As we will see, irony is a form of reasoning that can reach a more holistic point of view through the dialectical exchange of opposing identifications.[88]

Irony is not, however, the only critical force at work in passing. It is simply the primary critical force at work from a perspective that sees rhetoric as passing and passing as rhetoric. Tragedy also plays a starring role in the drama. Tragedy is a rhetorical genre devoted to playing out the intricate relationships among guilt and redemption, cause and effect.[89] Tragic descriptions of passing are based on historical anxieties about interracial heterosexual relationships and their offspring.[90] These anxieties are translated into a negative conception of multiracials as the products of personal and sexual sins, tragic mulattoes who are socially and biologically impure. Tragic mulattoes are victims of their own flawed natures and thus are alone responsible for the ill fates they suffer in passing. Yet they are compelled to pass because of their conflicted identities and deep longing for whiteness.[91] When passing becomes a tragic discourse, it cannot reward passers, because they appeal to forces that are beyond persuasion.[92] Tragedy is something passers were born with (i.e., multiracial ancestry) and not born into (i.e., an unjust racialized society).[93] The crime they commit is attempting to change their flawed natures by presenting acceptable monoracial personae to the world. In this context there is no choice but for passers to suffer, die, or go into exile. Society requires passers' suffering in order to avoid the disorder and impurity they carry by nature of who they are. It is important to note that on rare occasions passing becomes a tragic cautionary tale that preserves racial cohesion for marginalized groups. More often, however, tragic renditions of passing serve the same function as the Platonic dialogues mentioned above. Tragic accounts of passing work to conceal institutional constraints, shifting blame for any negative outcome onto passers as tragic mulattoes whose desire for whiteness leaves them no choice but to reject their blackness and multiraciality.

An updated take on tragic mulattoes would describe them as pathological, obsessed with monoracial identities and refusing multiracial identities. Tropes of pathology offer a critical rhetorical perspective on passing because they combine emotions and concerns about bodies with anxieties about and aspirations for increasing diversity, conceptions of wellness and disease and basic unexamined beliefs (or *doxa*) about "natural relationships" that are, in actuality, not so natural at all (constituted by *episteme*).[94] Pathological passers are beyond tragic mulattoes. They are racial traitors who have lost their racial inheritance and go on the attack, and consequently they deserve whatever befalls them. In historical and contemporary contexts pathological passers' conflicted racial identities, and not structural forces of oppression like racism, create stress and hostility toward identifying with nonwhite identities. The subversive enthymeme here is that the passer's multiracial background is solely to blame for his or her catastrophic life outcomes.[95] Pathological and tragic foci on passing distract us from exploring the possibility that institutionalized racism creates an environment of suffering that makes black and white into opposing and unequal social worlds, smothers expressions of multiracial identities in multiracial terms, and rewards passers' acceptable personae, dupes' ignorance, and the fourth personae's/in-group clairvoyant's silence.

Tragedy and pathology are not the only non-ironic contexts within which passing can be dramatized. As noted in the preceding discussion of rhetoric as passing, appropriation also proves valuable as stagecraft, underscoring synecdochic-metonymic representations of passers as either black or white.[96] Appropriation makes it possible to accuse passers of deliberately taking advantage of white or black identity without permission. Passers become criminals, undocumented aliens who cross social, and in some cases geographical, borders illegally. When we think of appropriation as the movement of words, ideas, and bodies from one place or position to another, then passing requires us to consider what movements are sustainable, what costs and benefits will be experienced, and what contextual limits exist.[97]

Returning to our example, let us suppose that Abby decides to continue her relationship with Dan. Then, years later, Abby decides to reveal the secret that she has been passing. Dan could perceive a violation or intrusion and say that Abby appropriated white racial identity in order to secure a place in his life. At the same time, Abby or Cindy could say that her ability to pass and Dan's inability to detect it are proof of the unreliability of racial categories. Thus, Abby's appropriation functions as a kind of submission and resistance. It is a kind of submission because her appropriation saturates every aspect of her life and forecloses opportunities for living and/or thinking differently. However, it is a kind of resistance because she embodies the social construction of race. Maintaining this delicate balance of submission and resistance makes appropriation different from synecdoche, irony, tragedy, and pathology. Because appropriation is a label placed on passing by the dupe once he or she realizes that he or she has been duped, passing is interpreted as thievery and not as a genuine pursuit of entitlement. Appropriation becomes the new subversive enthymeme, which replaces the original subversive enthymeme that convinced the dupe of the passer's acceptable persona. As the updated subversive enthymeme, appropriation requires the dupe to equate passing with identity theft, a criminal violation of privacy (the right to be free of unsanctioned intrusion) and self-ownership (the inalienable right to be the master of oneself and one's life chances). The dupe is forced to appeal to frameworks of privacy and self-ownership, the very same social frameworks upon which the passer relies to project her acceptable persona, to equate that acceptable persona with property the passer has stolen.[98] That passing could be a means of social protest or of humanization is not entertained.[99]

As our story of passing unfolds, we will see that passers rarely label their acts as appropriations, tragedies, or pathologies. Instead they rely on the descriptive trope of eloquence, which allows passers to accomplish practical goals by saying and doing things sincerely to express their social and political commitments. As it relates to passing, eloquence is the ability to help others see the world through our own eyes and respond to it in a way that resonates with us.[100] If, for instance, Abby describes passing in a way that allows Dan and his family to recognize their racism, then we can say that she was eloquent. Eloquence allows passers to develop inclusive frameworks for understanding, comparing, and contrasting black and white worldviews.[101] However, because Abby is always addressing two counterposed audiences, even if she is unable to change Dan's and his family's minds we can say that she has still been eloquent. Abby's announcement to Dan is eloquent because she has introduced her identity as multiracial, rebelling against the domination under which she has been held, which has heretofore been suppressed and distorted in monoracial terms.

Attention to the fourth persona affirms this outcome. In this moment Abby would be considered eloquent by Cindy, the fourth persona/in-group clairvoyant, who shares and understands Abby's experience as she has kept that understanding a secret. One of the secrets Cindy kept is that Abby passed because the vocabulary Abby needed to express her identity as multiracial exceeded that which could be phrased in monoracial terms. Thus, the fourth persona's/in-group clairvoyant's (Cindy's) silent eloquence also deserves consideration. This silence is not to be confused with weakness or failure to act. Rather, it is contextual and tactical, a form of preserving the pass, protecting the passer's privacy and protecting the passer from dupes' wrath, revenge, or disapproval. Passers' and fourth personae's/in-group clairvoyants' eloquence is rhetorical, regardless of what dupes think, because it affords opportunities for choosing and defining identities, whether it be to identify as either white or black or as white and black through different experiences and situations over time. In spite of their eloquence, historical evidence suggests that passers' and fourth personae's/in-group clairvoyants' violations of dupes' expectations lower their credibility and result in decreased credibility for their personae and rhetorical actions.

As it happens, eloquence implies discursive depth as well as stylistic ornament or beauty.[102] Eloquence means that our perceptions of who or what is eloquent are based largely on our exposure to rhetorical personae, situations, and sociopolitical values. So passers can speak eloquently when they demonstrate an ability to connect their words and ideals with the thoughts of dupes and the fourth persona/in-group clairvoyant. But speaking eloquently also means that passers may offend sociopolitical norms for proper identification, making them sound like tragic mulattoes, appropriators, or downright pathological cases. By shaping the available means of persuasion and perception through which we categorize and make sense out of identities, passing's tropes—synecdoche, metonymy, irony, tragedy, pathology and eloquence—direct our attention to certain parts of identities and make other parts less visible. Tropes of passing offer a particularly powerful rhetorical strategy because they organize identity categories such as race, gender, class, and ability according to human experience.[103] The diverse cases of passing reviewed in the following chapters explore each of these tropes, suggesting that neither rhetoric nor passing is transparent, and thus both are keeping secrets that need telling. We have located some of these secrets where rhetorical tropes, texts, and personae "intersect" to dramatize intrapersonal, interpersonal, communal, and structural relations.[104] These intersections provide a sense of the claims rhetoric makes about passing and reveal

Password Five

Biracial passing ends as an "intersectional" process through which tropes, personae, and texts combine to mark social place (institutional categories) and discursive space (passers within institutional categories).[105]

Rather than thinking of passing as passé, *Password Five* reveals that passing represents part of the contingent and ongoing process of persuasion in constituting rhetoric and enacting identity. *Password Five* also serves a summative function. It reminds us that every act of passing is a claim regarding status and sincerity (*Password One*) that persuades based on intersecting personae—passers, dupes, and in-group clairvoyants (*Password Two*). Persuasion is enhanced when passers use synecdoche and metonymy to create monoracial identifications (*Passwords Three, Four*). Some acts of passing also persuade by engaging irony, others use appropriation or eloquence as their medium, and others use tragedy or pathology to communicate what happens when distinctions between passers and personae can no longer be detected (*Password Five*). The *passwords* I have introduced are, in conjunction with the phenomenon of passing itself, of significance to exploring the parameters of identity, especially as it intersects with issues of racial politics, multiracial discourse and rhetorical communication today.[106]

The theoretical understanding of passing I have outlined is a starting point that indicates roles played by personae, tropes, and texts in the process of projecting and interpreting identifications. And, our theoretical understanding is also a sign that more of passing's secrets remain hidden. Once revealed, some of these secrets will remind us of the experience produced by the Guess My Race iPad application with which this chapter began, pointing to the ongoing possibilities and problems of racial identification in the twenty-first century. Other secrets will shed light on how identities are actually coded and valued by passers, dupes, and fourth personae/in-group clairvoyants alike. These secrets will chart out a trajectory of passing in spite of marked gains in social and political equality. Most importantly, secrets will take the form of additional *passwords* that provide a more thorough understanding of how rhetoric intersects with life to define who we have been and who we now are and to discover and mobilize who we might become for the purpose of positive change.

CHAPTER TWO

Passing as Power

In December 1848, Ellen and William Craft ended their lifelong search for answers. Ellen was at her master's plantation, and William was busy at work as a cabinetmaker. Until this moment it seemed as though they sustained only one conversation for months, even years. Nothing else mattered: How could they determine their own fates? How could they ensure they would always be together? How could they guarantee that no one else in their families would be enslaved? There was only one answer. Escape. Telling no one, the couple thought of countless ways that might be tried. Finally it dawned on William and Ellen that "slaveholders have the privilege of taking their slaves to any part of the country they think proper." Under these circumstances it was possible that as Ellen "was nearly white," she could "disguise herself as an invalid gentleman and assume to be" William's "master, while [he] could attend as . . . slave," and in that way they could "effect [their] escape."[1]

The couple's plan, while tempting, would not be without its difficulties. Ellen and William heard of only one other plan as daring—of Henry "Box" Brown, a Virginia slave who was boxed up and shipped to Philadelphia by abolitionist Samuel A. Smith in 1849.[2] Like Brown's and Smith's plan, the Crafts' escape required intricate planning and the obvious crossing of physical and geographic boundaries from South to North. But there the similarities ended. The Crafts' escape plan would require them to travel in plain sight and cross many other symbolic boundaries that were just as dangerous—gender, race, class, health, ability, and the separations between "us" and "them."[3] Escape meant passing. Passing meant power. Power meant bending conventional boundaries of rhetoric and culture.

Ellen and William Craft wanted this kind of power. They wanted to live as human beings with all the rights and privileges thereof and not to be "held as chattels."[4] They wanted to keep and spend their earnings as they saw fit and not to enable "tyrants . . . to live in idleness and luxury."[5] They wanted a right to "life, liberty and the pursuit of happiness." They needed to steal themselves away from their wrongful owners and become the rightful owners of "the bones and sinews that God gave" them.[6] They wanted to stop suppressing their rage and start asserting their dignity. They wanted, more than anything, an intact family and not to look on helplessly in submission to another's "power to tear from [their] cradle the new-born babe and sell it in the shambles like a brute."[7] They wanted to direct, enable, and energize their lives. Ultimately, Ellen and William wanted freedom from slavery's totalizing domination. They wanted to be whomever God made them to be without suffering mortal risk.

The Crafts' case forms a starting point for exploring passing as an act of power.[8] Passing is connected to power and rhetoric as a way to impact audiences by maintaining and transgressing boundaries—a prerequisite for understanding the major historical facts of the Crafts' story.[9] It is then possible to see how passing empowered the Crafts and their audiences within a network of dominant power relationships that were double-sided, prevailing yet contestable. The Crafts' case, in the end, allows us to expand on the relevance and irony of power to contemporary expressions of passing and enslavement.

"CRAFTING" A PASS

By definition, power is the capacity to direct or influence actions in a relational network.[10] Power is both stifling and liberating, involving institutional structures of domination (i.e., enslavement) and cultural practices of resistance (i.e., escape, passing). And power is also rhetorical. Rhetorical power is the capacity of discourse to direct or influence behavior inside and outside of traditional discursive constraints.[11] Rhetorical power can be measured by comparing the communication and behaviors of subordinates and dominant groups.[12] To use the critical vocabulary of passing, rhetorical power can be assessed by comparing passers' encounters with dupes to passers' encounters with in-group clairvoyants (*Password Two*). Ellen and William's passing makes these comparisons explicit and demonstrates how audiences, tropes, and texts intersect and exhibit force on each other and on society (*Password Five*).

For instance, the couple's escape plan was developed secretly and quickly and became more mysterious and complicated. Even in their own imaginations Ellen and William encountered domination in many forms, anticipating the many intersecting prejudices they faced based on class, race, gender, health, and ability. They would have to guard against being recognized by dupes, figure out where to stop along the way, and overcome the disability of compulsory illiteracy. Above all, they would have to do all of this in the presence of a hostile white audience so that they could travel together. One thing was certain. They would have to pass and, in passing, manipulate identity's codes of meaning. In order to pass, the Crafts had to create a lead character, and the rhetoric to support it, whose legitimacy would not be questioned. Racial conventions that privileged whiteness dictated that Ellen would have to play the leading role because of her white skin color.

The obvious first step was for Ellen to employ synecdoche by depending upon the white part of her racial identity to stand for the whole and pass as white (*Password Four*). However, the Crafts knew that even if she passed as a white woman, cultural convention forbade the pair to travel together on a public conveyance, reinforcing the idea that passing is an intersectional process that grapples with social place as well as discursive and physical spaces (*Password Five*). Railroad travel was segregated by gender and race, with white women and children in the first-class car, unattended white men in the smoker car, and black slaves in what was sometimes referred to as the second-class car but was, in reality, the baggage car.[13] Ellen and William overcame these logistical obstacles by "creating a costume," "a persona" in classical rhetorical terms, that transformed Ellen into a white man. But common sense (*doxa*) dictated that Ellen could not become just any white man. She had to become Mr. Johnson, "a most respectable looking gentleman."[14] Mr. Johnson's "respectable" class status presented additional obstacles that needed to be overcome. His appearance needed to justify why someone of his background could not write his name and why he needed the assistance of a slave in order to survive the journey.[15]

Ellen dressed elegantly in a stylish man's suit and cut her hair square at the back of the neck, the style usually worn by young white men at the time. Then the couple realized that Ellen's beardless face would give them away, so she made a poultice ("a moist, usually heated mass of a substance with a soft, pasty consistency, applied to the skin, usually by means of a bandage or dressing, in order to promote healing, reduce swelling, relieve pain, etc.").[16] Ellen placed the poultice "in a white handkerchief to be worn under the chin, up the cheeks, and to tie over the head. This nearly hid the expression of the countenance, as well as the beardless chin."[17] The poultice also created a muffling effect so that, as much as possible, Ellen could avoid conversation with white travelers. Speaking to whites entailed the possibilities of outing and return to slavery, as well as psychological stress. Ellen also used a sling to conceal her illiteracy. By feigning physical disability, she could rely on others to sign Mr. Johnson's name for her at checkpoints. As final touches Ellen wore a top hat to add height and a pair of green glasses, which obscured any eye contact she would inevitably make with passengers, passersby, or officials (figure 2.1). With these disguises in place Ellen's transformation into Mr. Johnson was complete and William had a reason to accompany her from Georgia to Philadelphia as slave and caretaker.

Each of Ellen's disguises demonstrates how one identity affects and is affected by others (race-gender-class-disability). Symbolically, each disguise challenges an *episteme* that privileges and empowers single, clear parts of identity that stand for wholes. In addition to questioning epistemic essentialism, Ellen's and William's combined disguises dramatize how passers struggle for actual power (*Password One*). Ellen's disability exposes domination experienced on the bases of race and class discrimination.[18] Ellen concealed some disabilities (illiteracy and enslavement) by revealing another (ill health).[19] Ellen's physical disability was produced symbolically by the poultices and slings that represented it and also gestured toward domination that enforced the learning

FIGURE 2.1
Ellen Craft, depicted in the clothes she wore for her escape
disguised as a man

disability of illiteracy.[20] Ellen's passing demonstrates how literacy was one more source of protection for whiteness and its privileges, such as the ability to sign for and identify oneself legally and the physical privileges of not being beaten, disabled, and enslaved. More obviously, it directed attention away from Ellen's prepassing race, class, ability, and gender identities (*aletheia*). So when Mr. Johnson's disabled body moved into the social space aboard the train, it made a way for Ellen's (and William's) physically abled, yet enslaved and stigmatized, bodies to be inserted into that space and travel to freedom, thereby transforming their class status.

Once Ellen's acceptable persona, Mr. Johnson, was fully formed, Ellen and William had to enact one final symbolic gesture: to secure permission from their masters to be away from their respective plantations for a few days. "So after no little amount of perseverance . . . [Ellen] obtained a pass from her mistress."[21] William obtained a pass from his owner-employer shortly thereafter, and the pair was off, "stepping out as softly as 'moonlight upon the water.' "[22] Mr. Johnson and William boarded separate cars and like method actors immersed themselves into the role of moneyed white male slaveholder and his property. William recounts: "[I] got into the negro car in which I knew I should have to ride, but my master (as I will now call my wife) took a longer way around. . . . He obtained a ticket for himself and one for his slave to Savannah, the first port, which was two hundred miles off. My master then had the luggage stowed away, and stepped into one of the best carriages."[23] After a series of harrowing encounters aboard trains, boats, and carriage rides over the course of four days, the Crafts arrived in Philadelphia, and from there went on to Boston and eventually to London with the help of William Lloyd Garrison's abolitionist network. "Scarcely had they arrived on free soil when the rheumatism departed—the right arm was unslung—the toothache was gone—the beardless face was unmuffled—the deaf heard and spoke—the blind saw—and the lame leaped" for joy.[24]

Neither Ellen nor William could know it as these events unfolded, but they would tell this story many times over the course of their lives. Once the couple reached Philadelphia, they became what we might now call "reality stars" as they garnered media attention from antislavery literary circles[25] and press.[26] They presented their story to abolitionist audiences in the North and in the United Kingdom and Africa. At one of the Crafts' final presentations in the United States before expatriating to the United Kingdom, the *Liberator* reported, "a lady in the audience wanted to know of Ellen if "they called her 'a nigger' at the South." Ellen replied, "Oh, yes, they didn't call me anything else; they said it would make me proud."[27] The lady's question suggests that perceptions of multiracial individuals (*doxa*), which tend to mirror the prevailing racial hierarchy (*episteme*), can be challenged when audiences encounter passers who violate expectations. Ellen's response underscores how racial identifications that pass as *episteme* are really cultural habits developed through frequent use (*doxa*). With generations of interracial mixing between black and white people and the vague definition of blackness designated to multiracial people by the one-drop rule, audiences discovered that they could not tell the difference between black and white (at least in Ellen's case).[28] Audiences made an epistemological leap when they realized that in Ellen they were seeing someone whose racial identity was ambiguous and changeable (*Password One*).[29]

Audiences saw one persona, only to find out that another one lay behind it, and behind it another one. In Ellen's hands, passing introduces a different concept of depth in which identities exist simultaneously and contingently. Thus, the audiences' struggle to understand Ellen's racial identity mirrored the social struggle for power at the heart of passing and signaled a struggle for interpretive power that can be viewed simultaneously from various competing perspectives—the passer's, the dupe's, and the in-group clairvoyant's (*Password Two*). Just as Ellen and William struggled for actual control over their own lives in passing, audiences struggled for interpretive power as they witnessed passing and began the transformation from dupes into in-group clairvoyants. Audiences were forced to question whether Ellen was passing as white to escape from slavery in 1848 or passing as black thereafter to add drama to the story she and William told (*Password Three*).[30] The subversive enthymeme in the minds of these dupes-in-transition, of course, is that there is a more likely vision of a slave, one whose race, ability, or respectability contrasts with Ellen's. Emphasizing the contrast between myths about and realities of multiracial identities and interracial relations in the context of slavery functioned effectively to challenge beliefs about the nature of race as grounds for enslavement. In fact, the Crafts presented enslavement itself as the grounds for race, racial categories, racism, and passing.

The Crafts' presentations and publicity also created an international readership that was hungry for a firsthand literary account.[31] They satisfied their audiences by providing the details in their autobiography, *Running a Thousand Miles for Freedom*. The narrative was sold by London's William Tweedie, and revenues went to further the abolitionist cause. The book was read widely, and a second edition was published in 1861.[32] It is to this account that we now turn.

POWER ON PAGE

Ellen's and William's literary account in *Running* allows us to more fully experience the rhetorical power witnessed in their presentations. The Crafts begin by discussing the repressive power and irony inherent in the Declaration of Independence. In the preface William appeals to a higher authority than human government when he cites the phrase "God made of one blood all nations of men" from Acts 17:26. He continues,

> Having heard while in slavery that . . . the American Declaration of Independence says that "We hold these truths to be self-evident, that all men are created equal; that they are endowed by their Creator with certain inalienable rights that among these are life, liberty and the pursuit of happiness;" we could not understand by what right we were held as "chattels." Therefore we felt perfectly justified in undertaking the dangerous and exciting task of "running a thousand miles for freedom" in order to obtain those rights which are so vividly set forth in the Declaration.[33]

The Crafts illustrate effectively that "life, liberty and the pursuit of happiness" are terms formed ironically because they were never meant to include the enslaved. The creation of a new persona, Mr. Johnson, was needed to make them real. The obvious enthymeme here is that the Crafts' identities disqualified them from enjoying "inalienable rights." Also note that William and Ellen "heard" and did not read about the Declaration and its truths. The repressive power of slavery outlawed literacy for the enslaved and made it virtually impossible for this group to apply the Declaration's words and worldviews to their lives.[34]

Highlighting this irony is more than a literary introduction. It introduces readers to their own impairment because of power relations by which they have been privileged. Readers begin the story unable to interpret their own society and soon realize that Ellen and William are not the only passers in this narrative. The United States is passing as a free and pious country. At the outset dupes believe that inalienable rights are enjoyed by all who deserve them. Dupes-in-transition see that this is not the case. Ellen and William reinforce readers' literacy training by highlighting the ironies inherent in contradictory state laws devoted to defining and maintaining racial distinctions. They discuss the ways in which it was possible, for instance, to be legally black in one state but not another, or to be white in one decade and not the next, or to become differently raced by moving from one region or even one situation to the next.

Readers find a physical description of Ellen from William's perspective on the second page of *Running* to reinforce the irony and their burgeoning critical perspective. Here readers begin to see that Ellen's passing challenged the epistemological concept of hypodescent (the idea that "one drop" of black blood makes a person black and look black) and the presupposition that "every coloured person's complexion is *prima facie* evidence of his being a slave" and not "the rightful owner of himself."[35] William explains: "Notwithstanding my wife being of African extraction on her mother's side—she is almost white. In fact, she is so nearly so that the tyrannical old lady to whom she first belonged became so annoyed at finding her mistaken for a child of the family, that she gave her when eleven years of age to a daughter, as a wedding present. This separated my wife from her mother, and also from several other dear friends."[36]

With the reality of miscegenation in the slavery context, Ellen's appearance posed a problem to the strict borders between black and white. It was unclear where she belonged or whether she was free or enslaved. The *partus sequitur ventrem* (birth follows the belly) legal doctrine, through which offspring follow the condition of their mothers, clarified things by making slaves out of virtually all multiracial persons born to enslaved mothers.[37] The doctrine implied that free white men could engage in sexual relations with black female slaves at will, and often by force.[38] The law also made Ellen a monetary asset to her owner-father. She was "legally the property of the man, who stands in the anomalous relation . . . of father as well as master" and could have been taken or sold at any time to settle any of his debts, as could any of her children.[39] Her indeterminate status and "almost white" appearance made her more valuable in comparison to other black slaves, garnering at least double at slave auctions.[40] Ellen's white slave status was materially valuable and symbolically rich because the enslaved were not thought to be white.[41] Ellen's body is submitted as evidence of the horror of slavery least often discussed—compulsory miscegenation—and the paradoxical status of the white slave.

Ellen and William mine the depths of a white slave persona as both a motive for escape and resource of their story. On one level, the white slave persona reveals dupes' leap from correlation to causation. Generally dupes assumed that because people with black ancestry were enslaved, blackness was the cause and reason for enslavement. To reduce this kind of logic ad absurdum, the Crafts use the white slave persona and passing to discredit racial appearance as an accurate measure of racial identity. But on another level race itself becomes a false representation and a false shield from enslavement. After introducing Ellen as a white slave, the Crafts continue by recounting cases of enslaved white and white-looking multiracial children who were abducted and whose appearances were altered by tanning and staining.[42] William reports to have "conversed with several slaves who told [him] that their parents were white and free; but that they were stolen away from them and sold when quite young. As they could not tell their address, and also as the parents did not know what had become of their lost and dear little ones, of course all traces of each other were gone."[43] Depicting Ellen as multiracial and in the same category as these known white slaves proved to be an ingenious rhetorical move, allowing her pass to achieve the desired effect of subverting slavery while reinforcing white audiences' pride in white identity (*Password Three*). Ellen and William convinced their audiences that slavery was evil by simultaneously staying within and transgressing cultural conventions. Some audience members would support the abolition of slavery based on its inherent evils and sins against humanity, while audiences that were unconvinced of the evils of slavery as they pertained to black people would be persuaded that the institution should be abolished on the grounds that whites (who neither deserved nor required enslavement) were enslaved.[44] In either scenario the Crafts' argument for abolition is an example of rhetorical power because it conformed to and broke with cultural and rhetorical norms. The power of their argument rested on the ironic presumption that whites would be more outraged that other whites could be enslaved than they would be by the injustice of institutional discrimination against anyone with black ancestry.[45]

But the Crafts transgressed cultural and rhetorical convention when Ellen's audiences could not discern her racial identity or distinguish definitively between white and black (*Password One*). The ironies highlighted forced audiences to resolve their confusion by abolishing the institution of slavery and gave them an in-group clairvoyant's perspective. For the irony to succeed, readers who begin as dupes must be absorbed into the process so that they may feel and share its intensity as in-group clairvoyants. As in-group clairvoyants, readers are absorbed further into the drama as they watch one of their own, the Crafts and, in particular Ellen, put one over on every dupe in the text. Readers are now not simply invited but empowered and compelled to question the stability of race when it is invoked later by dupes in the text as authority or *episteme*. Because readers are now in-group clairvoyants, subsequent exchanges become more complex, involving race-gender-class-ability, which readers must note and question to release the full irony and make the ideological point.

Running represents passing as a series of conversations between author and readers as well as among the personae that cross paths as the journey unfolds. The Crafts' conversational rendition of passing suggests that conversation—rhetoric—makes change possible. Readers, who may start out as dupes or spectators, are invited to become in-group clairvoyant participants in the pass by evaluating a series of ideologies or worldviews that are presented ironically as exchanges the Crafts either participate in or overhear. The next set of exchanges occurs between Mr. Johnson and fellow white male travelers aboard the train, allowing readers to find out what dominant group members talk about in the absence of subordinates—"namely, Niggers, Cotton, and the Abolitionists."[46] These topics serve as the basis for conversations that justify control of the enslaved, suggest that mastery (read power) is the natural endowment of whiteness, and reinforce hierarchical order. By recounting these conversations, the Crafts subvert existing power relations and reveal what may lie beneath the surface.

A slave dealer informs Mr. Johnson that he is making a grave mistake by taking William to the North, that black people and freedom did not mix, and that instead he should sell William. "If you have made up your mind to sell that ere nigger, I am your man; just mention your price."[47] Mr. Johnson's reply is simple: "I don't wish to sell, sir; I cannot get on well without him."[48] This could not have been a truer statement. Ellen's passing is destined to fail without the cooperation of William as the in-group clairvoyant, the silent observant who controls the outcome of any pass (*Password Two*). Then a young military officer eating breakfast next to Mr. Johnson offers the following insight: "You will excuse me, Sir, for saying I think you are very likely to spoil your boy by saying 'thank you' to him. I assure you, sir, nothing spoils a slave so soon as saying, thank you' . . . to him. The only way to make a nigger toe the mark, and to keep him in his place, is to storm at him like thunder, and keep him trembling like a leaf. . . . If every nigger was drilled in this manner they would . . . never dare to run away."[49] This exchange, and all others like it,[50] affirms masters' superiority and provides the occasion to display their power and group cohesion. Exchanges like these also show the Crafts exactly how unjust their subordination is. Ellen and William learn how to recognize and rebut opponents' arguments by exposing enthymemes and fallacies that dupe them into believing they are indeed superior: that black people are childlike and savage and so need to be cared for and controlled as slaves. White slaveholders feared that the enslaved would escape if taken north and were convinced that they would be incapable of handling life if they did so. The Crafts understood what white slaveholders feared most: the humanity of the enslaved. Thus, Mr. Johnson's saying "thank you" acknowledges William's humanity publicly and challenges white supremacy.[51] These exchanges suggest that for the Crafts passing was as much a matter of expedience as it was morality.

Interspersed among Mr. Johnson's encounters with white men are William's encounters with others who are enslaved. A "shrewd son of African parents" from South Carolina begins questioning William in dialect while ordering his master's dinner and polishing his shoes. He asks where William is going, and if he knows that Philadelphia is free territory, and encourages him to leave Mr. Johnson and escape. William says that his master is good and that he is not interested in escape. The irony, of course, is that the act of rebellion William disavows here he later confirms. But at the moment, the reader is simply called to notice the constraints of William's communication as in-group clairvoyant. He is sworn to secrecy on all fronts. Thereafter, another enslaved man tells William that Mr. Johnson is "a gentleman of distinction" because Mr. Johnson tipped him after being served dinner. Tipping is noteworthy because it means that Johnson acknowledges the slave and his labor, and perhaps even his humanity, rather than taking these for granted. Johnson's act, if transposed to the context of his prepassing persona, would represent an act of rebellion. William, constrained by the limits of the in-group clairvoyant, affirms the enslaved servant's assessment but is unable to express the hidden irony.

The tables now turn. William's narration provides an ideal distance from the events in order to crystallize the critical consciousness of an in-group clairvoyant perspective for the reader. An in-group clairvoyant perspective emphasizes the radical difference between masters and the enslaved, between those who suffer and those who do not, and the theatrical character of their relationship. For instance, William's excellent care of his master ensures that Mr. Johnson will receive the best service available and also the most sympathy, even as William himself is treated horribly. On several occasions he puts Mr. Johnson to bed and then has nowhere to rest his own head. Though William's performance is virtually flawless, he makes clear that hiding in plain sight was difficult, uncertain, and anxiety-ridden for him. He writes:

> For the purpose of somewhat disguising myself, I bought and wore a very good second-hand white beaver. . . . [But] an uncouth planter, who had been watching me very closely, said to my master, "I reckon, stranger, you are '*spiling*' that ere nigger of yourn, by letting him wear such a devilish fine hat. . . . It always makes me itch all over, from head to toe, to get a hold of every d—d nigger I see dressed like a white man.[52]

The irony here is compelling. The reader, from having taken on his or her ultimate role as critic and in-group clairvoyant, knows that Ellen is the one "dressed like a white man," yet William is the one accused of racial passing. This is no accident. Readers' critical literacy skills are being tested as they encounter a dupe who suspects he is being duped, accuses William of passing, and makes Ellen the silent in-group clairvoyant. The racism is on the surface of the discourse, but readers begin to see a rhetoric of classism beneath. William's hat is read as a signal of his desire to transcend slave status, which means transcending blackness according to his accuser.[53] The race-class passing correlation exists because passing is motivated by a desire for economic opportunity and social mobility available to members of the dominant group but described (by the dominant group) as being motivated by a desire for the dominant group's racial identity.[54] Indeed, class often passes as race and gender, and its effects are experienced differently. The most powerful effect of passing here is the change it makes in the Crafts' class status—from enslaved chattel to free human beings who generate income for themselves.

But class is not the only terrain upon which the Crafts' effort is threatened with exposure and return to slavery, and its cruel retribution. As the couple was boarding the last leg of their train trip from Baltimore to Philadelphia, William was stopped by an officer who thought he was trying to stow away. The officer made

William retrieve Mr. Johnson in order to authenticate his presence. Mr. Johnson left the white-only carriage and met the officer.

> On entering the room we found the principal man, to whom my master said, "Do you wish to see me, sir?" "Yes," said this eagle-eyed officer; and he added, "It is against our rules, sir, to allow any person to take a slave out of Baltimore into Philadelphia, unless he can satisfy us that he has the right to take him along." "Why is that?" asked my master, with more firmness than could be expected. "Because, sir," continued he, in a voice and manner that almost chilled our blood, "if we should suffer any gentleman to take a slave past here into Philadelphia; and should the gentleman with whom the slave might be travelling turn out not to be his rightful owner; and should the proper master come and prove that his slave escaped on our road, we shall have him to pay for; and therefore, we cannot let any slave pass here without receiving security to show, and to satisfy us, that it is all right."[55]

Hearing this, several travelers assemble to find out what will happen. Some of them express sympathy for Mr. Johnson because of his disabilities and suggest he be detained no longer. The officer is unmoved. He asks Mr. Johnson if he knows any man in Baltimore who can verify his story. Mr. Johnson answers, "No, I bought tickets in Charleston to pass us through to Philadelphia, and therefore you have no right to detain us here."[56] Mr. Johnson's use of the word "pass" here is significant because it constitutes a "wink" to the in-group clairvoyant who is aware of the many physical and social borders being crossed by the purchase of their traveling passes. It is also a reminder that the couple is, in fact, breaking the law by passing and escaping from slavery. Mr. Johnson's confident persona as master is then juxtaposed with and justified by William's melodramatic and impotent reaction. William, "believing that [they] were caught, . . . shrank into a corner, turned [his] face from the door, and expected in a moment to be dragged out." Suddenly, just when it seems that the Crafts are going to be exposed, the officer lets them go.[57] Mr. Johnson and William climb aboard, to white-only and baggage cars, respectively, and complete their journey.

Mr. Johnson's encounter with the conductor demonstrates the importance of the presence of a dupe that supplies the subversive enthymeme and accepts Mr. Johnson as acceptable persona (*Password Two*). Mr. Johnson's fellow white travelers, also dupes, invite the conductor to become a part of their audience by embodying the subversive enthymeme. The subversive enthymeme for the conductor is that if the white passengers (also slaveholders) believe that Mr. Johnson really is a white man accompanied by his slave, then he should believe it as well. Of course, this enthymeme also works in the minds of readers-audiences. The subversive enthymeme for the passengers is that Mr. Johnson's disabilities are evidence of his need to get to Philadelphia with William and thus should excuse him from this harsh line of questioning. Fortunately for Ellen and William, the dupes are persuaded by these enthymemes and their escape is successful. Readers also experience the good fortune of understanding how passing takes on meaning, form, and power through rhetorical encounters that animate every character in their range (*Password Two*). By the time the Crafts make it to Philadelphia, readers are skilled in finding inconsistencies, breaking down differences, and overturning hierarchies. The United States becomes the home of the enslaved, the enslaved become masters, and the enslaved become free. The dangers of passing performed on stage and on page overturn subtle appearance-based ideologies of race, class, and ability while leaving the more obvious appearance-based ideology of gender relatively intact.

Though gender presents an obstacle to Ellen's passing that Mr. Johnson ultimately overcomes, gender remains the only aspect of identity that keeps Ellen from being entirely ambiguous and unplaceable. Throughout the narrative William describes Ellen as a woman and Mr. Johnson as a man. Ellen's gender as woman is underscored by the fact that William constructs Ellen's transformation to Mr. Johnson by then refusing to call her his wife. In fact, for nearly two-dozen pages, the literary length of their escape, William refers to Ellen as "my master" and with male pronouns only.[58] As opposed to the critical position Ellen plays in the plan as Mr. Johnson, she is described and introduced as a woman who does not speak unless spoken to or otherwise addressed directly. Further, Ellen dons Mr. Johnson's attire when she appears on stage or when posing for an engraved likeness sold as a souvenir. Even her body language, her curtsy after each presentation, is a gendered sign that connotes femininity.[59] She is, because of her racially ambiguous identity, a form of physical proof that the escape actually took place. However, her gender remains concrete, real, and essential while her race, class, and ability are conjectural and deconstructed. In this way, power is both subverted and reinforced in the Crafts' passing and its retelling. Still unexplored is how irony fuels this power struggle.

IRONY, THE POWER OF PASSING

As a multidimensional means of subverting and reinforcing power, the Crafts' passing is riddled with irony. Irony explains what happens when the passer invites dupes to become in-group clairvoyants.[60] Put in terms of "effective irony," the Crafts' passing takes on another rhetorical layer represented by three participants—"(1) the speaker or ironist, (2) the hearer or victim and (3) an audience or evaluator."[61] Each participant brings to the event an attitude formed by cultural, experiential, and rhetorical standards that identifies and distinguishes between words uttered and their meanings.[62] As ironists, passers are required to speak and audiences are required to listen and assess. Like the in-group clairvoyant, the evaluator in an ironic moment must be capable of differentiating between actual and apparent meanings whether (s)he announces the difference or not (*Password Two*).

In this ironic model, a passer's persona is made meaningful only insofar as it is allowed to exist by the evaluator or in-group clairvoyant, who must note the apparent meaning and its mask along with the contradictory meanings that lie beneath the surface. For dupes, Ellen's truer racial identity is black and female. For the in-group clairvoyant, Ellen's racial identity is associated with and affected by her gender, class, and ability statuses. A visual representation makes this clearer.

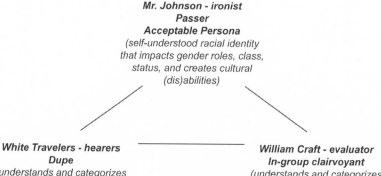

FIGURE 2.2
Irony and the Triangulated Dramatic Theater of Passing

As the figure illustrates, *Running* is not only inviting dupes to become in-group clairvoyants. The text challenges the privileged dupe's gaze by "winking" at readers who are already in the know. The Crafts' story proved persuasive because it solidified in-group clairvoyants' worldviews, teaching them to become more effective change agents and how to exercise their newfound agentive force.[63] Readers are urged to do more than purchase the book to exercise power and effect social change. They are empowered to align the knowledge gained as in-group members with actions as democratic citizens. Along the way readers are also introduced to

Password Six

Passing is agonistic (operating inside and outside of rhetorical and cultural conventions) and transformative (using irony-synecdoche-metonymy to transform dupes into in-group clairvoyants).

Passing empowered the Crafts and their readers to escape external restraints without losing control over their own representations and appealed to mainstream democratic and Christian values of equality to abolish slavery and the values upon which it was based.

The power of irony comes to the fore when the Crafts position and address their audiences as the in-group clairvoyant so that multiple interpretations can be made possible and visible. The discrepancies audiences pick up are ironies carried beneath outward appearances. That is, the connection between Ellen, William, Mr. Johnson, and audiences is based on substitution, concealment, and revelation (*aletheia*). Audiences can locate what is said by dominant and subordinate group members in each other's presence and absence so that they can apprehend contradicting truths: because of the Crafts' identities and experiences as slaves, they are not qualified for freedom and citizenship; because of their identities and experiences as slaves who emancipated themselves in passing, they are qualified for freedom and citizenship. These ironic dialectics are at work throughout the narrative. Slavery made the Crafts illiterate, yet it also authorized them to write their story once they were freed and learned how to write in the United Kingdom. Racism expressed by dupes along the way solidified the couple's perspective as in-group clairvoyants and showed them how to appeal to and transform dupes into future in-group clairvoyants.

Ironies become more complex as we understand the deeper rhetorical principles upon which they are based. A case of "true irony," for instance, relies on ambiguity and emphasizes consubstantial relationships.[64] Rhetors and passers who employ true irony understand that domination and resistance live within us and outside of us. Ellen's experience is an obvious demonstration of true irony. Because of Ellen's historical relationships with her family as black and white as well as daughter and slave, thematic tensions and oppositional character groups within this dramatic plot resemble a predictable ironic reversal, wherein multiracial, black, enslaved, and impoverished becomes white, free, and wealthy. Ellen's prepassing description as a white slave makes her a natural counterfeit, correlating her multiracial ancestry and illegitimate family status to the forgery of Mr. Johnson's signature in particular and to notions of authentic identity and recognition writ large.[65]

A more subtle yet equally complex demonstration of true irony is the dominant group–centered version of critical literacy the Crafts engage. Consider the following exchange that begins between Mr. Johnson and a pious Christian widow aboard the train. The widow's husband emancipated their slaves upon his death, but she and her "good Christian minister" son altered the will to prevent this from happening. "Did you mean, madam," asks Mr. Johnson, "that willing the slaves free was unjust to yourself, or unkind to them?" "I mean that it was decidedly unkind to the servants themselves." Another passenger's ears perk up when the widow later reports that at least ten of her slaves ran away that year alone. The woman continues, "My son . . . has always told me that they were much better off than free niggers in the North." "You are quite mistaken, madam," the passenger responded. "For instance, my own widowed mother, before she died, emancipated all her slaves and sent them to Ohio, where they are getting along well."[66] The Crafts are undoubtedly satirizing and criticizing misinterpretations of Christian teaching and legal breaches. But the irony reaches full force when the Crafts reach out to readers, suggesting that there are good and bad white people. There are those who use religion to justify sin—sinners passing as saints—and those who have not been so converted. Good white people might even be willing to speak out and fight for the abolitionist cause. Readers are invited to side with Mr. Johnson and the unnamed white male passenger and against the pious white widow and her son and the institution of slavery in which they are invested.

By focusing on cultural intersections and conversations throughout *Running*, the Crafts tap into their audiences' imaginations and create identifications. Readers-audiences are transformed from dupes to trained ironists and in-group clairvoyants because they can now see added dimensions to the pass. Images of who could be and who actually was enslaved are altered by Ellen's display of her pre- and post-passing personae. Together Ellen, William, Mr. Johnson, and their readers-auditors become a unified in-group clairvoyant that sees the abolitionist cause as an urgent one. Though they begin as illiterate, Ellen and William teach audiences how to read. In this way, the Crafts' passing can stand out as not just a series of ironic moments but a powerful moment of refiguring identity.

A look at the ironic intersections of passing also allows the critic to draw valuable and progressive conclusions. Most obviously, we can conclude that irony is a powerful tool of connection and disconnection. We have seen that there is a time for ironic disconnection and a time for a return to reality, and the Crafts have shown us that there is power in learning how to tell one time from the other. Audiences connect with Mr. Johnson, an ironic character who, when juxtaposed with Ellen, causes audiences to disconnect and question race as the basis for liberty and justice. Embodying an in-group clairvoyant's perspective not only accounts for insiders' perspectives, but allows for reconnection and the possibility of being an outsider (or dupe) who gains an insider's (or in-group clairvoyant's) point of view. An insider's point of view allows audiences to observe their own inconsistencies and prejudices and then, hopefully, rectify them. It also encourages audiences that are already in the know to keep fighting for the cause, to keep working to create a culture of inclusivity, awareness, and equality.

Exploring the many cultural and rhetorical intersections of the Crafts' case reveals passing to be a democratic sensibility for acting powerfully in the world. It also reveals that race is a dangerous social construct, that women endure particular indignation and oppression in slavery, that passing's true subversion is in changing passers' class status, and that forced illiteracy is forced disability. In Ellen's and William's capable hands, passing is a form of rhetoric that uses irony to resist the singularity of rhetorical forms or identities. The growing intensity of resistance requires the Crafts and their audiences to recognize rhetorical appeals to false authorities (i.e., the law and its racial distinctions; slaveholding Christianity) and to expand their vision to take in at least two perspectives simultaneously (i.e., their own as passers and dupes-in-transition and Ellen's and William's as in-group clairvoyants). The Crafts' ironic rhetoric also helps to extract meaning from acts of passing that occurred after the abolition of slavery in the United States and abroad, which are similarly expressive of unique agencies in the face of new and different personae and structural constraints.

POSTSCRIPT

The Crafts' story of enslavement and passing does not end when readers close the book or with the Emancipation Proclamation. Enslavement and passing are still occurring in the United States and across the globe, and are taking on forms the Crafts might not have imagined. To begin with, there are more slaves today than there were during the Crafts' lifetime. According to the U.S. State Department's 2011 *Trafficking in Persons Report*, up to one hundred thousand people in the United States are in bondage and perhaps 27 million people worldwide, of which an estimated 9 million are children. Approximately 80 percent of this population is made up of women and girls.[67] The enslaved population continues to grow, with an estimated six hundred thousand to eight hundred thousand children, women, and men trafficked across international borders annually.[68] "Modern-day slaves face brutal conditions in rock quarries, rice mills, brick kilns, fisheries, garment factories, and many other industries around the world."[69] Like the Crafts, today's enslaved are deprived of freedom of movement, unable to leave the facilities where they are forced to labor, and unable to seek employment elsewhere.

Forced laborers (especially women and children) suffer the added brutalities of rape and vicious beatings.[70] Sreypov Chan is an example. When she was seven years old in Cambodia, Sreypov was sold into sex slavery until she finally escaped at age ten, with HIV.[71] While enslaved, Sreypov passed as a domestic worker at the same time that she was forced to work in a nearby brothel, sleeping with up to twenty clients daily. After Sreypov ran away, she passed as a person who had not been enslaved or infected by disease. Only now, after a decade of freedom and treatment, has Sreypov made the decision to speak out. She has described the horrors of her experiences and explained how the trade of "rape for profit thrives in the absence of robust law enforcement to ensure the protection of the law for vulnerable children and women."[72] Sreypov has also shared a few of the ways she and others used passing as a survival tactic before and after their escapes. Like the Crafts, she now tells her story to further the abolitionist cause. But Sreypov is careful not to divulge too much about passing as a survival tactic, so that she does not spoil it as a means of eluding death and enslavement for those whom it can help.

Sreypov Chan is not the only modern-day figure whose story parallels the Crafts' in significant ways. A *New York Times* article entitled "Afghan Boys Are Prized So Girls Live the Part" details how, for generations, girls have passed as boys in Afghanistan in order to bring honor to their families, to escape social criticism, and often to bring much needed economic support. Though extant statistics are unavailable concerning the number of Afghan girls who pass as boys, narrative evidence abounds. "Afghans of several generations can often tell a story of a female relative, friend, neighbor or co-worker who grew up disguised as a boy. To those who know, these children are often referred to as neither 'daughter' nor 'son' in conversation, but as 'bacha posh,' which literally means 'dressed up as a boy' in Dari. . . . In most cases, a return to womanhood takes place when the child enters puberty. The parents almost always make that decision." Like the Crafts' passing, *bacha posh* passing is about much more than masquerade. Acts of passing are about opening a space to understand how raced, gendered, classed, and cultural identities are constructed within specific historical and geographical situations. From this perspective, the similarities of *bacha posh* passers and Ellen Craft are astounding. Obviously, both stories involve females passing as males. Like Mr. Johnson, Ellen's acceptable persona, a *bacha posh* enjoys all the freedoms afforded to a male in her culture, including the right to have a job, to play sports, and to travel freely. Despite the clear crossing of gendered boundaries evident in these cases, other types of boundary crossing are performed rather than stated—class, political freedom, (dis)ability, race, and ethnicity. Additionally, both types of passing share the exigencies of segregation and social inequality. In the Crafts' case there is racial segregation and enslavement experienced differently on the bases of color and sex/gender. In *bacha posh* cases there is sex/gender segregation and discrimination. Ellen's and *bacha posh* girls' forays into boyhood and manhood have end points, from a few days to a few years. Ellen passed for four days to escape enslavement. *Bacha posh* girls pass for months or years to avoid the social stigma of girl-only families and to bring much-needed income into the home from the work they do as boys.

Additional parallels exist. Passing as a respectable young gentleman is an anxiety-ridden process. For instance, Ellen developed physical disabilities whenever there was a possibility for outing. She pretended to be deaf to avoid an acquaintance of her slave master's, she feigned rheumatism when white people became too friendly, and she fainted when two white ladies got too close for comfort and began to flirt with Mr. Johnson. And in 2010 Miina, a *bacha posh* passer, "is also nervous that she will be found out if one of her classmates recognizes her at the store. 'Every day she complains,' said her mother. 'I'm not comfortable around the boys in the store,' she says. 'I am a girl.' "[73] Ellen's reactions and Miina's statement are particularly telling of the separation between sex, gender, and resources in their worlds. On one hand, Afghan girls do not appear to face the same degree of legal or physical risk by passing that the Crafts did—including forced return to slavery and separation, fines, and physical punishment. On the other hand, we should not underestimate the fact that being shamed frightens *bacha posh* passers like Miina to their cores. Though it often goes unspoken, a rhetoric of shame suggests that all *bacha posh* passers are subject to a larger project of "social control" that generates and maintains socioeconomic differences along the axes of gender, race, and ability.[74] Miina's comment also suggests that shame and fear are connected to normative definitions of femininity and masculinity that need to be challenged.[75]

And here is where passing becomes subversive. Like Ellen Craft, former *bacha posh* passers understand that the traits of femininity, the very symbols that are used to make second class citizens out of women and diminish the quality of their lives, are socially constructed.[76] However, it would be wrong to say that the moral of their stories is for women to "act like men" in order to obtain their goals. A more accurate interpretation of Ellen Craft's and *bacha posh* passers' stories is that many women remain unable fully to express or represent themselves as women, and are therefore unable to bring lasting change to macrocultural traditions that minimize their roles.[77] What is more, Ellen Craft's and *bacha posh* passers' stories embody another subversive enthymeme: if society recognizes that a change of clothes and behavior can be enough to win a woman honor and freedom, perhaps that society will also recognize that no viable justification can be made for imposing social hierarchies that differentiate, enslave, shame and otherwise interfere with women's life chances.[78]

Some recognize and are now teaching lessons learned from Ellen Craft and *bacha posh* passers. Gender-neutral parenting and educating are gaining notoriety as radical child-rearing methods in the twenty-first century.[79] Those who advocate gender neutrality eschew the usual pink or blue color schemes, avoid gender-based language by referring to boys and girls as "friends," provide toy trucks and baby dolls to all children, and ultimately refuse to disclose children's biological sex.[80] Take Canadian parents Kathy Witterick and David Stocker as an example. The couple garnered mainstream media attention in the spring of 2011 when they announced the birth of their third child, Storm, and did not include any information about Storm's sex. The parents say that they want Storm to decide the gender with which he or she will ultimately identify over time.[81] Many people applaud the couple's decision. Others have expressed outrage over the decision and believe withholding gender identity information is a form of child abuse. Detractors are so outraged that some have threatened to report the parents to child welfare. The "storm" created by Witterick's and Stocker's decision suggests that gender-neutral parenting, like passing, may have its limitations and risks and also carries possibilities for challenging gender hierarchy.

The controversy over the disclosure of Storm's sex can also be seen as the latest chapter in an ongoing narrative of passing that extends from the Crafts' era to our own. Passing, a process that hinges on ambiguity, proves that legal and cultural prohibitions based on race and gender can be subverted. Passing also proves that enslaved, daughter-only, and gender-neutral families are unable to assert themselves as whole human beings under their existing social hierarchies. Passers' experiences allow us to envision options for different life outcomes under different circumstances. And passers' careful adaptations to legal and cultural prohibitions ultimately remind us of the great irony that passing requires the recurrence of boundaries and hierarchies in spite of all the suffering and misery they impose.

As Ellen and William Craft have demonstrated, the opportunity for progress is best seized after passers return to their pre-passing (and non-gender-neutral) identities. When the time for passing is over, one wonders how easy or difficult the transition to daily life will be. One also wonders if passing and gender-neutrality will change masculinity or femininity in any sustainable fashion. And one wonders to what extent today's race- and gender-bending passers will experience retribution or return to enslavement. Given the Crafts' example, one cannot be sure. Despite this uncertainty, the Crafts have made clear that none will be more able to answer these questions than the passers themselves—that is, if they are allowed to voice their rhetorical power freely and in their own words once they come out of the closet.

CHAPTER THREE

Passing as Property

Forty-six years after the Crafts boarded a train in Georgia to use passing as power, Homer A. Plessy boarded a train in Louisiana to use passing as property.[1] The plan was simple: imbue passing with a new meaning that would be exploited to challenge section 2 of Act 111 of the 1890 Louisiana legislature, An Act to Promote the Comfort of Passengers, or the Separate Car Act.[2] The new meaning was property. The challenge was simple enough: Pass as white. Purchase the ticket. Board the train. Pass as black. Ensure arrest. Get political.[3] On June 7, 1892, Plessy executed the first five parts of the plan. He passed as white in order to get the ticket and get on the train. He then passed as black in order to get arrested and booked. With the help of attorneys Albion Tourgée, James C. Walker, and Samuel F. Phillips, Plessy got political and fought the charges all the way to the U.S. Supreme Court in 1896. Plessy's legal team hoped to dismantle dominant racial categories and oppose the legitimacy of segregation by exposing a case of circular cause and consequence— the Court constructed the very racial categories on whose behalf its law claimed to act.[4] When Plessy lost the case, the effects reverberated throughout the nation, and segregation was institutionalized.[5] This chapter aims to figure out why the promise of Plessy's passing resulted in the penalty of segregation.[6]

Critics offer many explanations for Plessy's loss based on legal and historical context.[7] Because the case was argued on the basis of the Fourteenth Amendment's Equal Protection Clause[8] and was considered in the context of the precedent of the *Dred Scott* decision,[9] many maintain that *Plessy v. Ferguson* was just one of countless legislative cruelties toward nonwhite people. Other explanations blame the loss on capitalist priorities because this Supreme Court was the same one that protected corporations as "persons" under the Fourteenth Amendment.[10] Still other explanations suggest that Plessy lost due to lack of public awareness and outrage. Black newspapers such as the *Crusader* and the *Parsons Weekly Blade* covered and critiqued the case extensively, yet the mainstream press barely mentioned it;[11] the *New York Times*, for instance, covered the decision in its railway column.[12] What is suggested less often, however, is that Plessy lost because the Court transformed his passing into a theft of identity—the assumption of another's identity in order to break the law and acquire goods and services.[13]

Plessy's pass was a political act designed to disassemble dominant racial categories and challenge the utility of any law for which they are the basis. Reading Justice Henry Billings Brown's majority opinion as a response to Plessy's challenge explains how the Court eschews an in-group clairvoyant perspective and likens Plessy's passing to a theft of racial identity.[14] In so doing the Court embodies what I will call a "defensive dupe" persona. A defensive dupe is too invested in and empowered by racial hierarchy to take on an in-group clairvoyant perspective. As defensive dupe the Court reinscribes Plessy as "colored" and labels his passing as an appropriation—"making a thing private property, whether another's or one's own."[15] I liken the Court's institutionalization of segregation to a firewall, or security measure installed to defuse the political panic that multiracial identities and passing induce. The striking resemblance between the Court's take on Plessy's passing and what we now call identity theft holds valuable implications for contemporary culture wars and conceptions of identity in a networked world.

PLESSY'S PASSING

Practically every phase of the plan that culminated in *Plessy v. Ferguson* was touched by issues of multiracial identities and passing—from its location in New Orleans and its Creole context, to the activist group involved and its carefully chosen passer, to legal arguments presented before and made by the Court.[16] Historians describe New Orleans's late nineteenth-century Creole community as not exactly white or black and not exactly free or enslaved.[17] New Orleans operated in a three-tiered system with whites at the top, Creoles in the middle, and blacks at the bottom.[18] But there was one complication: an observer could not necessarily determine the race to which a face belonged.[19] Racial indeterminacy created a cultural and epistemological crisis and provided a context for considering the insurgent properties of passing. First, passing could be exploited to challenge the assumption that obvious and distinct biological racial lines existed. Second, passing proved a person could not be classified racially based on appearance and that society was actually classifying people by law. The Separate Car Act of 1890, because it sought to solidify dominant racial categories and erase the middle, especially threatened members of the Creole community. Segregation law called forth a new *episteme* that would only recognize a black-white racial dichotomy—no ambiguities allowed.[20] Yet it is incorrect to assume that Creoles opposed the Act simply because it threatened their relatively privileged place between blacks and whites in the racial hierarchy. Rather, the Creole community realized that the Act was part of a larger imposed "Americanization" of their region and erasure of their unique culture.[21] Far from using it in an attempt to expand white privilege, the Creole community deployed passing to challenge white supremacy by undermining the epistemological security and constitutionality of racial categories and, by consequence, the legality of racial segregation.

Prominent Creole citizens of Louisiana joined forces in protest of the Separate Car Act and created the Comité des Citoyens in September 1891.[22] The Comité sought to test the constitutionality of the Act by staging violations of the law. The East Louisiana Railroad Company supported the Comité's efforts because it found that maintaining separate facilities for white and colored passengers would be expensive. With corporate and political sponsorship in place, Plessy's pass emerged as the second of two plans formulated to test the interstate and intrastate features of the Act.[23] Plessy, a shoemaker from New Orleans's Treme neighborhood, was the perfect passer. Self-identified as an "octoroon" (seven-eighths European and one-eighth African ancestry), Plessy was selected specifically because his racial ambiguity could be read as an exception to the one-drop rule of hypodescent.[24] Hypodescent consigned multiracial individuals to the "colored" group, thereby appearing to resolve the dilemmas of miscegenation and categorization by forcing people to pass as black. Plessy's willingness and ability to pass were used as instruments of protest against hypodescent and laws for which it served as bedrock.

The protest began June 7, 1892. Passing as white, Plessy bought a one-way ticket aboard the East Louisiana Railway, boarding in New Orleans and headed toward Covington (*Password Four*). Reminiscent of Ellen Craft, Plessy paid the higher fare and dressed appropriately in a suit and hat, giving him the appearance of a respectable gentleman who was used to traveling in first-class accommodations.[25] Plessy then "entered a passenger train and took possession of a vacant seat in a coach where passengers of the white race were accommodated."[26] As the train moved away from the station, its white conductor, J. J. Dowling, collected tickets. When Dowling reached Plessy's seat he paused and asked, "Are you a colored man?" Plessy answered yes (*Password Two*). Dowling told Plessy to remove himself and take a seat in the colored car where he belonged. Plessy refused, stating that he was a U.S. citizen who had purchased a first-class ticket and expected to ride in the first-class car. Dowling again asked Plessy to leave, and he would not.

Dowling stopped the train, disembarked, and returned a few minutes later with Detective Christopher C. Cain to handle the situation. Cain informed Plessy that he should ride in the colored car. Again, Plessy refused and added that he would rather be arrested and imprisoned than leave his seat. And so it was. Plessy was arrested publicly and charged with Violating section 2 of the Separate Car Act.[27] Few realized that Cain had been hired as the railroad company's in-group clairvoyant to make the arrest and forcibly remove Plessy from the train after Plessy admitted that he was "colored" (*Password Two*).[28] Plessy was released the following day on a five-hundred-dollar bond and was later represented by Tourgée and associates at trial.

TOURGÉE'S ARGUMENT

When the case reached the Supreme Court in April 1896, Tourgée presented Plessy's passing as a challenge to the legal construction of dominant racial categories. Articulating an in-group clairvoyant perspective and suggesting that passing makes dupes out of us all, Tourgée argued that the very concept of racial identity (or *episteme*) could not be divorced from the institutions that assign it (*Password One*). By focusing on the unstable and arbitrary process of racial classification, proven by the fact that passers and dupes exist, he hoped to use Plessy's passing as a way to void all racial categories (*Password Two*). Tourgée's brief before the Court explains:

> The act in question . . . proceeds upon the hypothesis that the State has the right to authorize and require the officers of a railway to assort the citizens who engage in passage on its lines. . . . The gist of our case is the unconstitutionality of the assortment. . . . The question is not as to the equality of the privileges enjoyed, but the right of the State to label one citizen as white and another as colored in the common enjoyment of a common highway.[29]

Equality was not the issue for Tourgée. Rather, the issue was the legal right to racial assignment along the "common highway," which emphasized the identifications and divisions inherent in racial determination. Tourgée's arguments proved as much when he later declared that interracial romantic relationships and multiracial identities were matters of fact. The fact that individuals like Plessy existed, Tourgée argued, proved that racial intermixture would not result in the end of civilization. It would only result in the inability to "label one citizen as white and another as colored." Tourgée's argument was based on the idea of getting around the "common highway" afforded Plessy by a history of racial intermixture and intermarriage.[30] Tourgée implied that an individual like Plessy simply could not define himself in monoracial terms and thus had not breached any law by taking a seat in the first-class car.[31]

With prescience, Tourgée went on to note the law's efforts to consolidate multiracial identities and dislocate intrinsic notions of self onto the exterior mechanisms of skin color, property, and privacy. Tourgée urged the Court to acknowledge and correct these efforts when he introduced the concept of property and offered the following scenario for consideration:

> How much would it be worth to a young man entering upon the practice of law to be regarded as a *white* man rather than a colored one? Six-sevenths of the population are white. Nineteenth-twentieths of the property of the country is owned by white people. . . . Under

these conditions, is it possible to conclude that the reputation of being white is not property? Indeed, is it not the most valuable sort of property, being the master-key that unlocks the golden door of opportunity?[32]

Tourgée doubted racial identity was as much a part of one's internal consciousness as it was a performance of ownership regulated by judicial rhetoric (*Password One*). He painted Plessy's apparent whiteness as a valuable commodity because whiteness "unlocks the golden door of opportunity." Tourgée thereby implied that the devaluation of blackness can be traced to slavery, wherein blacks were actually treated as property. To solidify the point, Tourgée attempted to demonstrate that a whites-only space was already privileged as a basis for property rights.[33] He argued that if a white person was required to sit in a colored car, then he or she should sue for damages because his or her white privilege was denied and reputation was stained. Whiteness, according to Tourgée, is like an American Express card—something one should never leave home without. Clearly meaning this remark as a sarcastic take on the instability of racial categories and as a connection to the economics of racial categorization and hierarchy, Tourgée did not foresee that it was precisely on these grounds that the Court would ultimately deny Plessy's right to "own" white identity.

The Court supported the presupposition that a person's reputation as white could afford that person property rights to possess, use, enjoy, and own white privilege.[34] But it denied that right and its expressions to Plessy because he could pass as white and as "colored" (*Password Three*).[35] Thus, Plessy's biracial passing was both the condition and the resolution of the case. Plessy began by appropriating passing as a way to show that racial categories were not givens but symbolic social constructions (*Password One*). By taking one part of his identity for the whole, in two distinct and related instances as white and then as black, Plessy occupied a space the law said he could not occupy—a racial identity that was "colored" white. Plessy's passing thereby challenged dominant racial categories, dissolving their apparently seamless, natural integrity into disparate bits and pieces of customs, attitudes, and legalese.[36]

Tourgée concluded by arguing that even if definitive racial categorization were attainable, its deployment to segregate the populace would be unconstitutional and unethical. In his argument he affirmed the authority of juridical rhetoric in constructing racial categories and identities and respectfully requested that the Court dismantle dominant racial categories and laws such categories upheld. The Court responded to Plessy and Tourgée by transforming Plessy's passing into an actual identity crime based on immorality, impurity, and appropriation (*Password Five*). It is to these transformations that we now turn.

MAJORITY DECISION TO CONTAIN PLESSY'S THREAT

While Tourgée argued for the insecurity of racial categories based on the subversive qualities of passing as white and as black, the Court sought a way to address the weakness exposed and resecure dominant racial categories (*Passwords One, Three, Six*). Acting as a defensive dupe—a persona too entrenched in and privileged by dominant racial hierarchy to consider undoing it—the Court needed to secure the nation's racial borders and counteract the threat of Plessy's passing. And if whiteness did carry a property interest, as Tourgée suggested, then the Court could assert that whiteness was subject to theft and needed to be protected. It is precisely in terms of protecting the property interest in whiteness, and appropriating the logic of Plessy's passing, that Justice Brown delivered the Court's majority opinion (*Password Five*).

Brown began by situating his response in terms of nature, and the natures of political and social equalities. "Political equality" refers to the realms of government and representation. "Social equality" is shorthand for interracial contact, typified by sexual intimacy, and evidenced by Plessy's ancestry and ability to pass as white and as black (*Password Three*).[37] He declared,

> The object of the [Fourteenth] amendment was undoubtedly to enforce the absolute equality of the two races before the law, but in the nature of things it could not have been intended to abolish distinctions based upon color, or to enforce social, as distinguished from political equality, or a commingling of the two races upon terms unsatisfactory to either. Laws permitting, and even requiring, their separation in places where they are liable to be brought into contact do not necessarily imply the inferiority of either race to the other, and have been generally, if not universally, recognized as within the competency of the state legislatures in the exercise of their police power.... The [Plaintiff in Error's] argument also assumes that social prejudices may be overcome by legislation, and that equal rights cannot be secured to the negro except by an enforced commingling of

the two races. We cannot accept this proposition. If the two races are
to meet upon terms of social equality, it must be the result of natural
affinities, a mutual appreciation of each other's merits and a voluntary consent of individuals.[38]

Brown's position was simple. Political rights were in the Court's
domain. Social rights were in the domain of nature. Thus, Plessy
and Tourgée were not necessarily wrong but had embarked on a
wrongheaded political project. Segregation was not an institution
to be forced upon the nation by the Court's authority, but was part
of a natural order that the Court was compelled to preserve or rel-
egate to the "reasonable" sensibilities of each state and "voluntary
consent of individuals." Aware that a closer reading revealed the
states' varying formulas for calculating racial difference, Brown
dismissed the variances as being "not properly put at issue" by
Tourgée.[39] Brown's appeal to individuals' "voluntary consent"
also strengthened the *Dred Scott* decision (1857), which ruled that
"colored" people had no rights that white people were bound to
respect. What "colored" people desired was of no consequence.
Only the "voluntary consent" of white individuals mattered.
Therefore, Brown's dismissal denied "colored" persons equal protection at the federal level and left them without redress in fighting
for citizenship at the state level. The dismissal had the simultaneous effect of protecting the exclusive nature of white identity,
thereby setting a precedent that was not rejected fully until the
Civil Rights Acts of 1964 and 1968.

Brown added biology to his discussion of nature to appeal to
what the Court declared was right, proper, legal, and fair. The
opinion plays on fears of social equality (read miscegenation) by
defining Plessy's racial identity as an "octoroon" with an ambiguous racial appearance. Concentrating on Plessy's racial ambiguity
reinforces white supremacy and suggests that the taboo of interracial heterosexual sex must be further contained because it yields a
blackness that is not necessarily visible. Brown then appropriated
the logic of Plessy's passing—that race is a social construction that
privileges whiteness—to preserve racial distinctions and the properties of natural order.

> It is claimed by the plaintiff in error that, in any mixed community,
> the reputation of belonging to the dominant race, in this instance the
> white race, is property, in the same sense that a right of action, or of
> inheritance, is property. Conceding this to be so, for the purposes

of this case, we are unable to see how this statute deprives him of, or in any way affects his right to, such property. If he be a white man and assigned to a colored coach, he may have his action for damages against the company for being deprived of his so called property. Upon the other hand, if he be a colored man and be so assigned, he has been deprived of no property, since he is not lawfully entitled to the reputation of being a white man.[40]

Appropriating the logic of Plessy's passing and Tourgée's argument serves several functions. First, it positions the white race as normative and dominant and therefore allows whiteness to assume a dominant and uncontested position.[41] The Court framed white identity as natural and not social or rhetorical, implying that we need not explain why or how it came to be so.[42] The Court appealed to nature as *episteme,* declaring that white dominance is a fact and we all already *know* it. However, naturalized dominance bears mentioning as part of the Court's strategy to assert the power of whiteness rhetorically before it can be justified and enacted socially. The naturalization of whiteness as an empowered and entitled property served to enhance the Court's authority on challenges to segregation based on passing and multiracial identities but limit the Court's power to challenge natural racial hierarchy. Brown summarized:

> So far, then . . . the case reduces itself to the question whether the statute of Louisiana is a reasonable regulation, and with respect to this there must necessarily be a large discretion on the part of the legislature. In determining the question of reasonableness it is at liberty to act with reference to the established usages, customs and traditions of the people, and with a view to the promotion of their comfort, and the preservation of the public peace and good order. Gauged by this standard, we cannot say that a law which authorizes or even requires the separation of the two races in public conveyances is unreasonable.[43]

Translating the Court's earlier "natural" and "dominant" vocabulary of whiteness into a cultural vocabulary of "established uses, customs, and traditions" for the people's "comfort," Brown began to construct whiteness as a zone of privacy ordered by nature and, therefore, naturally resistant to legal interference.[44] As a zone of privacy whiteness becomes entitled to unobservability (not being watched or scrutinized), self-determination (that whiteness could only be used in ways that white people approve and understand), and "comfort" (the right to be left alone in "private").[45] The only power the Court rightfully held was to uphold the natural order of white supremacy and therefore to uphold segregation on that basis.

Second, the Court's concession that whiteness is private, protected property reified the relation between racial identity and the ownership one has to oneself.[46] The Court appropriated the logic of Plessy's passing to argue that passing is proof of the value of whiteness as ascribed by natural law and that whiteness had to be protected by the Court as separate, private, first-class accommodation. The Court's decision rests on notions of biological purity and uniqueness, suggesting that white identity is private in its "natural" state and unspoiled by any other lines of blood. The high value of white identity is solidified by institutionalizing segregation to maintain white racial purity and increase the value of white over black. Segregation then becomes increasingly valuable as a way to augment and maintain white identity's high property values. And so rights to own, protect, and privatize whiteness are institutionalized.

Next, the Court equated passing with a renunciation of the property rights to whiteness. The Court claimed that Plessy's ability to pass as white and black meant that he did not own an unspoiled natural whiteness. Plessy's whiteness was white in appearance only and therefore painted as impure and artificial. In contrast, and from an in-group clairvoyant's perspective, Tourgée argued that the Court stole Plessy's property interest in his white appearance when it determined his racial identity metonymically by way of the one-drop rule. Nevertheless, as a defensive dupe (a dupe who realizes he has been duped and refuses to take on an in-group clairvoyant's perspective), the Court took great pains to emphasize that if Plessy truly "owned" his whiteness, then he would not have been passing in the first place. And Plessy certainly would not have admitted that he was passing (as white). Rather, it was Plessy's "one eighth African blood" that motivated his pass and ensured that he would not partake of white privilege.[47] Removing Plessy's right to white identity served two functions for maintaining the Court's defensive dupe perspective. It solidified the belief in white dominance by locating the flaw of Plessy's racial identity in the taints of "African blood" and multiracial ancestry. It also upheld the belief that the Court's system for racial categorization and resource allocation was equitable and fair, allowing defensive dupes to purge any guilt that might be felt over ignoring how white racial dominance was maintained.

The Court added insult to injury when it opined that in passing, Plessy also violated his relationship to his true (devalued) identity as "colored," removing his ground for self-ownership of either white or black identity. Brown masterfully reversed the logic of passing that allowed passers to express multiracial identities in monoracial terms (*Password Three*). To do this he relied on hypodescent to make multiracial identities valuable only in terms of the "colored" identities for which they could be exchanged (*Password Three*). Adding multiracial identities to the "colored" category meant that whiteness remained dominant, natural, pure, private, and increasingly valuable. The threat of Plessy's passing was neutralized, and the Court was now free to institutionalize segregation as a way to keep "colored" people out of whiteness and out of the private spaces white people occupied and dominated. As the defensive dupe, the Court transformed Plessy's passing from political tool of dissent into a political tool that upheld dominant racial categories and justified segregation.

To use the critical vocabulary of passing, Plessy's biracial passing (*Password Four*) was meant to transform dupes into in-group clairvoyants and to empower in-group clairvoyants throughout the nation (*Password Six*). In this case it did the opposite and caused dupes to become defensive dupes. As a defensive dupe, the Court imbued white and "colored" racial categories with symbolic meaning, making the latter inferior to the former, and institutionalized that inferiority by creating two mutually evolving and separate social worlds whose borders required continual maintenance.[48] Racial borders were maintained by linking an individual's natural rights to her "natural" racial identity and place in the natural racial and social order.

The Court's claims to uphold unalterable "natural" racial identity, order, and rights were subsidized by its depiction of Plessy's passing and right to white identity as appropriations—"invasions of privacy whereby one person takes the name or likeness of another for . . . gain."[49] In short, the Court asserted that Plessy deliberately acquired whiteness without the permission of the dominant white group.[50] Passing became a violation of privacy because Plessy used and enjoyed whiteness and its privileges to obtain special treatment as a "colored" person.[51] The threat of such use and enjoyment was profound because it meant that every white persona a passer projected was a violation of privacy and a theft, a means of unauthorized access to different social, cultural, and economic spaces (*Passwords Three, Four*). In defensive dupes' hands, racial categories became identity cards that protected whiteness by indicating how socioeconomic privileges were distributed.[52] In Plessy's hands passing became a form of property, an experiment with a new form of subjectivity, and Plessy became suspect in the eyes of the Court for exactly that reason. Ultimately, the Court's majority opinion appropriated the logic of Plessy's passing as a call to dismantle dominant racial categories and reframed it as an actual identity crime—an illegal appropriation of whiteness in the contexts of controlled access and private property.

HARLAN'S DISSENT

A small glimmer of hope was provided by Justice John Harlan's dissent when he wrote that "our Constitution is color-blind, and neither knows nor tolerates classes among citizens. In respect of civil rights, all citizens are equal before the law."[53] Historians and legal scholars speculate that Harlan's appeal to color-blindness might have been related to his relationship with his half-black half brother, Robert Harlan.[54] But any hope of living up to a color-blind ideal was dashed by closer examination of the dissent, in which Harlan succumbed to white supremacist thinking and proved that interracial social contact within families was not a panacea for racism. Harlan explained, "The white race deems itself to be the dominant race in this country. And so it is. . . . So, I doubt not, it will continue to be for all time, if it remains true to its great heritage."[55] Because Harlan introduced the concept of color-blindness only after he appealed to white superiority and dominance, his color-blind interpretation of the Constitution actually completed the work of the Court as defensive dupe. Not only did Harlan's rhetoric legitimize the social, economic, and political aspects of white privilege, it also further cemented the link between passing and illegal appropriation.[56]

First, Harlan conceded that the white race was naturally dominant and required zones of privacy whose borders were enforced. This left nonwhite groups with no other recourse but to demand equality by entering private white spaces even while it remained an act of white privilege to grant entrance and equality. In no way did this aspect of Harlan's dissent contradict the majority opinion offered by the Court. In fact, it bolstered the Court's position as defensive dupe and its authority to perpetuate racial subordination by labeling passing as an act of appropriation.[57] Second, rather than explaining what racial jargon such as "white" and "colored" actually meant, Harlan continued to disguise the Court's role in the creation of such categories. The closest Harlan came to providing racial definitions was when he positioned dominant racial categories as different from each other and similarly opposed to Chinese. For Harlan, Chinese are the "race so different . . . that we do not permit those belonging to it to become citizens of the United States. Persons belonging to it are, with few exceptions, absolutely excluded from our country."[58] Harlan's anti-Chinese xenophobic rhetoric reinforced the conception of Chinese as the "yellow peril" and supported the Court's earlier decision to uphold the Chinese Exclusion Act (1884).[59] In addition, it proved that racial formation in the United States had never been a strictly black-and-white conversation.[60] Neither Harlan nor the Court held that people should be treated equally regardless of their racial backgrounds and nations of origin. The Court's opinion ruled despite the Constitution's alleged color-blindness. The key feature of Harlan's dissent, then, was its embodiment of a defensive dupe persona and its refusal to grant social equality on the basis of natural white supremacy.

Finally, Harlan's position of white dominance and his defensive dupe persona simultaneously acknowledged, privatized, and contained racialist assumptions within the space of social rather than political rights.[61] Harlan's appeal to privacy was a pernicious and subtle affront to liberty and justice as well as a powerful mode of justifying savage inequalities.[62] As in the majority decision, Harlan's dissent exploited and succumbed to fears of social equality (i.e., interracial sexual contact), and his argument therefore would not eradicate racial categories, private racial spaces, or define passing as anything other than an appropriation or breach of privacy and security of dominant racial categories.

The majority decision and dissent used the trope of appropriation to reverse the (synecdochic and metonymic) logic of Plessy's pass and embody a defensive dupe persona (*Password Five*). Because the Court connected racial identity to property and natural order, its interpretation of Plessy's passing can be viewed as a forerunner to the crime of identity theft. To introduce this claim, I have explained how Tourgée used passing to posit racial identity as external both to the consciousness of the self and to biology, challenging the Court's natural and accepted usage of the concept. I then explained how the Court defined racial identity as property worth protecting from passers by taking on a defensive dupe persona. Now it is necessary to make the comparison between the Court's interpretation of Plessy's passing and identity theft explicit.[63]

PLESSY'S PASSING AND THE THREAT OF IDENTITY THEFT

The Court's depiction of Plessy's passing bears a striking resemblance to the contemporary crime of identity theft. The Federal Trade Commission defines identity theft as the appropriation of an individual's personal information to provide access to goods and services under an assumed identity.[64] As with passing, individuals attempt to gain access to private social spaces to enjoy members' exclusive rights and privileges. As in *Plessy v. Ferguson*, today's law defines identity as a form of property used by individuals to refer to themselves as persons and used by others to identify them as "unique and particular persons."[65] The law also defines identity as private. A private conception of identity relates less to an individual's conscious self-concept and more to the ability of others to distinguish and recognize that person as a unique entity. Thus, to learn or establish a person's identity involves reference to some set of institutional or socially agreed upon identifying factors that authenticate a person's uniqueness in relation to others. In the case of passing such factors are certain kinds of appearances and bloodlines that are required for systemic representation. In the case of identity theft, factors include birthdates, names, social security numbers, passwords, contacts, and geographical locations.[66] Identifying factors are utilized to authenticate identity and, therefore, become a crucial gauge of socioeconomic value by transforming appropriation into theft.

Let us return to the Court's interpretation of Plessy's passing to make the point clear. Legally, Plessy exercised a right to which he was not entitled because he was not white. This raises the question of whether racial identity can be reclaimed, recouped, and reestablished. My reading of the majority opinion and dissent in *Plessy v. Ferguson* suggests that the answer is yes. Plessy's passing undergoes a four-stage process in the Court's majority ruling consistent with the stages of identity theft outlined by the Federal Trade Commission: an acquisition of white identity through a breach of privacy; the appropriation and unauthorized use of said identity for socioeconomic gain or privilege; the transformation and discovery of appropriated identity; and finally, the repair of identity (recouping losses, reestablishing reputation and status quo).[67] From the passer's and in-group clairvoyants' perspectives, Plessy's pass began as political protest against segregation. It was interpreted by the Court as a theft of white racial identity and as a circumvention of natural law protected by the Constitution. The Court had to shore up the power it lost by acknowledging Plessy's multiracial ancestry, which exposed the Court and not nature as the authorizing force behind the propertied racial self and its commodification.

As an antecedent form of identity theft, Plessy's passing provided an occasion for the law to tighten security around zones of privacy by creating tracking devices that located and authenticated information about people. Today we would call these tracking devices legal documents, passwords, identification numbers, or biometrics. In the *Plessy* case ancestry, race, and skin color functioned as biometric tracking devices that provided proof of a person's identity. The Court considered Plessy's pass a simple identity theft because he took hold of whiteness without authorization to break the law and invade a private whites-only space. The Court's argument relies on a specific definition of identity that can be appropriated if the passer knows the password.

Password Seven

Passing reveals whose identities are valued as property, how much they are worth, and what defensive dupes will do to protect them.

Password Seven is consistent with the property-oriented pattern of American jurisprudence that informed the Court's decision in *Plessy v. Ferguson* and consistent with the Identity Theft and Assumption Deterrence Act of 1998, its 2004 amendment, and the Real ID Act of 2005.[68] *Plessy v. Ferguson* and identity theft laws simultaneously create and identify citizens, making particular identities the measures by which opportunity, privilege, and power are accessed. Appropriations of identity are labeled invasions. Like the Court's ruling in *Plessy v. Ferguson*, today's identity theft and REAL ID laws cement identity as a matter of property value and consider appropriation as invasion.

Legal definitions of identity as private property and appropriation as invasion are not the only qualities the Court's interpretation of Plessy's passing and legal definitions of identity theft share. Length of time is also a critical factor. As in part-time passing, the "duration" of identity theft can range from a single incident lasting only moments to the lifelong use of another's personal information—passing full-time as someone else.[69] Duration of the pass or theft is often associated with the "level of immersion."[70] Permanent identity theft characteristically involves a greater penetration into another's personal details than a one-time incident.[71] The level of immersion refers to the depth with which the identity thief delves into another's private identity and to the range and extent of the personal details that are appropriated. Like passing, identity theft can result from the possession of the most basic details about an individual, such as race, name, and date of birth, to more complex cases involving a deeper level of immersion whereby a host of personal and financial details are uncovered to prolong the act (i.e., employment history, education, social security number, and bank account details).[72]

Like part-time and full-time passing, duration and level of immersion provide a basis for establishing a twofold categorization of identity theft. A permanent adoption of all the victim's personal details is classified as "total identity theft," while the temporary use of some of the victim's personal details could be more appropriately termed "partial identity theft."[73] Typically, partial identity theft and part-time passing involve the transient adoption of an aspect of identity to the extent that is necessary to cross some social or legal boundary (i.e., national border, PIN number, or racial segregation). This is epitomized by the property-oriented approach taken to passing in *Plessy v. Ferguson* and to identity theft taken in the Identity Theft and Assumption Deterrence Act of 1998, which makes it an offense to "knowingly transfer or use, without lawful authority, a means of identification of another person with the intent to commit, or aid and abet, any unlawful activity."[74] This approach clearly limits the parameters of identity theft to the deliberate use of another's personal information—identity— in order to break the law. Total identity theft, however, provides a way in which an individual can perhaps escape from an unsatisfying life experience and begin anew.[75] The impulse to rewrite one's identity may stem from a general sense of dissatisfaction with one's own identity or may be a way to escape from some particularly problematic aspect of life (i.e., segregation). It has been theorized that total identity theft, like full-time passing, can provide a material and symbolic respite from a stigmatized identity by enabling the individual to escape the stigma and acquire a legal identity that is in accord with his or her desired life outcomes.[76]

The final characteristic that the Court's interpretation of Plessy's passing and identity theft laws share is the reliance on personae and detection (*Password Two*). Like passing, identity theft requires three major participants: "the impostor, the creditor, and the credit bureau."[77] The impostor can be likened to the passer, and the creditor can be likened to the dupe. By adopting a different identity, the passer or identity thief increases his or her chances of avoiding detection with the help of another persona—the credit bureau.

The credit bureau, however, is not easily likened to the in-group clairvoyant, though it serves a similar function. The role of the credit bureau is debated. For the purposes of our discussion, we must concede that the credit bureau is not necessarily in collusion with the identity thief in the way that the in-group clairvoyant is typically in collusion with the passer to protect his or her privacy. However, analysts argue that the success of identity theft depends on whether the credit bureau finds and reports theft to the victim and creditor. Bureau officials argue that the credit bureau cannot be in collusion with the identity thief because bureaus are often exploited by consumers even when there is no identity theft.[78] Activists argue that credit bureaus are in collusion with identity theft because they are not protecting consumers but making it easier for thieves to access personal information. For instance, credit bureaus share consumer information with credit card companies unless consumers opt out. Moreover, increasing instances of identity theft create a new market of account security alerts from which credit bureaus earn profit. But there is another party to consider: the victim of identity theft. For even if the victim is able to establish that he or she has been impersonated, this generally leaves authorities with few clues to point them in the direction of the perpetrator. The greater the damage and loss of privacy, the sooner the theft is recognized. Similarly, the Court saw itself as the entity which authorized racial identities and victim of Plessy's passing. Consequently, Plessy's passing became an invasion that could only be recognized when detected and that had to be stopped as soon as it was detected. Because detection is so critical to the success of Plessy's passing and to identity theft, we can see how both acts rely on multiple audiences who acknowledge contradictory rhetorics of identification (*Password Two*).

As a result of the definitions, duration, level of immersion, and detection shared by the Court's interpretation of Plessy's passing and how we think about identity theft today, a correlation can be made between the high values of disembodied flow of personal information online and the high value placed on fluid racial identifications afforded by an ambiguous racial appearance. Just as the Federal Trade Commission warns that identity thieves are abetted by the social mobility, anonymity, and discursive nature of the Internet, the *New York Times* reports that "both in the mainstream and at the high end of the marketplace, what is perceived as good, desirable, successful is often a face whose heritage is hard to pin down."[79] From a defensive dupe's perspective racially ambiguous passers like Plessy are comparable to today's identity thieves because of the fluid nature of identity they (dis)embody. Plessy's passing and identity theft crimes have provided the law with occasions to differentiate and consolidate identities at the same time.[80] Disembodied personal information and racial ambiguity mean that we cannot tell who is who by simple ocular proof. Instead, the ability to tell who is who is fused to a legal rhetoric that defines identity as private property worth protecting and passing as a theft of racial identity.

IMPLICATIONS FOR PASSING AND IDENTITY THEFT IN THE TWENTY-FIRST CENTURY

Growing concerns over identity theft and passing present broad implications for political life, particularly in a post–September 11 digital age. Increasing rates of identity theft have resulted in a popular desire for heightened security and policies and laws reforming national intelligence, and a variety of identification categories.[81] In terms of racial identification and public policy, neoconservative Ward Connerly employed racially ambiguous and rights-oriented rhetoric to protect racial privacy rights by ending racially based legal initiatives.[82] Connerly's infamous Proposition 54, Classification by Race, Ethnicity, Color or National Origin, also known as the Racial Privacy Initiative, proposed that "the state shall not classify any individual by race, ethnicity, color or national origin in the operation of public education, public contracting or public employment."[83] In support of this proposition, Connerly argued that race is a form of private property that should not be disclosed (i.e., should be protected) because it has no bearing on an individual's character or qualification. Connerly called on "color-blindness" as the antidote to racism because he equated race with racism—the use of phenotype in the interests of negative discrimination.[84] In order to make this argument, Connerly conveniently ignored what played out so dramatically in the *Plessy* ruling and dissent: (1) Color-blindness serves the interests of white supremacy and privilege. (2) Oppressive policies can appeal to color-blindness by dismissing race as either a fixed natural construction or as an unfixed symbolic social construction that can be appropriated.[85] (3) Privatizing racial identity upholds rather than undoes structural and institutional inequalities. As in the *Plessy* ruling, racial privacy initiatives protect state interests and not citizens' rights by preserving a context in which white supremacy goes unchallenged.[86]

We have seen new iterations of laws that link identity, property, privacy, and security in Arizona's SB 1070, Mississippi's SB 2179, South Carolina's SB 20, and Georgia's and Utah's newly passed immigration laws, measures that allow law enforcement officers to verify a person's immigration status during a routine traffic stop or while enforcing other laws. Alabama's HB 56 takes matters a step further by requiring schools, landlords, and businesses to verify the immigration status of their students, tenants, and employees, respectively. It also makes giving a ride to an undocumented immigrant in the state of Alabama a crime.[87] As indicated in Harlan's dissent, negotiating black-white racial identity in the United States always operates in conjunction with those races and ethnicities considered foreign, represented by an underclass that often immigrates for the purposes of labor. In Plessy's time this underclass was the Chinese, who were subject to various legal restrictions, including prohibitions on obtaining education, entering licensed professions, and owning real property. Heightened security measures imposed by contemporary anti-immigration laws place similar restrictions

on undocumented immigrants as "illegal aliens" (i.e., stereotypi-
cally considered Central and South American Hispanic populations). These similarities suggest that the threats of passing as a
U.S. citizen are proportionate with the threat Plessy posed to the
Court as a racial identity thief, making passing an ongoing issue
of public policy and public value. Enacting rights and privileges of
U.S. citizenship is precisely the property right Plessy and his attorneys set out to make available to all by appealing to the Fourteenth
Amendment.

Plessy's example of using passing to expose political hypocrisy
is also followed by today's immigration activists. In an autobiographical exposé in the *New York Times* entitled "My Life as an
Undocumented Immigrant," Jose Antonio Vargas explains how
passing as a U.S. citizen since the age of twelve affected his life
and work as a reporter for the *Washington Post*. Vargas may not
be considered the stereotypical "illegal alien," which is one reason why his story resonates so profoundly with mainstream audiences. He describes his eighteen-year experience as "an odd sort of
dance: I was trying to stand out in a highly competitive newsroom,
yet I was terrified that if I stood out too much, I'd invite unwanted
scrutiny. I tried to compartmentalize my fears, distract myself by
reporting on the lives of other people, but there was no escaping
the central conflict in my life. [Passing] for so long distorts your
sense of self. You start wondering who you've become, and why."[88]
Like all full-time passers, and the in-group clairvoyants who keep
their secrets, Vargas wondered what would happen if dupes found
out (*Password Two*). He became downright paranoid, especially
after he won the Pulitzer Prize in 2008. Vargas wondered if he
would be fired, deported, or worse: arrested and tried as someone
who stole the rights and privileges of U.S. citizenship. The answer
is currently unknown. Despite this uncertainty, Vargas, like Plessy
and his lawyers, publicly embodied the role of in-group clairvoyant and took the risk of outing himself. Like Plessy, Vargas will
work with legal counsel and hopes that the consequence of telling
his story will be to better the lives of those who share his social
location. Like Plessy's, Vargas's passing is about having enough
agency to feel a sense of control over who he is, how he communicates that information, and how, as a result of his communication,
others come to understand him. Like Plessy, Vargas hopes that
his passing and outing will be seen more as a form of courageous

political protest and less as a sociopolitical threat. Like Plessy, Vargas may not get the outcome he desires. Yet to stop there is to miss the full impact of the Court's interpretation of Plessy's passing and the privileges of U.S. citizenship in our increasingly networked present-day context.

The threat of Plessy's passing as it pertains to property, privacy, and identity theft continues to rear its head in controversies over advertising content and personal data–capturing algorithms embedded in mobile technology applications.[89] In 2010 the *Wall Street Journal* reported that popular mobile application games such as Angry Birds and game applications developed for social networks like MySpace and Facebook were merely private information (read identity)–grabbing devices passing as entertainment.[90] Angry Birds, the most notorious offender, is a ninety-nine-cent game that has captivated millions by asking them to participate in a revenge fantasy against "the green pigs who stole the Birds' eggs."[91] The game has been downloaded upwards of 12 million times since its release in December 2009 and reaped incredible financial rewards for its creators, Finnish studio Rovio Mobile.[92] But according to Peter Vesterbacka, the CEO of Rovio, "Angry Birds to us is more than a game."[93] The *Wall Street Journal* agreed when it reported that Angry Birds was the most serious privacy violator it found, alleged to be transmitting the most types of private information to third parties for profit—users' locations, ages, and genders, users' contact lists, phone numbers, and phone identification numbers.[94] It seems that "collective intelligence" and "digital fingerprints" left by billions of netizens may be finishing what the *Plessy v. Ferguson* decision started by replacing individual privacy with institutional privacy.[95]

Based on the law's broad concept of identity as a form of private property established in *Plessy v. Ferguson*, these applications appear to be violating users' privacy by appropriating their identifying information for a profit. Though such use would seem illegal in the context of our discussion of passing and identity theft, it is not because corporations also have a right to privacy. Software development firms' corporate appropriation of users' identities is not illegal and therefore not considered identity theft. Corporate appropriation is legal because corporations have been awarded full rights of personhood by the U.S. Supreme Court and because our internet security laws focus on data collection, not data usage.[96]

Therefore, corporations are obligated to make users aware (usually quite subtly) that their personal information will be screened but are not obligated to make users aware that their information will be pieced together and sold to behavioral marketers.[97] It seems the onus falls hardest on users to stay vigilant and look out for their own interests. Unfortunately, current models of privacy are overly obsessed with individuals and individual harm.[98] As a result, and exemplified in the *Plessy v. Ferguson* decision, today's identity theft law still fails to address the institutions that create the problem. Instead, it focuses only on individuals as lone rangers who breach security. Based on this legal perspective, I can introduce

Password Eight

Passers are treated historically as individual bad persons and not as part of a larger society that treats people unequally based on who they are and appear to be.

We are now seeing an appropriation of *Password Eight* and a global focus on privacy breaches made explicit in the age of "hacktivism" and the enduring WikiLeaks controversy. Governments and corporations are now preoccupied not just with citizens' and consumers' private information but with their own. Now under debate are issues of how the push for more openness and transparency conflicts with legitimate security concerns and a right to privacy, the responsibilities of online organizations like WikiLeaks[99] who distribute information from whistle-blowers in the wake of *The Pentagon Papers* and "Cablegate," and distributed denial-of-service attacks (DDoS) by hacktivist ensembles such as Anonymous and LulzSec as a new force for social justice.[100] Recently these groups claimed responsibility for hacking or defacing websites belonging to Gawker, Amazon, MasterCard, HBGary, Sony, Nintendo, PBS, the city of Orlando, Florida, NATO, the CIA, the U.S. Senate, and Canada's Conservative Party. Governments and corporations are now figuring out when to conceal and when to reveal in the face of in-group clairvoyants that are trying to make such expressions of privacy obsolete.[101] However, today's security breaches also force us to question whether an organization like WikiLeaks, because it profits from leaked information that it does not own and obtains "illegally," is serving an authentic journalistic and democratic service as a media insurgent or simply violating privacy to enhance the reputations of its owner, the Sunshine Press, and creator, Julian Assange, and dupe its audiences.[102]

The many faces of identity theft exploit instabilities in today's policy, geography, and technology just as Plessy's passing exploited instabilities in yesterday's dominant racial categories and legal rhetoric.[103] However, the ownership Plessy sought over his social situation should not be simply equated with control exercised over technology or government forms. The type of ownership Plessy sought when he used passing as property is more far-reaching than what passes as ownership when we edit privacy settings online and leave boxes (un)checked on official documents. The type of ownership Plessy sought requires a deep understanding of institutional standards and limitations, of who is watching or listening and for what reason, and of whose identities are valued most and why (*Passwords Two, Four, Five, Seven*).[104] As a result, Plessy's passing carries today's concerns along with the ongoing presence of the past (*Passwords Three, Eight*). Because Plessy appropriated passing to challenge racial boundaries and identifications, we can see how passing requires persuasive communication to ensure that others believe us when we say who we are or are not (*Password One*). We can also see how passing exposes the law's rhetorical construction and imposition of dominant racial categories and invites dupes to become in-group clairvoyants (*Password Six*). And we can see what happens when the insurgent properties of passing are appropriated by defensive dupes out to maintain the status quo (*Password Seven*). Hence, we can see that the foremost challenge to passing as property is its dependence on a racial *episteme* and an institutionalized racist hierarchy.[105] As a result, we have a clearer picture of why Plessy lost, why his passing was appropriated, equated with an invasion of privacy, and why Plessy's passing became the first case of identity theft.

CHAPTER FOUR

Passing as Principle

Iola and Harry Leroy grew up thinking they were white. Their father was white. Their mother was white. Their grandparents and aunts and uncles were white. Their family even owned slaves. But as the Civil War approached, Iola and Harry found out that they were not white after all. Frances E. W. Harper brings this scenario to life in her novel *Iola Leroy, or, Shadows Uplifted*, demonstrating how passing eloquently connects the realities of fiction to the fictions of reality. Through Iola's and Harry's experiences Harper shows that access to reality is sometimes based on fiction rather than fact and that identities are understood best in terms of the stories we tell about who we are. Harper reveals how fiction can sometimes ring more "true" than fact and that what we call facts are sometimes simply eloquent and persuasive fictions— fictions we deem most reasonable and expedient.[1]

Harper's protagonists, Iola and Harry Leroy, discover the relation between fact, fiction, and passing when their sister and father die suddenly of yellow fever and their "true" racial identities are revealed. After spending their lives growing up in an upper-class white slave-owning family in the South, the siblings find out they and their mother are multiracial and, because of hypodescent, considered black. The discovery changes everything. It changes where and how they live, what they own, who they love, and what they can expect for themselves and from society. Most important, it sets them on a journey to uncover and discover themselves, their roots, their family, and the difficult and complex story of racial identities in the slavery, Civil War, and Reconstruction eras. The road is rocky and the conflicts are profound. Like the nation itself, Iola and Harry experience unions, break-ups, compromises, battles, and displacement.

As Harper narrates it, many years pass before Iola and Harry reunite. When Harry boards a train en route to meet with Iola, he sits in the "colored" car. But after several hours, and because he is no longer in his hometown, things change. "A colored man entered the car, and, mistaking [Harry] for a white man, asked the conductor to have [him] removed."[2] Harry insists that he is "colored" in order to remain in the "colored" car with his black traveling companion and girlfriend, Miss Delaney. When things calm down, he turns to Miss Delaney and groans, "It would be

FIGURE 4.1
Frances E. W. Harper, author of *Iola Leroy, or, Shadows Uplifted*

ludicrous, if it were not vexatious, . . . to be too white to be black, and too black to be white."[3]

Harry's sharp and critical commentary is a direct response to the notion that people are not who they say they are. Interestingly, Harper herself was accused publicly of passing as both black and female. For example, after speaking engagements it was noted that "she was so articulate and engaging as a public speaker, audiences concluded that she couldn't possibly be a black woman. Some even speculated that she must be a man, while others reasoned that she was painted to look black."[4] Critical disbelief and alienation followed Harper in her life and in her writing as a function of racial *episteme*, which created collective identities and evidentiary standards that required extrinsic authentication. These standards are the determining factors of public knowledge, creating identities, identifications, and divisions. Because of such standards, it is no surprise that Harper's major rhetorical constraint and inspiration was found in passing—in relations between fiction and reality and in conversations among passers, dupes, and in-group clairvoyants, navigating between multiple audiences and their attendant perspectives. Harper made her characters as eloquent as possible and attributed their eloquence to blackness in order to prove she too was black.[5] Further, Harper's eloquent characters created a space in which blackness could be so eloquent that it expressed possibilities for interracial relationships and multiracial identities.

Harper uses her characters, "too white to be black, and too black to be white," to expand the social imaginary. Not only does she make room for herself as an eloquent black author, but she also exposes the few options made available to multiracial people in an unimaginative, tradition-bound society. Thanks to hypodescent, multiracial people lived in a world where a drop of black blood made them black and entitled them to few, if any, of the rights afforded to those considered white. But Harper's prose does more than state the obvious. It rewrites the narrative of racial identification. It asks readers to consider new possibilities, including the possibility of deciding to pass as black during an era in which racism and discrimination against black people were blatant. For Harper and her characters, passing as black is the product of a principled social imaginary that seems to contradict both *episteme* (objective truth) and *doxa* (common sense) of the time. In *Iola Leroy*, Harper presents passing as black as one way to embody a multiracial identity.[6] Passing as black is also part of her larger project of questioning patterns of interracial contact and perceptions of multiracial individuals that often wind up reflecting the existing hierarchy. She challenges the structure of racial hierarchy by redefining passing as principle, a choice to speak eloquently, act sincerely and in accordance with morality, and show recognition of right and wrong. For Harper, passing as black is an opportunity to make sociopolitical intentions public and at the same time to challenge prevailing conceptions of and motivations for racial identification. Harper's depiction of passing as black epitomizes race interpreted as a commitment rather than as a genetic calculation assigned by law or as a piece of private property. Harper privileges the intentions and motivations of the passer as a way to augment the in-group clairvoyant's perspective and devalue dupes' and defensive dupes' interpretations.

By articulating a heretofore underrepresented subjectivity— that of one who passes as black—Harper's principled renditions of passing reshape the social imaginary and the static terms in which passing has been depicted. They show particularly the motives, tactics, constraints, and outcomes of passing as black. Harper's uses of eloquence and sincerity support her characters' decisions to pass as black in terms of morality and to complicate relations between passers, dupes, and in-group clairvoyants.[7] Harper also refutes the contemporary claim that passing as black is a new phenomenon and that it is simply the reverse of passing as white.[8] Rather, according to Harper, passing as black calls for an acknowledgment of multiracial identities within the constraints of hypodescent that proves as urgent and vital today as it was at the turn of the twentieth century.

EXPANDING THE SOCIAL IMAGINARY

Iola Leroy, or, Shadows Uplifted is set in the southern United States from 1864 through 1867, with flashbacks to the 1840s.[9] The alternate titles serve several rhetorical functions, asking readers to consider whether the novel is passing under different names and thematic frameworks. On one level the novel is about Harper's struggle with accusations of passing, about proving that she is who she says she is—an eloquent black woman. On another level, the novel is about one family's struggle to figure out who they are and find their places in a rapidly changing world. The characters transcend life's circumstances through self-determination, eloquence, and sincerity. On yet another level, the novel is about its setting: one nation, divisible, without liberty and justice for all. The word "shadows" encompasses the full manifestation of unmeasured and unseen identities in a society brimming with secrets. The phrase "shadows uplifted" implies transgression, the passage of time as well as social and spatial movement. In addition, "shadows uplifted" implies that a space exists between lights and shadows, between fiction and reality, and between black and white. And, for Harper, the space between lights and shadows is as important as the liminal racial space her characters occupy. Harper brings her characters into eloquent dialogue, creating a space where identities are revealed and concealed and, consequently, where hybridity can be acknowledged.

Readers meet Harper's heroine, Iola Leroy, as a white slave, and become in-group clairvoyants when they find out that she is the daughter of Eugene and Marie Leroy, a wealthy white slave owner and his "quadroon" ex-slave wife. Eugene educated, emancipated, and wedded Marie. It is important to note that literacy and eloquent communication become the means by which Eugene and Marie unite. Both Eugene's (slave-owning) and Marie's (enslaved) families knew of Marie's multiracial (read black) identity. Because the couple eloquently explained their situation to their families, in-group clairvoyants, the families agreed to stay silent, and, as passers, the couple decided to keep Marie's racial identity a secret from any children they might have. Iola, one of their daughters, has white skin and blue eyes. She is described as "just as white as we are, as good as any girl in the land, and better educated than thousands of white girls."[10] Iola is reared to believe that she is white and articulates her whiteness when she defends slavery among many of her white classmates while attending school in the North: "Slavery can't be wrong . . . for my father is a slave-holder, and my mother is as good to our servants as she can be. My father often tells her that she spoils them, and lets them run over her. I never saw my father strike one of them. I love my mammy as much as I do my own mother, and I believe she loves us just as if we were her own children."[11] It is safe to say that at the start of her life Iola considers herself an unremarkable and uncomplicated white woman, though, through the information Harper later provides, the reader might conclude that she is passing as white. Or the reader might consider Iola to be the dupe of her own passing. Either way, from the start Harper presents passing as a question rather than an answer, a means to an end rather than an end in itself. Passing, for Harper, is a function of competing audience perspectives that often conflict with racial identifications and challenge distinctions between fiction and reality (*Password Two*). Characters and readers alike are forced to confront various standards for assigning racial identities—skin color, familial perceptions, genealogies, class status, scientific categorizations (*episteme*), common sense (*doxa*), and social commitments (*aletheia*) (*Password One*).

Black identity, understood metonymically via hypodescent, becomes real to Harper's characters insofar as it changes the ways they think and feel within a social framework they did not design and cannot readily control. For example, when Iola's mother, Marie, tells her teenage daughter that she is now considered black by law, Iola reframes the issue. Iola feels as though her white male relatives appropriated her racial property.[12] " 'I used to say that slavery is right.' I didn't know what I was talking about. Then, growing calmer, she said, 'Mother, who is at the bottom of this downright robbery?' "[13] This "robbery" involves a theft of Iola's material property as well as the loss of her legal claim to whiteness and its privileges. Informed that she is part black, and therefore legally eligible for enslavement, Iola is infuriated. "An expression of horror and anguish swept over Iola's face, and, turning deathly pale, she exclaimed, 'Oh, mother, it can't be so! you must be dreaming. . . . Almost wild with agony, Iola paced the floor as the fearful truth broke in crushing anguish upon her mind."[14] Note that Iola turns pale under the "crushing anguish" of being labeled black. Although she has a physical biological reaction Iola is not undergoing a psychological breakdown because she learns of her heritage. Rather, she sees the situation through the lenses of white privilege, racist bias, and inequality. Iola takes on an intersectional perspective, which recognizes that a change to her racial identity signals an immediate change of class status and loss of privilege. She attributes this change to the fact that her white racial identity and all that goes with it—claims to her father's estate and legacy, rights to a life lived on her own terms, and liberty—are no longer her own.[15] Anticipating the Supreme Court's opinion in *Plessy v. Ferguson* that whiteness is a form of private property that can be stolen, Harper frames Iola's newfound identity as an identity theft and as a manifestation of the changing character of domination and the constraints it seeks to impose (*Password Seven*).[16] The changing character of domination results from the fact that Iola, Harry, and their mother, Marie, cannot inherit their father's estate because they are now considered black by law (*Password Eight*). This "lawful" transformation is at the hand of Iola's nefarious cousin, Alfred Lorraine, after her father dies suddenly. Lorraine was an in-group clairvoyant who knew that Marie and the children were passing as white and took on a defensive dupe persona once Leroy died (*Passwords Three, Four*). Thereafter Alfred confiscates their estate, tricks Iola into returning, and sells the mother and daughter into slavery. Fortunately, Iola is able to warn Harry about these events and he does not return, thereby thwarting Lorraine's plan to sell him into slavery as well. Literacy and eloquence prove to be just as effective tools for the Leroy siblings as they were for their parents. Rather than mourning indefinitely, Iola becomes righteously indignant and takes a step toward passing as black. Through Iola, Harper inverts the stigma of blackness and stigmatizes whiteness, equating it with prejudice, oppression, and thievery.[17] Iola's desire to avoid a now stigmatized white identity constitutes her first motivation for passing as black. However, Harper is careful to clarify that Iola's choice is neither the effect of legal declaration that she is black nor the belief that she is somehow black inherently or internally. Because Iola is both white and black, but is unable to identify as such, she has a decision to make. Harper explains that Iola refuses to associate with the white race, which, in her experience, enslaves and steals from its own. Iola's choice to pass as black flies in the face of biological imperatives and instead is based on her own principled racial sincerity—her desire to become part of a black community with which she shares common interest (*Password One*). She announces her plans to enact her sincerity as a free woman: "I intend, when this conflict is over, to cast my lot with the freed people as a helper, teacher, and friend."[18] She understands that when she is free she can continue passing as white or pass as black, and takes pride in the latter, perceiving benefits in taking on important social roles for black women as nurse, teacher, and advocate.[19]

As promised, Iola devotes her labor and later her capital as a free woman and employed nurse to the cause of "reciprocal empowerment," supporting the causes of racial equality and uplift for others and for herself (*Password One*).[20] Her willingness to work cooperatively in a community to promote collective benefit further justifies her decision to pass as black in this historical context. In having Iola make this decision, Harper eschews a conception of multiracial identity as a void with no meaning on its own. Harper assigns meaning to multiracial identity within the legal, political, and social constraints of blackness. For Harper, Iola's decision to identify as black is a function of an intrinsic social and political *ethos*. By framing Iola's identity as a function of principle, Harper rebuts the law's authority to assign multiracial individuals to blackness as a function of its so-called impurity and degradation.

Despite its principled roots, Harper shows that passing as black proves to be just as complicated as passing as white, though it embodies a different set of constraints. For example, take Iola's personal and professional relationship with Gresham, a white Union hospital doctor, after she is freed from slavery and employed as a nurse. Dr. Gresham has feelings for Iola but raises an eyebrow at the way she nurses Tom Anderson, a black man and former slave who the reader knows helped her escape from slavery. Gresham despises miscegenation and attempts to suppress his emotions when he finds out about her multiracial ancestry and that she considers herself black. But Gresham proves unable to erase his feelings for Iola and eventually proposes to her. The reader learns that his growing attraction for Iola did not alter his true feelings about race and miscegenation when he tells Iola that he would prefer that she pass and live with him as a white woman. Iola refuses. Harper explains that although Iola found Gresham "the ideal of her soul exemplified," she could not bring herself to marry a man "of that race who had been so lately associated in her mind with horror, aversion, and disgust."[21] Whiteness is clearly the stigmatized racial identity for Iola. In refusing Grisham's proposal, Iola solidifies the rhetorical condition, and hence the possibility, of her persuasive and principled passing as black. Iola's response suggests a shift in how racial identities are valued. Morality is valued over materiality, and blackness is valued over whiteness. Gresham is not convinced. "She is one of the most refined and lady-like women I ever saw. . . . Her accent is slightly Southern but her manner is Northern. . . . I cannot understand how a Southern lady, whose education and manners stamped her as a woman of fine culture and good breeding, could consent to occupy the position she so faithfully holds. It is a mystery I cannot solve."[22] In expressing this sentiment, Gresham professes a belief in acceptance and equality but is unwilling to embody them through his actions toward Iola. Moreover, the fact that his proposal resounds with the language of possession—"Consent to be mine, as nothing on earth is mine"[23]—reveals his investment in whiteness and in the acquisition of social and cultural capital in Iola's gender. Instead of becoming an in-group clairvoyant who provides a safe space for Iola, Gresham becomes a defensive dupe (*Password Seven*). As such, he relies on his observations of Iola's appearance, behaviors, and verbal and nonverbal communication messages as indications of a racial identity he defines and would hope to contain by convincing Iola to pass as white. Iola's resistance to Gresham's definition reveals her own definition. Iola does not care about convincing a dupe that she is someone the law says she is not. Iola cares about believing in herself and aligning her identity with her own practical and principled goals. In doing so Iola reveals

Password Nine

When one is passing as black, dupes' conceptions are immaterial or at the very most devalued. Utmost value is placed on the passer and in-group clairvoyant, embodied by the passer's ability to justify the seemingly counterintuitive choice to pass as black.

Gresham's wish for Iola's silence emphasizes the normalized cultural perspective of passers as threatening, especially to dupes (*Passwords Seven, Eight*). This cultural perspective fears that passers who are multiracial, possess extensive and diversified social networks, and have learned proper manners can mobilize their actions toward attaining economic resources and social rewards allotted to white people only. In articulating this fear, Gresham proves unable to untangle the thickets of class and race. As a consequence he sees the opportunity for a better and freer life for Iola in whiteness only, and not in the upper-class background both he and Iola share. He is wrapped up so blindly in a racist sense of superiority that he is unable to understand why Iola would choose not to identify as white. His confusion is confirmed by his pause at the notion of offspring who might "show signs of color" and constitutes the end of his relationship with Iola.[24] Should Iola have succumbed to the temptation to pass as white, as occurs in many narratives of passing, it is highly probable that she would have met a tragic end because her motives would not have been socially sanctioned (e.g., interracial romance, family betrayal, domestic illegitimacy, and self-oriented achievement). Thus, Gresham symbolizes an unworthy solution to Iola's "ludicrous" and "vexatious" problem of multiracial identity. Marriage to him would quell racial anxieties, confound race with class, and shroud any transgressive and transformative effects of her passing beneath a shadow of imposed silence. Gresham makes her choice of racial identification a choice between whiteness and property, on the one hand, and blackness and sincerity, on the other. Harper imagines blackness as a form of racial and rhetorical sincerity rather than a form of property that can be owned.

Further analysis of Iola's romantic experiences demonstrates Harper's crucial contribution to a definition of passing (and of multiracial identity) that embraces rather than opposes blackness. We already know that Iola has refused the proposal of her white suitor, Dr. Gresham. Further dramatizing the constraints of gender on self-determination, Iola chooses to marry Dr. Latimer, another multiracial person passing as black, instead. Latimer is a man whose scholarship and personal philosophies resist racial stereotypes and emphasize his commitment to black racial uplift. Their union in marriage is a significant rhetorical move because it functions symbolically as a synecdoche for race itself, abetted by the synecdoche of passing (*Passwords Three, Four*). Take, as an example, Latimer's marriage proposal.

> "As a teacher, you will need strong health and calm nerves. You had better let me prescribe for you. You need," he added, with a merry twinkle in his eyes, "change of air, change of scene, and change of name."
>
> "Well, Doctor," said Iola, laughing, "that is the newest nostrum out. Had you not better apply for a patent?"
>
> "Oh," replied Dr. Latimer, with affected gravity, "you know you must have unlimited faith in your physician."
>
> "So you wish me to try the faith cure?" asked Iola, laughing.[25]

Latimer symbolizes the best available cure for Iola's "ludicrous" and "vexatious" racial identity.[26] As healer and husband he avows her pass as black and her sincere social transition into a black woman with a black family (as wife, daughter, and sister). The larger point is that for Iola's pass to be persuasive, she has to embrace her role in the raced and gendered familial and national hierarchies that initially concealed her under a layer of whiteness.[27] Though Iola does exercise agency in her choice of partner, Harper's larger comment is that any multiracial person's identity will be read as passing as either white or black and, consequently, in relation to her or his white or black spouse—unless one cannot tell whether the spouse is white or black either (*Password Three*). Because choosing a romantic partner becomes an expression of the passer's racial self-identification, Harper demonstrates that multiracial identities are imbued with racial value when they exist within a network of romantic relationships.[28]

In contrast to Iola's experience as a slave and then as a freed slave, Harper presents her brother's experience. When we last left Harry, he had received a letter from Iola that warned him of their cousin's trap. "As he read, he turned very pale; then a deep flush overspread his face and an angry light flashed from his eyes. As he read on, his face became still paler; he gasped for breath and fell into a swoon."[29] Like Iola, Harry turns pale with the newfound knowledge of black ancestry. He confides in his school's principal, who it turns out already knew the secret because Harry's father told him. Harry is confused. He does not understand how his parents' legal marriage could be undone posthumously and how his family could be denied their inheritance.

Harry decides to enlist in the army in order to fight against an institutional structure that destroyed his family. But when faced with the choice of serving in a white or "colored" regiment, he cringes. "He felt the reality of his situation as he never had before. It was as if two paths had suddenly opened before him and he had to choose between them."[30] He wavers initially about the decision to pass as black, unwilling to accept the lesser social status and privilege that accompany the choice. Like all passers, Harry struggles with the issue of selectively disclosing the black part of his racial identity in order to support his passing persona (*Password Three*). Eventually he joins a "colored" regiment of the Northern army because he thinks he will be better able to locate his mother and sister within a black social network. As events unfold, Harry becomes more assertive and confident in identifying himself partly, and then fully, as black. His identity is solidified when he marries Miss Delaney, a visibly identifiable black woman.

This is important for at least two reasons. First, Harry's marriage resets the racial recognition that he and Iola have so troubled by way of passing as white and then as black. Second, this marriage also makes a bold ideological critique of the one-drop rule. By pairing a couple of different complexions that is often (mis)taken for interracial, Harper inverts the term of value in hypodescent. She effectively undoes the typical assumption made in passing novels that marriage rights are only bestowed on those who refuse even the slightest hint of interracial association. So Harry's and Iola's marriages, and of course their parents' marriage, are in some ways passing too. Though legally considered monoracial, the couples are interracial. By presenting this possibility, Harper appeals to an in-group clairvoyant's perspective that does not strip interracial relationships and multiracial identities from characters within the black population. Rather, Harper grants the possibility for generational evidence of multiracial identities and interracial relationships within the symbolic and material constraints of blackness, the one-drop rule, and legalized segregation. Further, Harper presents the interracial unions and multiracial identities as empowered and as products of choices made by people who consider themselves political and social equals irrespective of how they are viewed by society at large.

Harper thus invokes passing as a principled response to the absence of fully representative categories of racial identity and the insecurities that ensue. It is a matter of principle to Harper that multiracial people acknowledge blackness, especially in the segregationist context.[31] Not only does passing as black provide Harper a platform for challenging the power imposed by metonymic logic of the one-drop rule, it widens the social imaginary by presenting white(-looking) persons who are committed sincerely to black political interests. Consequently, passing as black becomes a practice through which a multiracial person can benefit by exhorting the group into which he or she passes and thereby undoing inequalities among racial groups. In this case any achievements Harper's characters make are attributed to their choices to identify as black and not, as was commonly thought, to any amount of white blood coursing through their veins (*Password One*). In addition, Harper suggests that passing as black allows multiracial people to enact and engage an identity that can represent them as multiracial on their own terms and within the cultural constraints of monoracial logic. Finally, passing as black allows Harper to position herself through this literary revision as the in-group clairvoyant, who shifts the onus of racial reconciliation off of multiracials and on to all of us (*Passwords Two, Six*).

Harper's use of eloquence supports her depictions of passing as black and further destabilizes normalized monoracial categories. Traditional eloquence reinforces Harper's construction of passing in the novel. Indeed, transcendent eloquence and Harper's *conversazione* become tools for expanding the social imaginary and justifying her characters' decisions to pass as black.

FROM ELOQUENCE TO TRANSCENDENT ELOQUENCE

As established in the previous chapters, synecdoche (the part passing as the whole) and metonymy (the whole passing as the part) allow the passer to take a part of himself or herself for the whole and identify as either white or black (*Passwords Three, Four*). Synecdoche and metonymy meet eloquence, a trope rooted in the classical tradition and connoting outspokenness, in Harper's case, from the subject position of one who is (passing as) black.[32] Harper engages the transformative and transgressive effects of eloquence to create knowledge that alters the racial fictions and realities expressed in *episteme* and *doxa* (*Password One*). To understand Harper on these matters, I turn to two conceptions of eloquence that can be felt throughout her work.

The first defines eloquence as the highest moral condition and as the means of persuasive communication.[33] But the means are identified closely with the message, creating a positive correlation between eloquence and wisdom.[34] Harper uses Iola's eloquence both as a virtue and as a virtuous strategy. Harper's eloquence dispels the popular myth that multiracial and black women are incapable of moral virtue or sound deliberation. For instance, even after learning that Iola is passing as and decidedly black, Gresham is drawn to Iola's eloquence and in it locates "his ideal of the woman whom he was willing to marry."[35] As Gresham's ideal, Iola is far from the stereotype of the tragic mulatta as self-loathing vixen who threatens the white family structure. Instead, she embodies the perceived stability of the gendered roles of the cult of true womanhood—piety, purity, submission, and domesticity.[36] When Iola rebuffs his advances, Gresham discovers that she is not pious, submissive, or domesticated in the ways he imagined. By maintaining Iola's resolve, Harper shows her to be beholden only to her own sincerity, an eloquent and principled decision maker who cannot be swayed. Harper writes, Iola's "resolve was made. [Gresham's] words were powerless to swerve her from the purpose of her soul."[37]

A deeper understanding of Harper's deployment of eloquence comes from equating eloquence with wise speech.[38] The consistent theme is that the acquisition of knowledge should be followed by its eloquent conveyance to one's audiences. This view is extended when we consider eloquent speech effective because it is passionate and intellectual and because it sounds like who the speaker is.[39] Harper's eloquence, embodied in her characters' eloquence, always reflects identity. So Iola's and Harry's eloquence begins with expressions of stigmatized whiteness. But over time, and because of experiences in black and white worlds, they acknowledge all of who they are and no longer need to make use of synecdoche and metonymy, identifying themselves partly. Instead, they can identify themselves as black persons who are also multiracial. And, for Harper, wisdom and eloquence reside in such identifications. Iola's and Harry's acknowledgments and subsequent transformations support Harper's larger point that black people are exactly who they (eloquently) say they are. And that doing so does not make black people any less black or sincere or equal to white people. Through her characters Harper moves between contexts with eloquence, finding an individual place within a collective national narrative of self-discovery, discord, and unity provided by the backdrops of the Civil War and Reconstruction. In so doing, Harper uses passing to chart out a social place and discursive space as black and multiracial in a monoracial world (*Password Five*).

Harper's renditions of passing also engage eloquence as a way to accomplish practical goals by saying and doing things to express social and political commitments.[40] Goals are attained when audiences are transformed from dupes into in-group clairvoyants and empowered to abandon prejudices against passers and passing (*Password Six*). Harper demonstrates this high degree of eloquence through her version of a salon—the *conversazione* in chapter 30 of the novel—to create a context within which each participant's voice evokes a response, establishes personal relationships, and ultimately reinforces similarities and overcoming differences. This requires that passers display intelligence, imagination, and sound judgment, as well as a powerful command of language, delivery, and pronunciation. Harper employs eloquence to craft her argument about the nature of conflict, the virtues and dangers of cooperation, and the opportunities of identification and community in passing as black. In other words, the fictional characters and voices she invents and animates suggest real-life distinctions between intraracial and interracial social worlds and expressions. Hence, the novel is addressed to multiple audiences. It is addressed to dupes in order to ease prejudices against blacks, and it "winks" at in-group clairvoyants in order to provide strategies for racial uplift that search out means of representation and expression in the social imaginary (*Password Two*).

At this point it is important to reconsider Harper's passing protagonists in order to raise a key question: is it accurate, and more than that, is it just, to claim that Iola and Harry were passing as white if they were not aware of any aspect of their racial identity that was not white? A brief discussion of the language and look of passing is required in order to answer this question. Insofar as looks are concerned, passing is based on *episteme* (objective knowledge) that declares the visible to be a true and an accurate measure of identification and character. Dupes rely on this *episteme* as the subversive enthymeme (hidden information that prompts them to take the passer at face value) to believe that passers are either white or black but not white and black. *Episteme* is violated when passers alter their communication, behaviors, or relationships, thereby enhancing uncertainty and ambiguity as well as dissociating themselves from disadvantaged identities and associating themselves with privileged identities (i.e., passing as white). However, Harper "winks" at the reader as an in-group clairvoyant when she explains that monoracial identities as either white or black are privileged because they are recognized and have assigned (yet unequal) statuses. Multiracial is a nonprivileged identity because it goes unrecognized and therefore has no place from which persons so identified can speak out. Harper's passers create a space for multiracial identity by passing as black in order to become identifiable and master eloquence to speak out for transformative and transgressive effect. In this way passing marks social place and discursive space (*Password Five*).

The language of passing flows within rhetorical encounters among passers, dupes, and in-group clairvoyants (*Password Two*). Building on this idea, Harper constructs diegetic and exegetic audiences that add depth and dimension to her construction of passing from an in-group clairvoyant's perspective. If Iola and Harry are passing as white, then they and their associates are dupes. The in-group clairvoyants would be their parents as well as Harper and the readers. The multiple perspectives implicated here are important because they demonstrate that something exists beyond what is visible and because they highlight several dangers inherent in the question of unintentional and unconscious passing raised by Harper's text. One danger Harper suggests is the ease with which passing can be placed within a paradigm of deception regardless of intent or outcome. This negatively valenced labeling suggests that passing is always enacted in terms of falsification, equivocation, and concealment and that the message content of a pass depends entirely upon audiences' interpretations. Hence Harper's sarcastic comment that those who pass as black are best off wearing labels to explain their racial identities. In *Iola Leroy* passers' bodies will not confirm that they are black, so they must prove that they are black by eloquently expressing their sincere commitments to black sociopolitical causes.

As in *Plessy v. Ferguson*, dupes who refuse to be duped often accuse passers of falsification, or counterfeiting, forging, and lying (*Passwords Seven, Eight*). From an in-group clairvoyant's perspective it is more accurate to say that passers are equivocating, or selectively revealing aspects of their racial identities through what they do and say (*Passwords One, Two Six*). It can be argued that Eugene and Marie equivocate initially, and that Harry later equivocates when he enrolls in the army. The Leroy family's varied engagements with passing—as a white family, then as a black family—reframes passers as skilled rhetoricians who combine and reshape perspectives, tropes, and rhetorical forms in order to create and sustain identifications that reflect their sincerity and can influence audiences entrenched in social and moral conflicts (i.e., racism and segregation). A second danger of this question of unintentional passing is that it relies primarily on externally proscribed authenticity and assumes a subject-object relationship among rhetorical personae. In this paradigm the multiracial person is what I call an unidentifiable passing object, while the dupe and in-group clairvoyant are subjects who determine and evaluate her or his identity. In place of this demeaning subject-object relation, Harper engages racial sincerity, a method of interpolating identity that assumes a "subject-subject interaction" and allows for understanding of a passer's intent and motivations.[41] In this way passing is less a strategy or tactic of personal gain and more an eloquent argument that expresses identity as one's spiritual, emotional, and political commitments and actions. A sincere approach suggests that passing is not as simply characterized as we might think. Passing is not necessarily motivated by dreams of whiteness or blackness, but by practical goals of seeking equal opportunity in a racist society and seeking a community of common moral, social, and political interest.

Understood thusly, Harper expresses

Password Ten

Passing is an ongoing and eloquent drama of becoming more racially and rhetorically sincere.

As part of such a drama, identity can be performed as a set of earnest relations among subjects who share emotional and political ideologies and racial sensibilities. And so identity becomes who you say you are and what you have to say about who others say you are. This self-oriented description of identity formation and maintenance is consistent with the definitions of rhetorical eloquence employed by Harper and provided by the classical rhetorical tradition. Eloquence is used in passing as a means of highlighting or downplaying racial affiliations and can be linked with class background and exposure to diverse communities. Both identity and eloquence are situated performances and social constructions, but are nevertheless associated with race as if they were natural attributes. This association is why Harper's renditions of passing are based largely on eloquent communication and not on biology.

TRANSCENDENT ELOQUENCE IN ACTION

An opportunity to develop character and convince the audience that Harper and her characters are who they say they are comes at the end of the novel. The Leroy family (including the siblings' partners-spouses) associates with progressive Northern intellectuals and socializes with them at a salon or *conversazione* about how best to uplift blacks specifically and the nation generally in the wake of the Civil War. Unlike the rest of the story, which is told as a series of interpersonal flashbacks, the *conversazione* is a formal conversation in which participants deliver position papers that are discussed and debated. The interracial collective intends eloquently to persuade its audience about the nature of black humanity, and Iola's (now) husband, Dr. Latimer, outwits Dr. Latrobe, a white Southern man who doubts blacks' scholarly ability and therefore social status with respect to whites.

Other characters demonstrate eloquence in the *conversazione* through their abilities to speak folk dialect, standard English, as well as a hybrid combination of the two. This ability exemplifies a more type of eloquence called "transcendent" in contemporary terms because it bridges gaps among disparate communities.[42] Harper's use of "transcendent eloquence" presents passing as a moral difference rhetorically (passing as white versus passing as black) so as to build understanding and respect. Part of the process involves creating new categories against which the original monoracial categories can be measured, and developing a mixed or hybrid language to enable communication. The scene of the *conversazione* demonstrates several features of transcendent eloquence: philosophical, comparative, dialogic, critical, and transformative.

The *conversazione* is a rhetorical situation aimed at inventing and reviewing "subjects of vital interest to our welfare."[43] Harper presents five position papers that illustrate the in-between nature of multiracial identity (revealed in passing as black): "Negro Emigration," "Patriotism," "Rallying Cry," "Education of Mothers," and "Moral Progress of Race." Each paper demonstrates an element of transcendent eloquence. The first paper, concerning expatriation to Africa, is philosophical in that it explores several assumptions about knowledge, being, and values behind conflicting ideals of black identity in a postslavery context. On one hand Africa is presented as a comfort zone, a place where black people will no longer be alienated and repressed and can be identified as people and part of the majority population. The presence of American blacks on the continent will represent redemption and civilization, signaling the twin myth of Africa and Africans as savage and childlike. On the other hand, the United States is presented as a hostile home, a place where African Americans are called to bring about the true conditions of democracy by working to end racial prejudice. "America . . . is the best field for human development; the best place to settle down and work out our own salvation."[44] This shows that that those who identify as black are displaced and bifurcated, continually expressing their own senses of twoness or double consciousness in search of solid ground.

The second paper is comparative and presents an alternative argument concerning patriotism and assimilation. Delivered by a reverend, this paper portrays white people as superior, as more humane and pious than black or multiracial people. It strongly implies that it is "a privilege for colored man to be linked to his destiny and to live beneath the shadow of his power."[45] The reverend's rhetoric shows how narratives about race and religion are intertwined in ideals that suggest "a chosen people" and "a chosen nation." Specifically, America is framed as a chosen nation, and white Christians are framed as appropriating the status of "chosen people," which once belonged to Jews. However, the presence of black Christians in America complicates and at times opposes this narrative. The reverend's position is rebutted by Dr. Latimer, whose eloquence Harper uses to anticipate the *Plessy v. Ferguson* ruling. " 'Law,' he said, 'is the pivot on which the whole universe turns.' . . . We have had two evils by which our obedience to law has been tested—slavery and the liquor traffic."[46] Latimer appeals to morality as the ultimate law. True patriotism, he argues, is about surpassing the customary and legal limitations of institutionalized racism and discrimination in favor of identifying all racial groups as socially equal and equally visible. It is a call to a different and freer patria, a call for all U.S. citizens to live out their pledge of allegiance with absolute "liberty and justice for all."

The third paper is not a paper at all. It is a poem, "A Rallying Cry," written by an older woman named Mrs. Watson and read by Miss Delaney. This poem is dialogic and invitational because it aims beyond persuasion and conviction and at exploration. It begins,

Oh, children of the tropics,
Amid our pain and wrong
Have you no other mission
Than music, dance, and song?[47]

Written for a black audience, the poem opens a new perspective, an available opportunity, and does not make demands. The point is to invite audiences into a context where it is reasonable to talk about the nature of black identity and the responsibility of black people to take action to better their situations. This is why Harper does not address whites and white racism as an obstacle. Instead she uses the poem to illustrate a way to deal with the situation through a nationalist perspective built on what Barack Hussein Obama would later call "the audacity of hope."[48] Watson writes,

> In the pallor of that anguish
> I see the only light,
> To flood with peace and gladness
> Earth's sorrow, pain, and night.[49]

Rather than identifying against white supremacy, and risking its reinforcement as reality, the poem creates a context within which those who are ready to act in favor of black racial uplift can do so. It is offered as a pleasing ideal for excluded audiences and not for the sake of belittling or defeating them. We will see in the two papers that follow how this ideal is rejected for an approach that addresses structural inequities.

The fourth paper, written and delivered by Iola Leroy, is about family structure and gender role modeling. This paper is critical because it directly addresses the powers and limits of black and multiracial gendered identities. Iola discusses the interconnectedness between individuals, families, and communities. This is not surprising considering the events of Iola's own life. Her thesis is that people should see themselves as moved to create certain kinds of people. Consider the following response in support of its soundness: "I do not think . . . that we can begin too early to teach our boys to be manly and self-respecting and our girls to be useful and self-reliant."[50] It seems that Harper, through Iola, argues that the power of self-enrichment relies on how individuals negotiate the norms of existence. The ensuing conversation reveals her insistence on the fundamentally ontological role of rhetoric in cultivating an ideal identity. Signaling the ways in which gender norms are circulated and enforced, she provides eloquent evidence for the constraint of gender-race. Gender-race defines personhood and knowledge and places value on individuals according to a moral order that grants social access and opportunity to those who meet its standards of "the true strength of race . . . purity in women and uprightness in men."[51] Through Iola, Harper asserts that life—and its forms of resistance to oppression—are profoundly shaped by the simultaneity of race, class, gender, morality, and sexuality. She calls for a reorganization of black family structure that undoes the damage caused by enslavement. Her critique is that all audiences are potential agents of change with an obligation to recognize the seemingly unrelated factors that impact life experience. Therefore, they must adapt their methods of social action accordingly.

The fifth and final paper, on moral progress, is transformative because it changes the setting, expectations, and nature of the issues identified thus far. "Instead of narrowing our sympathies to mere racial questions," Harper writes, "let us broaden them to humanity's wider issues."[52] Harper steps outside the frame of the *conversazione* in search of a fresh perspective by firmly situating racial progress in the context of human history writ large. Through the voice of Reverend Carmichael, she addresses the social and rhetorical legacies of slavery that must be acknowledged. The social legacies include segregation and its effects— nihilism, self-loathing, miseducation, and increasing black imprisonment. The rhetorical legacy of slavery is embodied in the African American rhetorical gospels of hope, suffering, love, freedom, and justice that set the stage for the rhetorical situation of the *conversazione* itself.

Harper connects these legacies to slavery when Iola's and Harry's uncle Robert reminisces about these qualities in the hush harbor discourse of the enslaved: "how we used to go by stealth into lonely woods and gloomy swamps. To tell of our hopes and fears, sorrows and trials."[53] Historically, hush harbors were places where the enslaved gathered to plan escapes, worship, and hold unauthorized secret meetings. They were not merely physical locations, but also conceptual metaphors for strategies of passing, where the enslaved escaped the visible policing that identified them as enslaved, inferior, and inhuman. Hush harbor rhetoric, like the *conversazione*, allowed its participants to create an alternative public sphere within which they, otherwise disenfranchised, clarified their identities, ideologies, and commitments.[54]

The language dialects that many passers encounter and engage throughout the novel show that the normal discourse of one group does not necessarily match that of another or others. Moreover, these language differences illustrate that those who can neither code switch nor translate vernacular dialects into standard syntax are unable to travel socially. Therefore, in Harper's novel, passing is a means of eliciting and negotiating shared, as well as distinct, experiences between intraracial and interracial audiences. Take the shifting depiction of Uncle Robert's voice, which embodies several of the moral conflicts with which he grapples. As mentioned above, Robert speaks the standard English of the bourgeois *conversazione*. What is important here is that he links it to the folk dialect of the enslaved, indicative of the upward mobility evidenced in the events of his own life. Consequently, he can converse with rather than simply address multiple audiences. Robert embodies Harper's transgressive ideal of progress because he is someone who was a slave and has moved beyond it. Robert's ontology, along with Iola's and Harry's, is suggestive of an inclusive model of transcendent eloquence and passing. This model understands race and gender in conjunction with class and communication. It also demonstrates, somewhat problematically, how class serves as a corrective for the perils of an otherwise stigmatized black identity, while there is no corrective for a stigmatized white identity. Though Harper is often criticized for this stance, her ideological position is supported by the willingness of her characters to pass as black and support their decisions eloquently.

Harper's demonstrations of traditional and transcendent eloquence suggest that passing as black entails specific identity lessons taught sincerely through ideologies of racial uplift. Her eloquence also anticipates the "separate but equal" *Plessy* ruling and the institutionalization of segregation, exposing dichotomies that allow passers to travel within interracial and intraracial contexts so long as they identify as black. At times they provide some element of racial mediation, but this mediation is not based on biological ancestry (i.e., having one black parent and one white parent). Rather, Harper's characters have the potential for transcendent eloquence and mediation because of their experiences as passers traveling in and between racialized worlds. Harper's passers are unique because they believe they are white initially, are perceived as such by others, and benefit from white privilege. Then Harry makes the choice to renounce white privilege because it is the social force that entitled his uncle to sell Iola and Marie into enslavement. Iola avoids a now stigmatized white identity in order to fight for social equality after being freed. Passing as black within the contexts of slavery and segregation is not the reverse of passing as white, especially when one does not have to be an actual slave. Instead, it is about working with and as the marginalized for collective betterment. And this is Harper's principle of passing: to present the possibilities of identity in multiple moments of concealment and revelation (*aletheia*) in the interests of social critique and progress.

THE PRINCIPLES OF PASSING

We can measure the effectiveness of Harper's principle in terms of the results it generates for her characters. One result is that passing is intertwined with and identified in sexual terms. These terms privilege particular types of sexual behavior—heterosexual, monogamous, married, procreative—and reward them with respectability, legality, and mobility. In some ways Harper upholds a monoracial bias, but a deeper look in terms of the in-group clairvoyant exposes how Harper transgresses this bias with her depictions of interracial relationships in passing. Although categorized monoracially due to passing or the one-drop rule, Maria and Eugene Leroy (Iola and Harry's parents), Iola and Dr. Latimer, and Harry and Miss Delaney are all interracial heterosexual couples. Each couple manages visibility by passing as monoracial. Because her couples pass as monoracial, Harper demonstrates how racial dynamics operate to structure permissible sexual behaviors and identities. This is an especially important point to make in the context of slavery, Reconstruction, and segregation, when the racial-sexual boundaries between whites and blacks were most ferociously and legally policed. Often black women were constructed as overly sensual, possessing such an excessive sexuality that they could not be abused or refused. Black men were constructed similarly and violently, effusing so much sexual power that they would inevitably rape white women. In either case whites were constructed as innocent victims so that they could never be said to engage in aberrant sexual practices.[55] By concealing and revealing interracial relationships in passing, Harper argues against these constructions and against the conception that interracial marriage is necessarily emblematic of large-scale, interracial harmony. Further, passing allows Harper's characters to avoid a hostile context for interracial marriage.[56] Thus, passing provides a productive site for examining how multiple forms of privilege and marginalization collide and extend across generations, affecting conceptions and expressions of multiracial identities today.

Consequently, Harper's complex representations of passing highlight Reconstruction and the turn of the twentieth century as times of changing race relations and interracial politics.[57] Passing as black suggests a shift in how racial identities can become more valued and less stigmatized as a function of passers' considerable agency and conscious effort, which can be compared to the agency and effort of today's growing population of multiracial Americans. As more individuals claim multiracial identities as products of interracial unions, a look back at Harper forces us to ask whether these claims are new and qualitatively different from the experiences of her characters while passing as black. After all, today's multiracials are speaking out in order to find and build communities through which they can express their sincere racial identities.[58] Harper's eloquence also forces contemporary audiences to consider changing the question today's multiracials are so desperate to answer: What are you? Instead, she proposes we ask: Who are you? And, To what causes are you committed? Changing the question suggests that the solution to racism may not lie in adjusting racial *episteme* to include new groups but in rejecting biological concepts of race all together in favor of *aletheia* as sincerity.

But passing is not just a sincere personal choice for Harper or her characters. Passing is a principled response to individual and collective forms of discrimination and exclusion and strives to achieve new outcomes through racial sincerity and rhetorical sincerity (*aletheia*), concealment and revelation of racialized identities and personal intentions. This description supports Harper's larger representation of passing as black as a rhetorical and moral issue within the traditions and traditional constraints of an increasingly racialized and segregated world. Passing as black turns out not to be counterintuitive at all. Rather, passing as black expands the social imaginary because it capitalizes on the broad definition of blackness based on hypodescent, making it difficult for audiences to tell the difference between multiracial and black, or, for that matter, multiracial and white. Harper emphasizes this point through satire when, in the voice of a racist white physician, she announces to an in-group clairvoyant, "Oh, there are tricks of blood which always betray them. My eyes are more practiced than yours. I can always tell them."[59] The duped white physician cannot see what is obvious nonsense from an in-group clairvoyant's perspective: a biological notion of race and racial hierarchy cannot exist (*Password Two*).

Harper continues by teaching us how, as in-group clairvoyants, to discern the differences among multiracial, white, and black in terms of life chances and outcomes: the events if the multiracial individual were to take the privileged part for the whole and the events if said individual were to take the nonprivileged part for the whole (*Password Six*). In this sense the outcomes associated with passing are both eloquent and counterfactual but not biological. Every individual has potential outcomes under every set of circumstances, even though only one of these outcomes is typically observed or realized. The causal effect of interest to this chapter has been the differences between these potential outcomes enabled by Harper's eloquence and sincerity. That is, the effectiveness of passing as demonstrated in *aletheia*—characters' commitments to social, political, and rhetorical lifestyles and worldviews (*Password One*). The inability to observe both of these outcomes for a single individual is overcome by Harper's assessments and discussions of the outcomes of passing while her characters pass as white and then as black.

By presenting passing as a counterfactual problem that can be addressed eloquently, Harper demonstrates that sincere action will be to some extent diminished if one lacks an adequate supply of opportunity and community with which to identify. Someone who is unidentifiable racially, like a passer, and therefore without a social network will be unable to harness many opportunities for sincere activity or eloquent speech, and what little she can accomplish will not be profound. To some extent, then, living sincerely requires good fortune and good decisions. Iola's and Harry's experiences reveal that happenstance can rob anybody, even wealthy white slave-owning families, of security. Nonetheless, Harper insists, the highest good of sincerity is not something that comes to us by chance. It is an important social and rhetorical choice. Thus, the purpose of passing as black remains principled: to find a community and ensure that all individuals and communities can become more sincere. Passing becomes the means of expressing and exercising that sincerity eloquently by communicating sincerity and living out its implications.

Harper's representation of passing as principle suggests that behaviors and attitudes have meanings only within the context of specific selves, specific relationship networks, and specific situations. This being the case, Harper expands the social imaginary and the in-group clairvoyant's perspective through characters who pass as black, causing readers to examine their own collective and individual motivations based on the categories with which they identify. These reidentifications can lead to changes in *aletheia* as sincerity (i.e., moral, political, and ethical commitments) and, hopefully, changes in actions. Audiences are challenged to exercise their agencies by questioning how to relate and respond to a society in which people are told they are free, but are not necessarily free to be who they are. Iola and Harry's acts of passing accomplish exactly that by stigmatizing white identities and presenting social and moral benefits in identifying as black. What is most eloquent, however, is Harper's rhetorical move to eschew either-or identification in favor of an understated yet powerful third alternative—holding on to multiracial identity and passing as black. For it is in passing as black that both Iola and Harry find one way to acknowledge multiracial identities and resist the self-doubt and omnipresent readiness to retreat that precede traditional acts of passing as white in literature.[60] Time and again, and in varied settings, Harper refuses to animate the dread and revulsion accompanying forced confrontations with multiracial identity. She also refuses to imbue her characters with the shame of denial and deception. These refusals allow Harper's multiracial characters to identify with most blacks and most whites they encounter, though always with subtle and subversive effect. With malleable yet locatable identities, characters uplift shadows that have defined blackness in opposition to whiteness and as an inferior contaminant. By Harper's light we see more clearly into whiteness and blackness as identities that are all too often utterly and ruinously unacquainted with their in(ter)dependences.

CHAPTER FIVE

Passing as Pastime

Coleman Silk is not the only passer in *The Human Stain*. Crammed with passers of all sorts—racial, ethnic, class, professional, ability, mental health—the story is set during the months leading up to the Clinton presidential impeachment hearings in 1998 and during the postwar era of the 1940s and 1950s. Because lines of race and color are the most entrenched in these settings, and because Coleman is the only racial and ethnic passer, Coleman proves to be the one who causes the most trouble, not just for himself and the other characters in Philip Roth's novel (2000) and Robert Benton's film (2003)—his lovers, wife, children, siblings, parents, classmates, coworkers, students, and biographer— but for readers and moviegoers as well. Coleman's troublemaking is enhanced by the fact that he appears to be someone he is not. As a consequence, he sees himself differently than others do. And the more everyone sees, the less everyone knows. Where Coleman sees a black man, everyone else sees a white and Jewish man. Where Coleman sees a white and Jewish man, everyone else sees a black man. Everyone knows and no one knows. Everyone is a dupe and no one is a dupe. Everyone is an in-group clairvoyant and no one is an in-group clairvoyant (*Password Two*).

Appearance is not the only thing that fails Coleman in *The Human Stain*. Eventually language betrays him too. Consider how readers and moviegoers meet the passing protagonist, as a seventy-one-year-old classics professor and dean of faculty at Athena College in western Massachusetts. "Coleman had taken attendance . . . , [and] as there were still two names that failed to elicit a response by the fifth week of the semester, Coleman in the sixth week, opened the session by asking, "Does anyone know these people? Do they exist or are they spooks?"[1] Coleman's sarcasm, which Athena's administration ultimately condemns as a racist epithet, is the start of Coleman's end. It turns out that the missing students are black. When the students hear about Coleman's question, they file a complaint charging him with racism. Coleman explains that he used "spooks" literally as a synonym for phantoms and not as an insult. Despite a lack of realistic motive or proof that Coleman made a racist remark, no one at the college believes what Coleman says. No one believes him because no one knows that he is a black man passing as white and Jewish.[2] Readers and audiences expect Coleman's secret, if told, to exculpate him. Coleman disagrees. He thinks that his sincerity and character—not to mention the fact that he never saw the students and thus could not even guess their racial identities—should be enough to clear him of the ridiculous charge. Coleman maintains his position and keeps the secret of his passing, which results in his dismissal from Athena College and forced retirement.[3] And so from the very beginning *The Human Stain* presents Coleman's passing as tragic, a phenomenon based on secrecy that entertains in proportion to the amount of suffering ingroup clairvoyant audiences witness passers endure.[4]

As modes of entertainment, both the literary and cinematic versions of *The Human Stain* portray passing as updated versions of a classical theme—a tragic character's doomed attempt at liberation that reifies the tragic reality of a racial hierarchy. The novel boasts much critical acclaim, even a PEN-Faulkner award. The *New York Times* called it Roth's "most interesting book; its particular hero-fool [Coleman] is arguably the most socially intriguing character to whom Roth has ever devoted himself."[5] Readers take pleasure in negotiating reflections of themselves in the narrative and connecting to Coleman's true identity as they see it. In readers' imaginations Coleman looks like a light-skinned black man passing as white and Jewish. His choice to pass is considered a natural one given the value of whiteness in the monoracial caste system of segregation. Readers' expectations are met because they can out Coleman definitively as a passer and identify with and pity him on that basis.

Because film intervenes more directly in the relationship between image and audience, filmgoers often react differently to narratives than readers. Such is the case with the film version of *The Human Stain*. In fact, Miramax, the film's production company, tried to account for and prevent negative reactions to the film when it primed audiences and reviewers by distributing descriptions of "passing for white" and of Coleman as a "light-skinned black man" in advance of the film's release.[6] Unfortunately, Miramax's preemptive strategy failed. Film scholars suggest that the issue of bringing Coleman to life on screen made it exceedingly difficult to generate the textual wink required by in-group clairvoyant viewers no matter how much description was provided.[7] Movie critics agreed when they panned the film.[8] Reviews highlighted the inability to suspend disbelief and accept Sir Anthony Hopkins (cast as the elder Coleman) as an African American from New Jersey.[9] Critics were not convinced by Wentworth Miller III (cast as the young Coleman) playing a bona fide black man either.[10] The *New Yorker*'s review summarizes the problem succinctly. "In the new film 'The Human Stain,' . . . an actor named Wentworth Miller plays the young Coleman Silk—or, rather, the young Anthony Hopkins. (Hopkins, you see, plays the older Wentworth Miller.) . . . In real life, Hopkins is a Welshman (white, not Jewish), but Miller's origins are mixed. . . . Miller doesn't look black, whatever that means, but neither does Hopkins, or Silk. (Miller doesn't look anything like Hopkins, either)."[11] The actors' (and therefore the passer's) color, or lack of it, is striking. Reviews rightly draw attention to the actors' color as an absent presence in the film but miss a larger point. The actors' color, what is "not there," is a deliberate move that calls attention to what passers might actually look like if they were passing as white. Whereas readers envision themselves comfortably as in-group clairvoyants and Coleman as nonwhite, filmgoers' expectations are violated. Coleman (played by Hopkins and Miller) does not look like a black man passing as white and Jewish and therefore cannot be outed definitively as a passer. Because it lacks the textual wink required by in-group clairvoyants, the film's rendition of passing translates into an unsatisfying and bewildering experience. Filmgoers feel like dupes and seek the satisfactory ending that eludes them by generating justifications to support their negative responses to (the actors who play) passers they cannot out.

Juxtaposing critical receptions to passers and passing as represented in the literary and film versions of *The Human Stain* allows us to tease out a tragic formula for passing as pastime. This formula originates in the classical rhetorical tradition within which Coleman, *The Human Stain*'s passing protagonist, is steeped. As an updated take on classical themes of identification and tragedy, *The Human Stain* shows us how and why passing entertains when audiences can out passers and witness their suffering from a safe distance as omniscient in-group clairvoyants. The significance of developing this tragic formula and tracing its connections to classical rhetoric through *The Human Stain* is twofold. First, it allows us to determine what notions about race and identity underlie the foundation of passing in the modern imagination. Second, it allows us to understand how contemporary popular culture modernizes passing to see, read, feel, and discuss race and identity today.

THE PASSING CROW

Allusions to classical expressions of tragedy and identification abound in *The Human Stain*. Although less obvious than other classically tragic themes in the story, such as *Oedipus Rex*, significant roles are played throughout the novel and film by "The Crow and the Raven," an Aesopic fable to which the story cryptically alludes. In Aesop's fable the crow seeks to change its identity because it is considered a harbinger of doom and death.[12] The crow's dark appearance, unsettling caws, and appetite for carrion cause humans to react badly whenever it appears. Seeking acceptance by humans, and dissociating from a constraining identity, is the crow's motive for passing as a raven. The crow attempts to pass by presenting an acceptable raven persona. Unfortunately, her caws are unconvincing. This critical moment—as Aesop links eloquent speech to concealment and then to revelation (*aletheia*)—is the moment when the crow is outed. Aesop's fable suggests that it is possible to pass effectively insofar as what we say aligns with who we appear to be. But Aesop's crow actually fails as a passer because there is no dupe. Everyone is an in-group clairvoyant. And in-group clairvoyants can share the secret the passing crow can never keep.

Compare the frame for passing in Aesop's fable to the adaptations presented in *The Human Stain*. In the novel we meet the crow, named Prince, in a pet shop cage. Once he escapes, he passes as a wild crow and speaks the "crow language," in which he is not fluent. Prince, like Aesop's crow, proves to be utterly speechless, though he speaks incessantly. When he says the wrong thing he commits social suicide. He is attacked, nearly killed, and later banished from the community of wild crows because of his utterances. Prince cannot escape the constraints of appearance or language. Therefore, he is outed and fails as a passer. Prince returns to the pet shop and remains a jailbird because he cannot blend in with wild crows.

> The girl smiled and said . . . "Prince is the only bird that can fly. . . . He made a beeline for the door and went out into the trees. There were three or four other crows that came. Surrounded him in the tree. And they were going nuts. Harassing him. Hitting him on the back. Screaming. Smacking into him and stuff. They were there within minutes. He doesn't have the right voice. He doesn't know the crow language. They don't like him out there. Eventually he came down to me because I was out there. They would have killed him." "That's what comes from being hand-raised," said Faunia. "That's what comes of hanging around all his life with people like us. The human stain . . ." That's how it is.[13]

The novel's updated take on the Aesopic fable retains many of the themes associated with passing as a tragic classical expression: urgency, character conflicts, belief that words create and verify identities, and a consensus forged on partial truths. Only in Roth's novel the crow's ability to escape is the reason for his imprisonment, making him both a captive and an outsider. The crow's identity has been tainted by "the human stain," the crisis of identity we all struggle against to some degree or another, the actions we wish we could undo, and the preconceived notions that mark all aspects of our communication. Nevertheless, as in-group clairvoyants, we humans can pity the crow because we are assured his attempt at passing fails. Not only is no one duped, but would-be dupes within the vignette react violently and attempt to kill the passer. This violent outcome suggests that passers' attempts to defy their surroundings only lead them back to "the human stain," who and what society says they really are. Passers' tragic fates also suggest that audiences want passers to get caught. One reason could be that audiences are afforded power over passers as in-group clair-voyants and want to see that power expressed when passers are outed. Another reason could be that audiences have not been brave enough to pass, to remake themselves or overcome society's constraints in their own lives. Or audiences might want to enhance the connections between ocular and aural proofs and true identities. Or audiences could ultimately want to refasten racial loopholes.

In the film, we meet Prince in the same pet shop cage, only this time he converses with a character he knows well, Faunia Farley, a thirty-four-year-old white woman and troubled janitor at the university where Coleman taught who later becomes his girlfriend. Faunia recently escaped from her abusive and mentally ill Vietnam veteran ex-husband.

> Faunia: [*Breathes a sigh of relief when she sees Prince*]. Hey there.
>
> Prince: [*Squawks*]
>
> Faunia: Hey Prince. Hey.
>
> Prince: [*Squawks*]
>
> Faunia: Yeah, it's me. You remember me, don't you? It's Faunia. Did you forget me? I wanted to come and see you but I couldn't.
>
> Shopkeeper: [*To Faunia*] Hi. I haven't seen you in, it must be, three, four months. Prince missed you. He got out the other day. The other birds attacked him. They would've killed him. He doesn't have the right voice.
>
> Faunia: That's because he's hand-raised. Yeah. He's been hanging around people like us all his life.
>
> Prince: [*Squawks*]
>
> Faunia: A crow that doesn't know how to be a crow.

As in the novel, we find that ancestry, background, and language constitute three tragic marks to which "the human stain" refers. Prince is stained because of his personal relationships with those who raised him (his human family) and cannot assimilate with crows he looks like but whose backgrounds he does not share. Elsewhere in the novel and film we learn that Prince tries to erase his past by using his beak to tear down articles posted on the pet shop's wall that describe how he was hand-raised after his nest was destroyed. When that proves insufficient, in the attempt to remake his identity he escapes. In the film Prince is described as "a crow that does not know how to be a crow" because he does not know how to speak like a crow. For Prince, as a passer, it is speech and actions rather than appearance that makes a crow a crow. The difference between Prince, the would-be wild crow, and Prince, the domesticated crow, is less a difference in personality or appearance than it is a difference in speech. The same holds true for the difference between Prince and the wild crows that live in the trees. Thus, Prince's passing, a tragic personal choice, epitomizes the tragic reality of the society in which he lives. A society in which the opposite of a real and authentic racial identity is considered an artificial or appropriated one (*Password Eight*); a society that has trouble accepting options through which one chooses to identify sincerely, concealing and revealing oneself appropriately and eloquently (*Passwords One, Nine*).[14]

In Aesop's fable and in both iterations of *The Human Stain*, passing is disclosed quickly to ensure the success of passing as a pleasurable form of entertainment and ensure the failure and punishment of the passer. In the Aesopic rendering, the crow's voice confounds its appearance as a raven. Human audiences are not duped. In *The Human Stain*'s transcriptions, the crow's voice betrays the constraints of its domesticated upbringing around humans. Wild crows are not duped and go on the attack. In each case, the crow caws ineloquently with a voice that discloses his or her origins. These moments of revelation indicate that speech can be problematic when it is out of the speaker's control. These anecdotes suggest that passing is based as much on a passer's eloquence, representation, and believability as it is on an audience's willingness to become a character in the story, enter as a partner into social relations with other characters, and participate in the action in progress (*Passwords Two, Five*).[15] In *The Human Stain*, the metaphor of the crow frames passing as a series of rhetorical interactions in a racialized frame of reference that forces audiences to question the reassuring signs of ontological distinction they are accustomed to reading (*Password One*). And because of the literary significance of the crow as a bad omen, audiences are forewarned that passing is tragedy, clearly and completely.

Extending the deep analogy between Coleman and Prince (the figure of the passing crow) has important implications for the study of passing as pastime. In addition to connecting the passing protagonist to classical descriptions of passing as tragic act, the analogy allows us to identify the tragic formula for passing as a form of contemporary entertainment.

Password Eleven

Audiences must be able to identify passers as passers; identify dupes and potential dupes; identify themselves as in-group clairvoyants and share the secret with other in-group clairvoyants; pity passers' unfortunate circumstances and actions as a function of who they believe passers are; and derive pleasure from their own sympathetic responses to passers' suffering and outing.

Password Eleven ensures a pleasurable audience response to passing. When audiences' expectations are met, and they understand that certain claims are suppressed in the narrative, they dig deeper and make their own connections and conclusions where no material is provided. When audiences' expectations are violated, they correct violations and ease their displeasure by taking on a defensive dupe's persona and walking away from the narrative in search of answers to their unresolved questions.

Extending the analogy between Coleman and Prince allows us to track differences in and analyze critical responses to passing in the novel and film based on the entertainment formula (*Password Eleven*). And the metaphor of the passing crow allows us to chart the ongoing relevance of classical rhetoric as source of dignity and power through which passers can play with identity under conspicuous and indeterminate situational limits, even as dupes and in-group clairvoyants cast watchful eyes. We will now see that Coleman's reasons for passing are similar to the crow's and are confirmed by social encounters in which he is made to feel different because of what he says.

THE NOVEL

Because Coleman can be read as the crow passing in a Jim and Jane Crow environment, he is a synecdochic representative and a figure through which all identities in the novel can be interpreted.

He is at once a hero who defies racism and a tragic character slain for his defiance. Like all acts of passing, Coleman's begins at the intersection of synecdoche-metonymy (*Password Four*). His is merely one manifestation of the practice that stands in to represent the whole. Readers experience the tragic range of passing through the novel's dramatic style and content, its conclusion in Coleman's death and disaster, and the suffering and enlightenment that conclusion elicits. By the end everyone knows that Coleman is passing. Everyone is an in-group clairvoyant. No one is duped except, perhaps, for Coleman himself. Therein lies the tragedy. Although Coleman ultimately fails as a passer, his passing succeeds as literary entertainment.[16]

As the passing crow personified, Coleman stands in ambivalent relation to the tragedy of his historical and social setting. This scenic relationship is no coincidence. *The Human Stain* makes use of flashbacks to employ the past as agency, wherein any number of its parts are reincarnated in the present, and with them the whole dramas of racism and racial identification. For instance, Coleman's movements are described as "swooping, almost like birds do when they fly over land or sea and spy something moving, something bursting with life, and dive down . . . and seize upon it."[17] Swooping suggests passing quickly from one situation while hunting for new relationship networks. This strategy proves most effective when Coleman encounters constraints of Jim and Jane Crow segregation.

Coleman endures many unfortunate occurrences that cause suffering. Let us return to the unfortunate "spooks" utterance for which Coleman was banished from Athena College. At this point readers already know that Coleman is a passer. Hence the tragedy is that Coleman cannot denounce the charge without unveiling that very secret. In fact, his motives for saying "spooks" depend on his perceived racial status as black or white. If he is black, and assuming he is not the type of lighter-skinned black person who refers to darker-skinned black people as "spooks," then he must not be a racist and the word "spooks" is merely a synonym for "phantoms." If he is white, then he must be a racist and the word "spooks" means that because of their dark skin, these black students can blend into the night like ghosts. The "spooks" episode reverses the traditional tests of will and character assigned to his identity as passer. In a more traditional depiction, Coleman's passing would indicate that he is really black and racist against or ashamed of black people because he passes as white and Jewish. If he is true to his white and Jewish persona, then he is true to himself and has no obligation to anyone else, racist or not. In the end, he protects his white and Jewish identity by passing as a racist. He dies ironically at the hands of Faunia's ex-husband, who, as fate would have it, is a raging anti-Semite.[18] After a life invested in avoiding discrimination on the basis of one stigmatized identity, Coleman is tragically undone on the basis of the other.[19]

Coleman's murder, the "spooks" episode, and allusions to the passing crow are three among many symbolic offerings that make *The Human Stain* a prime candidate for the study of passing as a tragic pastime. Passing is framed as an epic conflict between (the part) "I" and (the whole) "we" that manifests as a series of deliberations and counterdeliberations (*Passwords Three, Four*). Coleman's passing can be considered an attempt to create his own individual identity under the ethnic category of Jewish and the racial category of white. His decision hinges on the fact that having white skin afforded him the privilege to choose not to identify with the values imposed upon him by black historical authenticity. Experiencing life through the eyes of his black family in New Jersey and later his black classmates at Howard University, he realized he could never be free to be what he wanted to be so long as he identified as black. This was confirmed when he experienced white racism and was called a "nigger" while away at college. To escape these situational constraints, he exercised the option to become what he saw as a "raw I" that could stand alone and apart from any "we."[20] Coleman later reflects on his situation:

> At Howard he'd discovered that he wasn't just a nigger to Washington, D.C. . . . Overnight the raw I was part of a we with all of the we's overbearing solidity, and he didn't want anything to do with It or with the next oppressive we that came along either. You finally leave home, the Ur of we, and you find *another we*? Another place that's just like that, the *substitute* for that? Growing up in East Orange, he was of course a Negro . . . down across the Newark line, he was, without thinking about it, everything else as well. He was Coleman, the greatest of the great *pioneers* of the I.[21]

Like many racially ambiguous adolescents, Coleman favors humanism and self-definition, sees the one-drop rule as a form of ancestor reverence and imprisonment and thus as an obstacle to representational freedom.[22] His passing is his flight away from and above the various "we" groups he is invited to join. Collective values inculcated by his family tell him to be proud of and assert his blackness, even though it is virtually invisible and stands as an obstacle to his individuality in the context of segregation.[23] In response, Coleman sets out to reinvent himself and eventually creates a new identity and family based on "his exhilarating notion of freedom."[24]

Tragedy is reintroduced when we learn that the very same forces abetting Coleman's self-identification as "raw I" are also those that structure his life around a "we," the collective values that limit opportunities for those who fall short of the ideal images of black and white.[25] For instance, many of Coleman's initial successful attempts at passing as white occur in the boxing ring. And, when asked why he disobeyed orders and defeated his final black opponent, named Beau Jack, in less than two minutes, he answers, "Because I don't carry no nigger."[26] Coleman's response aids his passing in two ways. First, it uses synecdoche to increase the distance between himself and his black opponent who stands in for all black men in Coleman's life. Second, in Coleman's mind, his response erases the distance between himself and those whites who would hurl the toxic term at him.[27] In order to maintain a low racial profile and avoid increasing scrutiny from dupes in the narrative, Coleman ultimately chooses Jewish identity as a beige buffer zone between the poles of blackness and whiteness.

Though Coleman is presented as the suffering victim in the tragedy, he is also presented as the agent of tragic developments that ensure his failure. Thus, Coleman's ambiguous racial appearance is implicated in the danger he poses to himself and to others. The novel's description of passing as Coleman's "first great crime" takes place in Coleman's teenage years. In October 1944, Coleman passed as eighteen and then as white in order to join the navy. He realized instantly that "he could easily lie about his age—to move his birth date back by a month from November 12 to October 12, was no problem at all. . . . It didn't immediately occur to him that, if he chose to, he could lie about his race as well. He could play his skin however he wanted, color himself just as he chose . . . it occurred first to his heart, which began banging away like the heart of someone on the brink of committing his first great crime."[28] Passing is Coleman's "first great crime" because it forces him to falsify his enlistment forms. Even more significantly, passing is a criminal event for Coleman because it exposes future options to get away with actions that would not be socially sanctioned for a black man by recreating identity through the power of communication. Making use of this power is the gateway to other "great crimes." But the question is, crimes against whom? Churning with anxiety about the ramifications of this "crime," Coleman tries to settle the question. The question is answered only as Coleman's persona as white and later as Jewish is constructed and undone and as incongruities among appearances, truths, and origins are exposed.

Coleman's passing is framed initially as a crime of identity committed in response to the larger crimes of structural racism and institutionalized segregation imposed upon him (*Passwords Seven, Eight*). And passing's powers are enhanced as Coleman learns how to adjust his persona in and through the interplay of language (*Passwords Five, Nine, Ten*). Such adjustments are supported and espoused first by Doc, Coleman's high school boxing coach, who presents him with a way out of having to go to an all-black college when interviewed by boxing coaches from Pitt. " 'If nothing comes up,' Doc said, 'you don't bring it up. You're neither one thing or the other . . . that's the deal.' "[29] This "deal" solidifies Coleman as an ambiguous agent who can pass through the rigid and static boundaries of racial identification. Doc tells Coleman that he is neither white nor black but "Silky Silk," a proper and uniquely individual name that represents his newfound acceptable persona. "Silky Silk" is an incarnation that is meant to help Coleman escape the limits of his environment and remove the human stain. But as fate would have it the human stain is inescapable. Therefore, the narrative is essentially tragic, presenting passing as a perpetual act of escape in which Coleman ironically remains a perpetual prisoner. Coleman, like Prince the crow, seeks a self-determined life without constraint; a life that is empowered rather than obstructed by legal and social custom. He explains that "all he wanted, from earliest childhood on, was to be free: not black, not even white— just on his own and free"; he equates freedom with racelessness and, ironically, with a Jewish ethnic identity suspended somewhere between whiteness and blackness.[30] Coleman's determination to be "free" culminates in tragedy as readers begin to construct him as the primary agent of his own demise.

Coleman fails to realize that true freedom is not available to him because he has not transcended race, but has traded one set of racial, ethnic, and behavioral constraints for another. His mother expresses this poetically when she laments that he "is white as snow and . . . think[s] like a slave."[31] Even without a master, Coleman is enslaved by the future he imagines for himself. Again identity is disconnected from appearance and historicity and connected to the language with which one thinks, discusses, and imagines the world and its future. In this scene, to underscore Coleman's ineloquence the novel draws on the figure of the passing crow that never seems to say the right thing. Readers see the tragedy in Coleman's ineloquence, thoughts, and character, and hence experience the tragedy in his passing. Readers respond to the tragedy directly by painting their own versions of what Coleman looks like in their imaginations. In coloring Coleman as they choose, readers identify him with self-interest, and their visions of race remain largely untested. In the absence of a challenge to what they know about race, readers can experience closure, identifying with Coleman's suffering at the expense of the pernicious nature of racism which causes it (*Password Eight*).

Because Coleman's passing fails repeatedly, and because every reader knows he is passing, the novel succeeds as a form of entertainment. The novel's critical acclaim stems from the sympathetic responses readers have to Coleman's painful existence and to the mental pictures of him they create and carry. Coleman exists exactly as readers imagine him, not quite black and definitely not white. Further, readers ultimately find pleasure in having their visions of Coleman confirmed. That is, the overwhelmingly positive response to the novel suggests a larger social connection among readers and characters, in-group clairvoyants, dupes, and passers. Those who judge the novel "a good read" are also approving of it as morally good, since disapproval would not generate the pleasurable response.[32] By this logic it can be considered morally good that the not-quite-black-and-definitely-not-white passer is outed and murdered. These tragic outcomes confirm readers' racial expectations and conceptions of passing as a tragic and costly ruse that only dupes the passer.

Though Coleman fails, readers derive pleasure from the confusion, sorrow, anxiety, and pity his passing arouses. The more readers are affected by Coleman's failures, first as a black man and then as a white and Jewish man, the more they are entertained; and as soon as the uneasiness and unpleasantness become too uncomfortable, the story is over and Coleman has passed on. So the more tragic the ending, the more satisfying passing becomes as a form of entertainment. It seems that readers of *The Human Stain* are ultimately entertained to the degree that they are affected by the tragic elements of Coleman's life, and are ultimately satisfied when the narrative fills them with sympathy and compassion for Coleman as the failed passer who engineered his own demise.[33] Of course, this reading also releases readers from the responsibility of imagining there was anything they or other in-group clairvoyants could have done to ensure an alternate ending. Everyone knows that what happens is Coleman's fault.

I now turn to the performance of passing and the appearances of passers in the film. The following section explores the film's mode of challenging the relation between identity and appearance and explains why it elicited an unpleasant and unentertaining response from viewers.

THE FILM

If the literary version of *The Human Stain* is a tragedy through which we imagine Coleman becomes invisible, then the cinematic version is a mystery through which we watch Coleman emerge. Coleman's emergence is no different than the emergence of any self-made person in the United States. But Coleman's outcomes are.[34] Outcomes unfold as a series of complex tragedies that hinge on discovery and an unexpected change of fortune or reverse of circumstances (*peripeteia*) through memory, and are awakened by something unveiled or spoken in the present moment (*aletheia*). Audiences observe Coleman's passing while his secret is divulged among dupes and in-group clairvoyants, who ultimately prove unable to grant him access to their social worlds.

As in the novel, audiences are asked to read racial passing as a tragic act. However, in the film audiences are also asked to read the passer's appearance as a challenge to the *doxa* (cultural common sense) that says a person must be categorized as and look black if he or she has any African ancestry.[35] The challenge to *doxa* posed by the passer's appearance in *The Human Stain* is something moviegoers cannot seem to wrap their minds around, even when Coleman stands before them as a black man who looks white.[36] Social anxiety over passing and ambiguous racial bodies ensures that Coleman suffers even more exclusion in the film than he does in the novel—exclusion from the white body politic, from the black community, from the realm of the living, and from successful entertainment. *The Human Stain* is set as Coleman's life unravels according to the template of the tragic mulatto, who, like the passing crow, is always made ridiculous by his desire to find acceptance as part of a flock that does not really exist. If the medium is the message, then the film displays something the novel does not dare whisper. When audiences cannot locate a passer's "true" racial identity as visually stained (read black or black-looking), they cannot believe that he would be a passer. In other words, passing fails to entertain when the passer actually succeeds in projecting his or her acceptable persona (*Password Eleven*).

FIGURE 5.1
Welshman Sir Anthony Hopkins as the elder
Coleman Silk in *The Human Stain*

While some critics saw casting Hopkins as daring and progressive,[37] most saw him as simply too white to portray a racial passer of Coleman's ilk.[38] In response, Robert Benton, the film's director, commented that this line of criticism is a function of medium: "In a novel, words evoke; images limit. And they are specific in a way you're stuck with."[39] Believing Hopkins's performance requires some casuistic stretching on the part of the audience. On one hand the audience watches the subversion of whiteness. On the other hand the audience sees nothing but whiteness. Benton suspends this tension by asking audiences to attend to a form of racial drag.[40] In this way they can take on a more active role as in-group clairvoyants and acknowledge that passing is not lost to history. And they can embrace Hopkins playing Coleman as black turned Jewish even though they know this is not his offscreen persona.

Not everyone saw it as Benton did. Rendering Coleman visible on screen is a symbolic gesture that some reviewers liken to a modern-day version of minstrelsy minus the blackface. For these reviewers, embracing Hopkins as Coleman would be akin to how many white and Jewish historical audiences embraced white and Jewish minstrels' performances (e.g., Al Jolson in *The Jazz Singer*).[41] Rendering Coleman's passing visible also dramatizes the larger issue of performance as a response to the demands of assimilation.[42] From this perspective all identities are rule-bound performances. Jewish American minstrel performers and African American passers then represent opposing sides of the "passing crow" story with which we began.[43] History supports such a read. For many Jewish immigrants in the early twentieth century, blackface was not interpreted as a denial of ethnicity but rather as a technique to translate it into American cultural terms. Some suggest that "blackface was a way for Jews to pass as Americans, making African American identity a synecdoche for American identity."[44] Although it is indisputable that blackface portrayals were and are demeaning to black historicity and its cultural expressions, minstrelsy proved to be one way of creating a unique cultural status for Jewish identity in America.[45] *The Human Stain* updates and reverses this classic theme by presenting Jewish American identity as a means of cultural translation for Coleman's black identity. In this way *The Human Stain* asks viewers to confront the processes of racial and ethnic formation for white, Jewish, and black groups simultaneously. And through the racially ambiguous figure of Coleman, encounters with blackness, whiteness, and Jewishness become increasingly intertwined and incommodious.

Ultimately Coleman's acceptable persona as Jewish, his intermediary strategy for racial identification rather than a strict ethnic nomenclature, becomes the cause for his murder at the hands of an anti-Semite. Like the passing crow, Coleman is ultimately unable to accomplish that which he most desires—to be understood on his own terms. He never reveals his prepassing persona to his Jewish family, colleagues, and friends, and he never reveals his in-passing persona to his black family (except for his younger sister, Ernestine). He is never able to say the right thing. He feels as though he is out on a limb, speaking ineloquently, all the while caged because he will never accurately predict exactly how his caws are read and interpreted. In attempting to fulfill his desires for freedom and esteem, Coleman sacrifices his ability to communicate. Like the crow, Coleman's nuanced appearance and speech fail precisely because they defy easy notions about identity.

FIGURE 5.2
Multiracial Wentworth Miller III as the younger
Coleman Silk in *The Human Stain*

The film mirrors its exegetic themes of identity formation, assimilation, and performance by connecting the younger Coleman's experiences as a black person during the segregation era to his present and future experiences as an older white and Jewish person.[46] The younger Coleman (played by Wentworth Miller III) appears within a series of spatial intermissions that teach the logic of passing—how to communicate eloquently with diverse audiences and ensure acceptance by dupes and cooperation from in-group clairvoyants (*Password Two*). Though some saw Miller as miscast because he did not look like Hopkins or like a member of a bona fide black family, several reviewers praised him for his credible performance as a confused passer. Such praise is due, in large part, to Miller's self-proclaimed multiracial identity, which allowed audiences to read him as a tragic mulatto with a divided heritage and loyalty.[47] As a consequence, audiences were able to accept his rendition of the comparisons (between passer and in-group clairvoyant, between black and white) that make passing meaningful.[48]

An example is the vignette in which the elder Coleman (played by Hopkins) remembers the time he and his white ex-girlfriend Steena went to a record store to purchase Rachmaninoff's Third Piano Concerto while he was studying at New York University. Framed as a flashback (from the elder Coleman's perspective as an in-group clairvoyant), this vignette is indicative of the passer's constant fear of being outed. As in-group clairvoyant, the elder Coleman looks back and remembers himself as the young Coleman (passer), who the audience watches enter the store in which a black saleswoman (in-group clairvoyant) immediately recognizes and stares at him incredulously. She approaches him and says:

Woman: Did you go to East Orange High?

Coleman: Yes.

Woman: I thought you looked familiar. Charlie Hamilton is my cousin.

Coleman: It's been a while. How is Charlie? How's he been?

Woman: Good. Actually, he's getting married.

Coleman: Good for him. Now, the Rachmaninoff please.

Woman: Is that your girlfriend?

Coleman: Yes. Yes it is. [*Change of tone*] Look. Maybe I
should come back some other time. Then we can talk.
Okay?

Woman: Fine. Here. That'll do the trick a lot better than
Rachmaninoff.
[*She glances over at Steena, summing her up in one fell
swoop, and hands him a jazz record instead.*]

This encounter reiterates the central theme of classical rhetoric's
passing crow: that Coleman's decision to protect his new identity as
white (and later as white and Jewish) depends on what he says and
upon who is able to see, hear, and understand him. Coleman's acts
of passing inevitably stain those around him by requiring either
their attention and complicity as in-group clairvoyants or their
ignorance and deception as dupes (*Password Two*). Accordingly,
the interaction is marked by Coleman's inability to sustain eye
contact with the black saleswoman because of her recognition. All
the while Steena stands behind them in a listening booth smoking
a cigarette and watching, unable to hear the interaction because
she wears headphones. Coleman's speech, Steena's deafness, and
the saleswoman's silence are all required to sustain the pass.

Steena cements her position as the dupe by reading Coleman
metonymically as a white and Jewish man (*Password Four*). Steena
reads Coleman's white appearance as the indicator of his authentic whiteness. The saleswoman, on the other hand, represents the
in-group clairvoyant who reads the tension between Coleman's
assumed authentic black identity and what she believes is his performance of white identity metonymically (*Password Four*). These
competing points of view are linked to each one's ability to hear
what Coleman says and ability to judge the image he presents
accordingly (*Password Two*). The elder Coleman represents the
larger audience of in-group clairvoyants, who keep the secret and
look on as he is later humiliated when Steena dumps him after
finding out he and his family are black.

Although the elder Coleman seemed secure in his persona,
audiences learn that he was merely passing as secure. Coleman's
inability to communicate openly with either his Jewish or his black
families is reminiscent of the passing crow that never seems to
say the right thing. The key to Coleman's passing, the inability of
what is said and seen to accurately represent reality, comes in a

precisely chosen word reminiscent of the younger Coleman's final interaction with his brother Walter and the familial pain passing caused the Silk family. Walter screamed, "*Never.* Don't you dare ever show your lily-white face around that house again!"[49] For the younger Coleman the term "lily-white" pierces the heart of his passing and the unstained acceptable persona he attempts to project for the rest of his life.

For the elder Coleman, the term "lily-white" rears its head during a consultation with his young attorney after being harassed by Faunia's violent and mentally unstable ex-husband. "Instead of the legal action [Coleman] expects, he finds himself on the receiving end of a presumptuous and condescending lecture, the gist of which is that he should end his affair with Faunia."[50] Because of the stain left on Coleman's reputation by the charges of racism after the "spooks" incident, the lawyer tells him he is inviting further tragedy into his life by being involved with this woman. Coleman appears to be listening calmly and then responds emotionally by telling the attorney, "I never again want to hear that self-admiring voice of yours or see your smug fucking lily-white face." Even though the lawyer (as Coleman's dupe) questions why Coleman would use the term "lily-white," Coleman knows why. He has finally exposed what was hidden for his entire adult life— that he is not "lily-white"—even if only to himself.

But the film's audiences cannot out Coleman as a passer based on this sly admission alone. Coleman's ambiguous appearance confounds the matter because he appears as a white and Jewish man—the identities into which he has passed. As supposed in-group clairvoyants, audiences expected a film about passing to validate racial identity as visible and authentic, making the passer a charlatan and passing a criminal offense deserving of tragic punishment (*Password One*). When audiences did not get what they expected, they panned the film and called it a sham.[51] By praising Hopkins and Miller for their performances yet depicting them as racially miscast, moviegoers corrected the violation. Audiences read Hopkins as white and not as a black man who could be white and Jewish. Audiences read Miller as a man who could be white and/or Jewish but not black. Or, to use the critical vocabulary of passing, filmgoers could not take the leap of faith required to embrace *aletheia* and question *episteme* or *doxa* (*Password One*). Instead, they dug their heels in, jeered at the film, and became defensive dupes. The subversive enthymeme: Race occupies no gray areas. There is no biracial passer. There is no history that could create a biracial passer. Therefore, white cannot be or look like black, and black cannot be or look like white. Filmgoers exercised their power to uphold the very racial and ethnic notions they were invited to challenge. Viewers transferred their discomfort and dissatisfaction with racial presumptions onto the passer. Their disapproval of the passer in *The Human Stain* suggests that passing is not a source of pleasurable entertainment when it operates critically and calls racial formation into question.[52] Passing entertains only when it is deployed to fix racial categories and uphold the status quo.

CONCLUSIONS

The Human Stain reincarnates classical themes of tragedy and identification to remind us that we can never truly leave the past behind. Coleman's personal history, U.S. history, and classical rhetorical history are manifest in his detection by readers and spectators, which reveals that the issues to which passing is a response—racism, freedom, and assimilation—have not passed on. In fact, readers' and filmgoers' reactions to Coleman help us better understand how consumers of popular culture experience passing today. For one thing, we have learned that images and narratives about passing are not just matters of entertainment. They are major liaisons in communication that affect how we think and talk about identity today.

Positive and pleasurable responses to passing as literary entertainment reveal that passing requires an audience that can empathize with the passer as a character of their own design and experience the passer's suffering from the relative security of an in-group clairvoyant's perspective (*Password Eleven*). Readers' pleasure is related to the passer's distress and sorrow and the language through which that distress and sorrow are rendered in Roth's novel. They are reminded of themselves and of the many masks they may have worn over the course of their lives. They identify with Coleman because they can paint his portrait in their imaginations. Because readers are not required to verify that image against alternative representations, the stability of racial structures and identities is maintained. Though things are not as they seem in the novel, things are as they seem when readers close the book. Coleman has pretended to be someone readers believe he is not and, therefore, made himself a pathetic and tragic figure. Readers are reassured.

The film's reception tells a different story, in part because its form causes viewers to question a simple voyeuristic consumption of racial ambiguity. Casting choices, meant to enhance the believability of passing and cultivate visual skepticism, backfired. Consequently, moviegoers missed an important opportunity to grapple with passing's epistemological, ontological, and existential dimensions in and out of the drama portrayed. Instead, as in *Plessy v. Ferguson*, audiences become defensive dupes who find passing too complex and confusing to decode (*Password Seven*). To simplify matters and attempt to ease discomfort over changing racial categories, film audiences exclude, vilify, and subordinate passers and deny passers' self-determination and unrestrained racial mobility. The film's poor reception suggests moviegoers' extreme discomfort with the relentless presence of the unstained human body and its relentless refusal to reveal racial truths.[53] Thus, as they embody Coleman, Hopkins and Miller become synecdoches, bodies that represent everything would be in-group clairvoyants can never really know about Coleman or about any passer. Because moviegoers cannot participate in the pass as in-group clairvoyants, and cannot out the passer, the film's rendition of passing fails to entertain. And *The Human Stain* becomes proof that we are as yet unable or unwilling to grapple seriously with certain kinds of racial ambiguity and the acts of passing they engender.[54]

Despite differing receptions, we must acknowledge that the novel and film use passing productively to emphasize the stains racial categories and hierarchies leave behind. Perhaps the truest tragedy evidenced by the competing receptions of *The Human Stain* is that passers are expected to fail and suffer at their own hands rather than challenge collective notions of racial identity and typecasting in contemporary popular culture. Instead of acknowledging *The Human Stain* as a constructive platform for updating the classical sophistic theme of the passing crow through the life of its protagonist, audiences interpret it through limited and antiquated frames of ocular proof required by Plato's *episteme*. The novel's rendition of passing succeeds because Coleman is always too black to be white. The film's rendition of passing fails because Coleman appears too white to be black. Neither of these reactions challenges the status quo or affords the passer an option to exist as a product of his or her own design. Instead these reactions further cloud much needed critical explorations of race, ethnicity, nationality and self-image.

Loving passing in the book and hating passing in the movie are the easy answers, for neither requires the hard work of rethinking racial fictions, challenging definitions of passing as deception and imposture, and confronting the realities of racial and ethnic formation in contemporary popular culture.[55] The hard work involves listening to the things said in passing, to the things that no one likes to talk about. Things like admitting that those who can pass as white men continue to accrue palpable advantages even after the Jim and Jane Crow era.[56] Things like acknowledging our ongoing perception of whiteness as unstained and of nonwhiteness as an odd deviation of form. Things like recognizing that enslavement, rape, duplicity, segregation, and discrimination happened and catalyzed the formation of African Americans as a racial group that is largely multiracial and is now expressing aspects of its contemporary relevance in multiracial terms.[57] Because audiences refuse to see how they are implicated in these things said in passing, they are unable to really see passers well either. From there the tragedy of passing in *The Human Stain* finds itself. And it appears to have found us as well.

CHAPTER SIX

Passing as Paradox

Many of us have been on jury duty hoping not to be selected to serve for trial. And if we have not been on jury duty or served as jurors, we have probably witnessed depictions of others who have. We endure and imagine ourselves enduring all kinds of questions about who we are and what we know. Lawyers ask, "Have you heard anything about the case from any source?" We answer, "No." Lawyers ask, "Do you know the defendant(s)?" Again, we answer, "No." Seeking out our hidden prejudices and sympathies, lawyers ask, "Is there anything about the nature of this case which might make it difficult for you to try the issues fairly and impartially without prejudice or bias?" "No, nothing I know of," we say. Usually this would be enough to guarantee a seat in the jury box. But in July of 2002 jurors who answered no to these questions faced many more, seventy-four more to be exact.[1] One by one the pool of three hundred potential jurors was whittled down to thirty-eight, and then to sixteen. They were asked things like "Have you or anyone with whom you have a relationship or friendship ever held the belief or espoused the position held by or been a member of the KKK, Aryan Nations, National Socialist Movement, National Alliance, or similar group which bases its doctrine on race or ethnicity?" And "Have you ever been a member of or donated funds to a civil rights organization like the NAACP?" And "What religion do you practice?" The questions went on and on.

It is safe to assume that as potential jurors many of us would be puzzled and troubled by the natures of these additional questions about our racial attitudes, religious beliefs, and political affiliations. We would be wondering who exactly was on trial. Was it the defendants or the jurors? We would also be wondering what exactly this case was really about. Hate crimes? Terrorism? Something else that would be less easy to determine? And so it was for the twelve jurors and four alternates selected to hear the case *U.S. v. Leo V. Felton and Erica Chase*. The defendants, Felton and Chase, were on trial for allegedly forming a "cell" of a self-described Aryan Order known as the White Order of Thule while seeking, by any means necessary, to rid the United States of non-whites and of perceived Jewish influence. The cell and its plot were funded with proceeds from counterfeiting. But there was something Felton's co-defendant and potential jury did not know. Something that would put their beliefs on trial as much as Felton's. Something that appeared in black and white on his Boston Police Department booking sheet when he was arrested in 2001: Name: Leo V. Felton. Age: 30. Race: Black. Suddenly the public was dumbfounded and drawn in. Anyone who, at some point in time, has discriminated against or been discriminated against based on race or ethnicity is implicated in Felton's case.[2] Reporters found themselves in a tight spot too—writing headlines such as "Black, White Past Clouded Felton's Identity" and "The Enemy Within"—attempting to explain the paradoxical case of a man who entered prison as an angry black man and exited as a white supremacist leader.

Leo Felton's case draws on the notion of paradox and explains how passing can bend racial boundaries only to prove that racial boundaries are indelible. Instead of defending or deploring Felton's actions, this chapter explores the case as a series of paradoxes. How Felton helped lead a violent movement that opposed his very existence. How he allowed himself a racial freedom that he refused to allow his victims.[3] How he could hate Jews and be hostile to all his mother represented. How Felton's father refused to believe his son, given his multiracial ancestry, could become a racist white supremacist.[4] How learning of Felton's multiracial identity caused his white supremacist girlfriend to end their relationship

FIGURE 6.1
Leo Felton's mug shot

and disavow her racism. The chapter continues by comparing the
mainstream media's attempts to resolve these paradoxes by framing Felton's passing as a mental health issue to Felton's own perspective on passing as a sane and principled choice.[5] The chapter
concludes by discussing how Felton's expression of a "beige" (read
nonwhite, nonblack) identity complicates and (mis)appropriates
passing to reproduce and restabilize the very concept of race he
purports to disavow.

THE CURIOUS CASE OF LEO FELTON

Leo V. Felton is the son of civil rights workers, a multiracial African
American architect named Calvin Felton and a white and Jewish
ex-nun named Corinne Vincelette. Like many interracial marriages,
Calvin's and Corinne's was short-lived.[6] The couple divorced in
1972 when Leo was only two years old. Calvin Felton stayed active
in his son's life and ensured that Leo and his five black half-siblings

were frequently in touch. Meanwhile, Vincelette entered a lesbian relationship with a Jewish woman named Nancy Clinch. Vincelette and Clinch went on to form, as the *New York Times Magazine* puts it, "perhaps the only family in the comfortable, mostly white suburb of Gaithersburg, Maryland, that had two white mothers, two white daughters, and a biracial son."[7] As Leo was part of a nontraditional family tree, it was assumed that he would develop a politically and socially progressive attitude. "He grew up in a family that was very much in favor of equal rights for everybody," one of his stepsisters told the *Boston Globe*, and the family was just as puzzled as the public over Leo's political choices.[8]

For Leo the natures of family and identity were not so simple. He became the protagonist in a twenty-first-century narrative of passing in 2001, when he and his girlfriend were arrested in Boston, Massachusetts, for attempting to pass off counterfeit money at a Dunkin' Donuts. But that was neither Leo's first attempt at passing nor his only crime. Leo was first institutionalized as a preadolescent after he reacted violently to being teased about his multiracial background. He chased a black classmate and friend named Corey with a knife and shouted, "I'll kill you" because Corey had called Leo a "half breed."[9] After a few months Leo was discharged from the institution, but his mother sent him back, against his father's wishes.[10] Leo was in and out of institutions until he was fourteen years old. Angry and callused, he found refuge in the DC Hardcore punk rock movement. He rebelled against his family and society—quitting school, hitchhiking twice across the country under assumed identities, committing robbery and assault, and tattooing "skin head" across his scalp.

When Leo was caught and fingerprinted, police discovered a pile of arrest warrants in his name. "Befitting his chameleon act, police records describe the many Feltons as different men."[11] Some reports describe him as a 200-pound black man with green eyes, and others depict him as a 150-pound male with a light complexion and brown eyes. But Leo did not realize his true identity as a white supremacist, he says, until he found himself immersed in the racially segregated New York prison system after assaulting an Afro-Cuban taxi driver in a road rage incident.[12] When Leo landed in the New York prison system, its population was 15 percent white and housed several black separatist and white supremacist groups.[13] There, in an environment whose racial dynamics were the reverse of mainstream society's, the gray-eyed Leo was identified by the state's Department of Correction as white. Leo allied with whites and immersed himself in white supremacist literature. Much of the literature proved unsatisfactory because it was rife with references to "mulatto zombies" and "half-White mongrels," attesting to a paradoxical attraction to and discomfort with multiracial identities.[14] Not to mention the obvious point that this kind of language excluded Leo's participation in the movement.

Nevertheless, Leo kept searching. He reached a turning point when he read Ulick Varange's *Imperium*, which characterizes race as an inherently emotional business and a form of *aletheia* based on personal belief and behavior, not on biological ancestry.[15] In Varange Leo found a kindred spirit. Not only was Varange passing too, since his real name was Francis Parker Yockey, but he wrote the racist and anti-Semitic opus while incarcerated and was rumored to be mentally unstable.[16] Leo's white supremacy gains its force precisely from the way he cites Varange and espouses a definition of race that challenges both *episteme* (objective racial knowledge) and *doxa* (everyday racial practices) through a commitment to white supremacy based on *aletheia* or sincerity (*Password One*). As a result, Leo escapes responsibility for creating the brand of white supremacy he enacts.[17] Instead, Leo says he was inspired by Varange. Inspiration led to an extension of his prison sentence when Leo attacked two fellow inmates, one black and the other Latino. While incarcerated Leo explored Greek Orthodoxy, married his nineteen-year-old pen pal Lisa Meetre, and began an emotional affair with another pen pal, white supremacist coconspirator Erica Chase.[18] Exchanging letters, Leo and Erica planned to rid the nation of all nonwhites, starting with people of Jewish and African descent.

Upon release from prison in January 2001, Leo and Erica met, joined forces, and used counterfeit cash to finance their domestic terrorist plot. They were, as a *Boston Magazine* writer put it, "busy stockpiling and preparing. Leo collected books on how to assume a new identity, carry out terrorist actions, and how to make explosives and silencers. Leo purchased computer résumé paper and a printer and churned out twelve hundred dollars" in counterfeit bills.[19] As outlined in Leo's handwritten notes and comic strips, he and Erica aimed to destroy violently various Jewish and/or African American monuments and symbols throughout

Boston as well as Washington, D.C.'s Holocaust Museum.[20] They also targeted "Jewish media moguls including Steven Spielberg, and black leaders such as the Rev. Jesse Jackson."[21] Before their plans were enacted, Leo was arrested and then outed as multiracial (i.e., black and white or black, depending on the newspaper) and multiethnic (i.e., Jewish and non-Jewish European). In what can only be described as a quest for an apology or an explanation, mainstream media coverage focused on Leo's public identity as a sadistic and brazen white supremacist and his private identity as multiracial and multiethnic. Leo was a paradox—painted as frank and insightful, offputting and scapegoating, and frightening in one way or another to any healthy or rational person.

FROM CURIOSITY TO PATHOLOGY

It is in this context that the newspaper-reading public meets Leo as the "marginal man"[22] of the new millennium, a man who does not exist in proper relation with himself or the antagonistic cocultures into which he is born.[23] A man who was afflicted at birth with a case of conflicted racial identity and bewailed his association with blackness while desiring in vain the full whiteness he could never attain.[24] As the press tells it, Leo's conflicted identity literally made him sick.[25] It caused structural and functional changes to what the media's *doxa* declared should have been a unified identity as multiracial and a liberal and socially progressive worldview. Interventions by Leo's family, by psychiatrists, and by law enforcement proved ineffective. No permanent cure was found for Leo's inner conflict. Article after article details that Leo loathed the nonwhite aspects of his identity to such an extent that he sought to blot them from the earth.[26] Leo's remorseless antisocial behavior is linked directly to his struggle with multiracial identity, underscoring the historical stereotype that multiracial individuals are unstable emotionally and prone to certain debilities—like passing—because they cannot integrate their racial identities.[27] Some reports speculate that Leo's intense personal struggle with multiracial identity created an intense longing for a white lover in order to validate or otherwise solidify his own claim to whiteness.[28] Other reports trace the roots of Leo's violence to feelings of alienation over never fitting in with either black or white social worlds.[29] Still other reports paint Leo's identification with whiteness and white culture as problems that could have been corrected if he had accepted and adopted an identity as black.[30] Regardless, Leo's multiracial ancestry was framed as the primary cause of conflict and, ultimately, his paradoxical position as a passer and white supremacist. Passing was read as synecdoche for his psychological health, and his psychological health was read as synecdoche for his passing.

Reports then turn to Leo's own words to set this frame. We learn that Leo once described himself as "1/4 English and 3/4 Italian" to a fellow white supremacist in early 2001. In 2002 he wrote that no prison sentence could compare to the agony he suffered when his racial identity became public. Leo seems to confirm this perspective in another letter addressed to a *Boston Globe* reporter during his trial. "For me, the drama has already occurred, and it had nothing to do with any court."[31] Perhaps "the drama" has to do with Leo's antisocial response to the revelation of his identity; a violent suicide attempt after being outed as multiracial and multiethnic and as a passer, an event he later described to reporters as an attempt at redemption and rebirth; as "some kind of blood offering. . . . Maybe to . . . My 'New' self. With these revelations about my lineage I could certainly never go back to what I had been."[32] The suicide attempt is framed as an attempt at change rather than as a sign of Leo's commitment to rid the world of one more black and Jewish person. And Leo's talking about what he was before and after the change is framed as his attempt to identify himself as changed. For instance, Leo now appears uncertain that he could be seen as an authentic white supremacist if others knew of the nonwhite aspects of his background. Reports indicate that he then internalizes his anxiety by lamenting the figurative drops of blood that render him black and Jewish despite all outward appearance and public declaration of white supremacy. "I'm Colored," he finally writes in anachronistic resignation to a reporter from the *Boston Globe*. "A Colored Guy."[33] According to news reports, Leo's misery stems from his complicated "colored" identity, which he ultimately refers to as neither black nor white but "beige."[34] This "beige" identity is framed carefully as a kinder, gentler, and somewhat wiser identity that reflects Leo's growing level of racial comfort. As mainstream news coverage reports it, Leo took steps away from his abnormal behavior and stance.[35] He has changed and is on his way to giving up white power. Leo is guilty of many transgressions, and appears to be ready to confess, apologize, and seek rehabilitation.[36]

This frame is broken almost immediately when Leo responds by declaring that he is sane, "beige," and genuinely sympathetic to the cause of white separatism, and thus will not apologize for his actions. Because Leo shows no signs of remorse, he is spun into a mental case.[37] The *New York Times Magazine* makes this explicit by running his story under the "Health" section. "He sounds like a typical antisocial case," reports the *Boston Globe*.[38] How could anyone sane, knowing that he had black and Jewish ancestors, become an unabashed white supremacist? It just could not be possible. Even Leo's own parents, who claimed to love and support their son in spite of his actions and beliefs, call him "confused about himself and his place in an integrated world" and "a sick man."[39] This view of Leo as multiracial, "confused," and "sick" is in line with the theory of the marginal man, which says that multiracials experience high levels of psychopathology.[40] The marginal man is not just physically, socially, and intellectually distinct from black and white racial groups, but also destined to live a depressed life midway between blacks and whites because of his distinctions.[41] Though no actual empirical evidence exists to link multiracial identities to high levels of pathology, several associations and assumptions are made and united to paint Leo as what I call the new millennial marginal man.[42]

The first association is that racial identity and the importance of racial group membership affect well-being. Belonging to a racial group is assumed to correlate with well-being, and not belonging to a racial group is assumed to correlate with unhappiness.[43] The second association casts unqualified loyalty to an ascribed multiracial racial identity as authentic. Disloyalty—read passing as either white or as black—is assumed to be the result of pathology. As pathology, passing becomes a problem of repression whose resolution is self-expression (i.e., outing). So, once Leo has admitted to his authentic multiracial identity, individual happiness and freedom should follow. The pathological assumption leads to the third association, which finally transforms Leo into the new millennial marginal man: that people who are true to their multiracial identities are naturally immune to racism. This booster shot comes by way of interracial families that serve a political and social purpose by directly challenging racial *episteme* and *doxa*.[44] Taking these assumptions as facts, it is no longer paradoxical that Leo would become antisocial and suffer from "feelings of shame, emotional isolation and depression,"[45] "neurotic behavior,"[46] and a "conflicted ambivalent, confused, and negative . . . identity."[47] After all, he failed to heed the call to achieve a healthy multiracial identity. He never resolved his own internal racial struggle. He went against his nature. He took part of himself for the whole and passed (*Passwords Three, Four*). He was, as he once put it to a *New York Times* reporter, his parents' failed "social experiment."[48] Apparently Leo's mixed racial background and racially ambiguous appearance were not signs of a postracial order. His was not the beige face that reflected the nation's desire for a newer, kinder and gentler, racial spirit.[49]

News reports rely on the aforementioned associations and assumptions when they frame Leo (*doxa*) as a psychotic deviant and refer to him consistently as "clouded," "in denial," "confused," "insane," "black," "biracial," and "sick."[50] The result is an understanding of Leo's story as an ever-escalating battle of alleged "neuroses and counter-neuroses in which group politics and identities," whether monoracial or multiracial, are privileged over any real interest in Leo's growth or well-being.[51] There is also no acknowledgment of race and racism as cultural norms. Instead, race and racism become personal private problems that are solved personally and in private. Ultimately, such framing conveniently paints society as Leo's innocent victim and thereby absolves society (and its racism) of any hand in his crimes (*Password Eight*). By locking Leo away and pathologizing him as a new millennial marginal man, we protect our preferred narrative of racial progress as a product of racial mixing.[52] Because Leo is a living expectancy violation, a man whose behavior deviates from standards of social and cultural appropriateness, liberal/progressive coverage of his story has to reconcile that violation by painting him as mentally ill. Leo's neurosis cannot be cured, or passed on. It can only be managed.

FROM PATHOLOGY TO MANAGEMENT

To clarify this point, it is useful to highlight the rhetoric that manages Leo's condition. This rhetoric effectively pathologizes Leo by juxtaposing his case with doxastic examples that associate multiracial and multiethnic individuals and families with antiracist progress. In this vision of the United States as a melting pot or "miscegeNation,"[53] we are reminded that multiracialism is not only our destiny but our reality and that Leo's stance is insane, hateful, and old-fashioned. Two visual images meant to fossilize Leo's views and usher in this view era of multiracial acceptance are virtual miscegenation in the form of a computer-generated "image of the new Eve" as "the new face of America" on the cover of a November 1993 issue of *Time Magazine* and the model of digital pastiche on the cover of *Mirabella* in September 1994. These are followed by Tiger Woods's 1997 proclamation to the world via the *Oprah Winfrey Show* that he was neither black nor white but "Cablinasian."[54] Most politically significant is the "check all that apply" option on the 2000 census, which made it possible for multiracials to identify their backgrounds and affiliations. Newspapers interpreted this change as a sign that multiracials, and especially multiracials who appear racially ambiguous, personify a new posttracial era in which the significance of race is either waning or no longer significant.[55] By 2005 the Associated Press reported that the media reflect demographic changes, promote social equality, and point toward political representation because "multiracial scenes are now common on TV ads."[56] In 2008 Barack Hussein Obama's status as multiracial icon and racial reconciler was solidified with his election to the presidency. And in 2010 the U.S. Census Bureau reported that the multiracial population has increased by 32 percent to approximately 9 million Americans.[57] Though those who identified on the 2010 census as multiracial make up less than 3 percent of the total U.S. population, the increasing visibility of a multiracial demographic has turned multiracial identities into a commodity that can be consumed repeatedly across a range of media platforms.[58] As a sociopolitical commodity, multiracial identities are deployed to justify the claim that the United States, a soon-to-be "majority-minority" nation, is no longer a racial or racist society.[59] And such claims are linked to the presumed racially ambiguous appearances of multiracial people in the United States.[60]

There are those who tell a different story. In 2003, at the height of Leo's popularity in mainstream press, art imitated life when renowned comedian and producer Dave Chappelle began his groundbreaking Comedy Central series, *Chappelle's Show*, with a controversial sketch entitled "Frontline: The Black White Supremacist." The sketch's protagonist, played by Chappelle, Clayton Bigsby, is a prominent white supremacist and Klansman who is not only black but physically blind to that fact and, by consequence, metaphysically blind to many others. Although Bigsby's blindness has not made him color-blind or unintelligent, it allows his audience, as in-group clairvoyants, to see that appearance and vision are red herrings when it comes to determining racial identities and politics. Audiences thus bear witness to Bigsby's white supremacist identity as a sincere performance that defines and describes intrapersonal, interpersonal, institutional, and structural relations. The sketch proceeds as a series of encounters between Bigsby and his dupes—racist white Southerners who are stupefied and silenced when he joins in on their racist rants. When Bigsby finally removes his hood at a Klan rally, he is officially outed and no longer welcome as a leader or member in the white supremacist movement. Later Bigsby divorces his blind white wife for entering into an interracial sexual relationship with him. Strikingly, no one Bigsby encounters within the sketch finds any humor in his experience. In fact, one onlooker's head literally explodes as he processes the paradoxical nature of Bigsby, blindness, blackness, white supremacy, and passing. It is only the sketch's televised audience, the in-group clairvoyant who looks on from a distance, who is in on the joke and can laugh at the seemingly preposterous scenario of a blind and black white supremacist.[61]

Not even the in-group clairvoyant can find a comic corrective in Leo's case, which, like Chappelle's sketch, reminds us that racial anxieties and charges of racism are always lurking to spoil the perfect picture of a postracial miscegeNation.[62] Consider what I call the contemporary "I can't be a racist because I am multiracial" defense as part of mainstream society's commitment to ensuring that Leo will always be considered pathological. This line of defense was deployed in the summer of 2010 by Sarah Palin to address the NAACP's charges of racism against herself and the Tea Party. In a Facebook post entitled "The Charge of Racism: It's Time to Bury the Divisive Politics of the Past," Palin calls on her own multiracial family as evidence of antiracism.

> I just spent a few beautiful Alaskan days with some beautiful Americans in my husband's birthplace—they are Todd's family and they are Yupik Eskimo. In the decades that our families have blended, I have never heard one proud, patriotic member judge another member based on skin color. Both Todd and I were raised to measure a person according to their capacity and willingness to love, work, forgive, contribute, and show good character. We're joined by the vast majority of Americans in this belief whereby we measure a man by

his character, not his color. Because of amazing efforts and accomplishments by those who came before my generation, it is foreign to us to consider condemning or condoning anyone's actions based on race. . . . Being with our diverse family in a melting pot that is a Native village just days ago reminded me of that. . . . No, the Tea Party is a beautiful movement, full of diverse people, diverse backgrounds. Folks of all walks of life who, for the most part, happen to oppose President Obama's policies. Not the color of his skin. They don't care that he's half white or half black.[63]

Here Palin launches a four-pronged defense against racism: (1) She married a man from a "beautiful," "patriotic," and "proud" multiracial and multiethnic family and lives in a "melting pot." Therefore, she is not a racist. (2) Because she married a man from a beautiful, patriotic, and proud multiracial and multiethnic family and lives in a melting pot, she can consider herself multiracial and multiethnic. Therefore, she is not a racist. (3) Because she and her beautiful, patriotic, and proud husband are multiracial and multiethnic and live in a melting pot, her children and grandchildren are also beautiful, patriotic, proud, multiracial, and multiethnic and live in a melting pot. Therefore, she is not a racist. (4) Because she and her beautiful, patriotic, and proud husband, children, and grandchildren are multiracial and multiethnic and live in a melting pot, and because she is a leader of the Tea Party, neither she nor the Tea Party is racist. For good measure, as beautiful, patriotic, and proud multiracial and multiethnic melting-pot dwellers, Palin and the Tea Party certainly cannot be racist against Obama, himself also a multiracial and multiethnic melting-pot dweller. According to Palin, racism and the prospect of racism emerge as bound to the personal history of national, racial, familial, gender, and heterosexual contact being detailed in the post. To be multiracial is to be beautiful, patriotic, proud, and diverse. To be with one's beautiful, patriotic, proud, and diverse multiracial family in a melting pot is to enjoy a state of perfect racial harmony and health, to be personally immune to racism. Here Palin imagines herself and the Tea Party as tolerant, above prejudice and the need to fixate on racial difference.[64] As "folks from all walks of life," Palin and the Tea Party construct themselves rhetorically as individuals first and foremost, and thus are absolved from needing to consider collectivity and systemic inequalities.[65]

The "I can't be a racist because I am multiracial" defense was not invented by Palin,[66] but she did make it so popular that Sharron

Angle appropriated it after telling a group of Latino/a students that they looked Asian in late 2010 and Charlie Sheen remixed it in early 2011 to ward off charges of anti-Semitism.[67] This line of defense is also absurd, especially in light of the fact that so-called biology neither justifies stereotypes of whites as super-humans and nonwhites as nonhumans nor creates a race of people immune to racism and anti-Semitism. The rhetoric of biology, however, when coupled with the tropes of nature and pathology, leads to

Password Twelve

In the twenty-first century, passing solidifies racial difference, plays on multiracial identities as a new racial formation, and makes racial hierarchy seem so natural that it goes unquestioned.[68]

Biological rhetoric laden with tropes of nature and pathology creates a context in which the "I can't be a racist because I am multiracial" defense is hardened and accepted uncritically as common sense or *doxa* by the press and blogosphere. As early as 1998, the *Washington Post* suggested that "mounting fears of ethnic divide are being answered by a force of potentially equal might: the enormous rate at which couples of different races and ethnicities are marrying one another."[69] The subversive enthymeme here is that interracial heterosexual couples will also be reproducing at an "enormous rate" and thereby creating multiracial offspring who will naturally erase race and racism. The *New York Times* made the enthymeme explicit when it reported that "Generation E(thnically) A(mbiguous)" is charting new social territory by expressing race and ethnicity differently than they have been expressed in prior generations.[70] In light of this sentiment more and more stories and opinion pieces focus on multiracials as proof of our nation's racial progress with headlines that read "In Census, Young Americans Increasingly Diverse" in the *New York Times,* "President Obama: Black and More So," "Where Interracials May Take Us" in the *Los Angeles Times*[71] and "Interracial Marriage, Hispanics Fuel Growth of Multiracial Population" in the *Orlando Sentinel,* as well as similar headlines in other major news outlets.[72] *Allure Magazine* reported that 64 percent of their readers now find mixed race faces the most beautiful.[73] *Time Magazine* went so far as to report that the nation's increasing numbers of multiracials who identify as multiracials are "better adjusted" than their monoracial counterparts.[74] Celebrating multiracials' enhanced physical beauty and psychological well-being is nothing short of objectification. What is more, this brand of objectification promotes the notion that multiracials inherit the best traits of all racial groups and are therefore both *post*-racialists and non-racists by nature. Such "cheerleading"[75] also contributes to

Password Thirteen

*Because of our nation's history of slavery, segregation, and interment (*episteme*), racism is conflated with physical separation on the basis of biological race (*doxa*). Therefore, racial progress is conflated with racial mixing via interracial heterosexual relations.*

Password Thirteen expresses the obvious but significant casting of racial reconciliation as a heterosexual family drama. In this drama multiracial individuals and interracial families, because of the biological and psychological adjustments created through miscegenation, are touted as icons of racial healing because they are thought to have special insights based on what they are, biologically mixed.[76] Multiracials who do not engage in racial reconciliation or share special insights into a positive postracial future can only be mixed up.[77]

FROM MANAGING FELTON'S PATHOLOGY TO FELTON'S PATHOLOGICAL PRINCIPLE

Being "mixed and mixed up"—a pathology that makes the (racist) multiracial self the very source of its illness—turns Leo's case into one of personal prejudice and offense, perpetrated by one pathological man (*Password Eight*).[78] Further, this news media "framing" offers a powerful resolution to the paradoxes of Leo's passing because it appeals to fear, desire, sexual mores and family values, notions of well-being and illness, and entrenched beliefs about "natural" and unnatural relationships. What is more, the trope of pathology offers a powerful metaphor for social perception on Leo's part. Pathology offers a way of perceiving the world as natural and normal and of perceiving Leo's deviation from a healthy or normal existence in the world as a function of his abnormality, his (mis)perception of multiracial identity and status as new millennial marginal man. It addresses the paradoxes enumerated above, especially how, despite his liberal upbringing and multiracial heritage, he could become a white supremacist. Leo's passing and white supremacist beliefs were not his parents' faults, they were outcomes of his pathology as a new millennial marginal man and signs of his inability to accept his own multiracial identity in an increasingly postracial world.

As the mainstream news coverage tells it, passing—a pathological response to a confused multiracial identity—drove Leo into a racial closet. This racial closet impelled him toward the radical remedy that is white supremacy, which in turn drove him into another kind of closet, the isolation he suffers in prison generally and in solitary confinement specifically as a result of his pathological choices. By framing Leo's case as pathological and as dysfunctional interracial family drama, the press coverage communicates that multiracial identities carry the genetic strands with which they are unraveled and rewoven. Tied up neatly in terms of an unraveled identity and mind, Leo's passing can be viewed as a symptom of his larger disease: conflicted identity as new millennial marginal man. To ensure against an outbreak, it becomes necessary to justify his isolation from the rest of normal society for our own general protection. Moreover, pathologizing Leo blinds society to the incongruities in its notions of race, racial progress, and multiracial identities. So blinded, society can then congratulate itself by locking Leo away in a prison cell and dismissing his perspective as a matter of multiracial madness. In the case of Leo Felton, any discussions of structural and institutional racism in the mainstream news coverage of his case gave way to a focus on the pathology and immorality of one new millennial marginal man.

Leo's identities as mixed and mixed up collided behind bars, where he looked around and wondered how the family, nation, and world into which he was born got so confused.[79] He was tired of being part of the problem, part of the pathology that seemed so intractable. He wanted to be part of the solution. For Leo the initial solution involved passing as white. In all honesty it was not a difficult decision. New York State registered him officially as white. And, as one witty blogger put it, there were not many nonwhite "mohawked, swastika flaunting, Ramone's idolizing skinheads in prison."[80] The more permanent solution involved redefining the very nature of race so that he would no longer feel like a passer, an inauthentic white man. Leo needed to disconnect race from biology, blood, and genes and even from social construction and performance, and connect it to a sincere feeling (*Password One*). Passing provided this connection by allowing identity politics and real politics to merge almost seamlessly. Almost, that is.

Leo forces us to resist the temptation of dismissing him as a mental health case and invites us to a closer reading that provides an important rhetorical critique of passing—as an act of *aletheia* embodied in words and deeds and not through biology and appearance. Leo confirmed his own racial feelings, his white supremacist "racial sincerity," with Varange's *Imperium* in order to justify his claims to white identity. *Imperium* gave Leo access to a new criterion of truth based on *aletheia* (*Password One*). By uncovering the true "sincere" nature of race as interiority and then committing to it with full force Leo could conceal the exteriority of racial identity (as what others think he is or what his parents and ancestors are). In this way, Leo's identity was always concealed first "in here" and only later revealed "out there."[81] And, paradoxically, it was also always revealed first "in here" and only later concealed "out there." These multiple concealments and revelations cannot be observed by conventional means. *Aletheia* and sincerity are revealed in rhetoric-as-passing and in the actions rhetoric-as-passing incites.

First, Leo talked his way out of seeing his body and background as indicators of racial identity. He rejected the metonymy of hypodescent, the notion that because his father was black he too was black or even biracial. Instead, using synecdoche, he took the non-Jewish white part of himself as the whole (*Password Four*). Then he cast a blind eye to all groups other than the one to which he had an affinity. Leo's rejection allowed him to disconnect from the environment of hate he would work to forge. Finally, he talked his way into whiteness and white supremacy, expressed most vividly in his letters, comic strips, and leadership role within the movement. He felt he had as much, if not more, claim to whiteness as any other white person because of *aletheia*, the extra effort and extreme sincerity he invested in passing, a process Leo later described as traveling a "circuitous route" to "becoming 'white,' in quotation marks."[82] For Leo passing was a "circuitous route" because it involved many concealments and revelations. "Becoming 'white' in quotation marks" connotes the special status Leo attributed to whiteness and to himself as white and his latent fear that it could slip away.

As proof of his *aletheia* and sincerity, and to guard against his own concealed anxieties, Leo sought out a new family that felt right. He married a white woman and later took a white supremacist girlfriend. He found brotherhood among a white power skinhead group whose logo he emblazoned on his skull and whose battle call to "rahowa," racial holy war, he adopted as his own. "The only people that I had anything in common with all happened to be white," he said. We were surrounded on all sides by an antagonistic alien [black] presence. We stuck together."[83] Leo frequently referred to his adversaries as "aliens" and as "unintelligent," flaunting his intelligence along with his white supremacist and nativist training as shields against those in-group clairvoyants who might dare to question him on racial grounds. Whiteness provided Leo with an identity that ensured resources, power, and protection in the mostly nonwhite prison environment.[84] White supremacist literature encouraged Leo to invest completely in whiteness and, in turn, to possess it in ways "that most people in the movement didn't . . . despite their blond hair and blue eyes."[85]

Questions remained. Could he ever be completely certain that he was white? Was he perpetrating an act of violence against himself? Could he be sure that his parents' union was unnatural and that his decision to exterminate anyone who was not an Aryan was correct and compulsory? Maybe, maybe not. To answer these questions, Leo developed a curriculum, facilitated study groups, and became a leader in the White Order of Thule, a selective group of racist pagans that he once described as a "graduate-level school of Aryan" ideology.[86]

FELTON'S WHITE SUPREMACY

Leo's principled and sincere white supremacist curriculum required "students" to learn Norse mythology and study works by Jung, Nietzsche, and other prominent nineteenth and twentieth-century philosophers. As the curriculum moved to cover the contemporary era, it adopted the language of a besieged minority group. Its vocabulary expressed high anxiety over people of color generally and multiracials specifically, suggesting that the mere presence of nonwhite people in any setting constituted discrimination against whites and justified white people's rights to ensure their existence by violent means. While Leo worked on his curriculum behind bars the U.S. Census Bureau projected that white people will become a minority by 2050, fueling racial anxiety in mainstream society.[87] This transition will not be a smooth process because of the fears that Leo embodies so sincerely—that whiteness will no longer represent the norm and hold the power, and therefore can no longer be considered pure, distinct, and more powerful than other racial groups. Much of this anxiety comes from sharing spaces with undesirables—nonwhite people (or "mud people" as Leo would call them). For those within the law, a solution might be enacted by way of racial privacy initiatives, anti-immigration, and racial/ethnic profiling legislation. But Leo was not inside the law. He was an outlaw. Thus, "the primary goal right now," he wrote, "is to foment revolution and inaugurate a natural order on the continent." [88] Leo's idealized "natural order" would be the same as Hitler's and Varange's. And, as he later noted, "The means by which we will attain this is quite simply war."[89] As a sincere white supremacist, Leo saw it necessary to wage a concerted campaign to end the injurious condition that was increasing ethnic and racial diversity.

Leo's high levels of self-efficacy, the perception that he had what it took to carry out "rahowa," were based on his knowledge of the cause and, more importantly, on his sincere devotion to whiteness and white supremacy. "I don't for one moment feel like I did anything wrong by choosing not to define myself according to the way other people wanted to define me," he said.[90] Leo did not see passing as a crime or as an indicator of mental illness based on marginal multiracial status. Instead, passing was an expression of *aletheia*—an internal constitution and principled intentionality based on divorcing racial identity from a verifiable authentic essence (*Password One*). "Those [authentic] definitions are not things in themselves. They're not a-priori true. They're legal fictions."[91] And so Leo corroborated the ideological verdict of *Plessy v. Ferguson*, that apparent whiteness is no guarantee of "authentic" whiteness. Here is the most powerful portion of Leo's critique—contradictory, paradoxical, self-deconstructed as it may be. Leo identified others' definitions of his racial identity as symptoms of cultural and legal and not personal neuroses, as large-scaled social fictions with no basis in reality. While attempting to disavow the "fictions" of racialized biology and appearance, he paradoxically and ironically sought out and attacked those he believed were black and Jewish on the very bases of biology and appearance (*Password Five*). The desire to lash out against these groups can be linked to a fear of in-group clairvoyants and their ability to out him and spoil his white supremacist agenda (*Password Two*). In-group clairvoyants must be exterminated because they act as sleuths who interrogate the claims made in passing and have the power to remain silent or express those claims as untrue.

Ironically, paradoxically even, Leo failed to acknowledge how his perspective also made everyone else's racial identity a fiction—even those non-Aryan in-group clairvoyants he sought to annihilate. Leo could see and feel that race itself was passing as both biology and social construction, and existed as more of a feeling or set of principles. However, he remained blind to the principle of race—to divide people into distinct categories, which exist hierarchically and become more socially palatable over time. The latter was a fact even his co-conspirator and girlfriend, Erica Chase, could not ignore. While in prison Erica, says, she "abandoned the racist cause" because "learning Felton's true racial identity had caused her to rethink everything. . . . It was something that undermined her concept of race."[92] As a result she brought her relationship with Leo to an end. This breakup befitted both Erica's newfound antiracism and Leo's deep-seated and sincere white supremacy.

Leo's sincerity was blinding. It obscured his ability to see that crying "my race is a fiction but yours is not" in a crowded prison is a faulty principle that cannot be applied universally. This incoherence is enhanced by the drawing fascinations of white supremacy and passing, a conceptual relation through which Leo fused identity and principle (*Password Ten*). For Leo passing did more than highlight the fictionalized "truths" that inform cultural and historical attitudes and actions. Passing allowed him to become who he believed himself to be. In passing he was identified as white and was able to become a white supremacist. And there is the paradox of passing—as it capitalizes on the artificiality and pliability of color lines, it also reinforces the naturalness and rigidity of those same lines. The paradox of Leo's passing is that it makes race an illusion and brings it to life, all at the same time. It proves that race is one of many fictional truths.[93] Understanding Leo's passing as a paradox that cannot be resolved via pathology or principle demonstrates a relationship to agency (or lack thereof) that becomes far more complicated than feelings or stereotypes like the new millennial marginal man lead us to believe. It is the paradox that makes Leo's passing so striking.

Consequently, it is also striking that after undergoing the humiliation of being tried in court, Leo now had to endure what seemed to be a larger ignominy—being outed as black and Jewish and as a passer. Leo cited being outed as an impetus for slashing "his wrists, neck and bicep" in a suicide attempt, which can be considered the only act of power he retained that would allow him to rid the world of one more black and Jewish person. For even as Leo was excluded by the very white supremacist ideology he espoused, he was also espousing it sincerely. In passing as paradox, then, we begin to see how difficult it is to alter how we allow ourselves to think, talk, and embody race. Of course, Leo demonstrates that it there is no basis in reality for a biological notion of race or the metonymic rule of hypodescent that it begets. That it is really crazy for us to call Leo black, Jewish, or multiracial because of a few drops of blood. But it will take a sharper and more sophisticated adjective than "crazy" to describe the society that encourages passing, not to mention the convergence of white supremacy and passing in the prison system that became the driving forces in Leo's life.[94]

FROM FELTON'S PRINCIPLE
TO FELTON'S PARADOX

In contrast to the versions of *aletheia*, sincerity, and passing presented by Frances E. W. Harper in *Iola Leroy, or, Shadows Uplifted* (chap. 4), the curious, pathological and principled case of Leo Felton animates the dread and revulsion accompanying forced confrontations with nonwhite and multiracial identities. Leo's story is imbued with the real fictions of race and with the shame of denial, deception, and separation that upheld these fictions when he was outed as multiracial and multiethnic. Where Harper tells a story of multiple acceptances, Leo tells a story of multiple rejections. Upon outing, Harper's characters embraced their identities, first as black and then as black with white ancestry. Upon outing, Leo rejected both white and black racial identities. The *New York Times* reported these rejections as Leo's desire to "fix [his] center of gravity in something Beige," a color that is neither black nor white but somewhere in between, as a mixture of yellow, brown, gray, and tan. Seemingly rejecting both black and white, Leo arrived at multiracial identity in a way that fascinates and frightens. His "beige" identity fascinates because it acts as a sign that Leo might finally have been racially rehabilitated. That he had seen the error of his ways. That he was remorseful and apologetic and willing to conform, albeit on his own liminal terms. One the other hand, his "beige" identity is frightening because it so vague, because it is presented as a racial state of being in and of itself. Beige represents the perfect blend. It is neutral, harmless, completely palatable. Most significantly, beige is not very dark.[95] Beige is fetishized as a step in the right direction, a (seemingly) happy end to Leo's story.

But a "beige center of gravity" was only passing as the end of Leo's story. A closer reading suggests that beige can also be considered Leo's new beginning, what he referred to as a kind of rebirth after the "blood sacrifice" offered by his suicide attempt. For Leo an identity as beige could be considered a calculated move within a biracial binary that served only to hold up its primary role in U.S. racial formation and continue a white supremacist agenda. Beige accomplishes this because of its apparent neutrality, which neither dismantles nor supersedes the black-white biracial binary. Beige merely reproduces the binary and increases the dangerous distance between the poles of black and white.[96] Considered carefully, beige reveals a lurking antagonism with blackness and Jewishness, an antagonism that still stood in Leo's way of being a white supremacist and explains why he continues to engage in passing. Only now, by fixing beige as its own distinct category, Leo made it possible to pass as multiracial and remain a white supremacist.[97] In this version of the story, Leo was not rehabilitated. He was recycled. He was ready to be used again to move forward with a reactionary agenda that was determined to undo the gains of the modern civil rights movement. And so the quandary of Leo's passing rears its head again.

While it is difficult to envision a resolution to the many paradoxes present in Leo's passing, it is important and necessary to explore what the paradoxes reveal. The first revelation is not a happy one, for in many ways we must realize that Leo outsmarted us. Beige was not his mode of redemption. It was not an evolution. And it was not a neutral stance that diffused the charge of white supremacy. Rather, it was a way for Leo to grasp the two poles on which our nation's racial hierarchy rests, brace himself against them and, using all his might, keep them as far apart as possible. In some ways Leo's beige can be considered the new " 'white' in quotation marks." This claim would make sense in so far as it empowered Leo to increase the distance between black and white and thereby increase the need and space for passing as either one and introduce the possibility of passing as multiracial. Unfortunately, for Leo at least, he did not acknowledge that his fixed beige position made him the consummate prisoner. He had to insert himself and remain fixed in the binary order to keep the poles apart. And this time Leo really did have no one to blame but himself. He chose to keep himself in the box, to continue his white supremacist agenda and stay true to his sincere identity as " 'white' in quotation marks."

The second revelation is no more cheerful. Leo's story brings the paradox of passing full circle. As we saw in the cases of Ellen Craft and Homer Plessy, passing starts as a way of expressing multiracial identity in monoracial terms (*Password Three*). This expression came about because there was no room for multiracial identities as multiracial in a black-white bipolar perspective on race. In this way passing began as a way to defy binary thinking and to detach superior or subordinate social statuses from distinct racial groups. In short, passing began as a challenge to white supremacy focused on sharing the in-group clairvoyant's perspective (*Password Six*). As time marches on, minds and laws begin to reflect social equality, and we expect motives for passing to decline. Yet we have seen exactly the opposite. Frances Harper showed us that it was not only possible but important to pass as black in a segregationist context (*Password Nine*), and Philip Roth and Robert Benton showed us that passing as white is as alive and well in the twenty-first century as it was during segregation and the Holocaust. Leo's case shows us that passing not only thrives but becomes more sophisticated in a society that is desperate to believe in the irrelevance of race and the actualization of social equality. By "fixing a center of gravity" in "beige," Leo became part of a larger movement to further stratify the black-white binary by transforming it into a black-beige-white triad. Rather than challenging white supremacy, this triad continues to assign superior and subordinate statuses to racial groups and promotes a multiracial exceptionalism that makes it desirable to pass as "beige." Passing as beige is a possibility many historical passers and multiracial individuals could never have envisioned. However, the fact that people are now passing as beige—and also passing in terms of gender, sexual orientation, nationality, ability, religion, physical, and mental health—tells us that some people are still considered more equal than others. Taken to the extreme, as in Leo's case, passing can no longer be considered a challenge to white supremacist thinking. Instead, passing is a sophisticated and ultimately antisocial phenomenon, which reminds us that so many categories we now consider natural became so through violent and malevolent means (*Passwords Seven, Eight*).

The third revelation is why Leo's racial sincerity and version of *aletheia* is distinct from the other versions presented in this book, and especially distinct from the version presented by Frances Harper in chapter 4. As we may recall, Harper's multiracial protagonists chose to pass as black in the context of enslavement and segregation. Like Leo, Harper articulated a choice that did not make sense to the world around her. Like Leo, Harper realized that passing was only a means to a much greater end. Like Leo, Harper argued that passing was a powerful and principled decision based on sincerity and *aletheia* (*Password One*). Unlike Leo, however, Harper saw a different kind of power, principle, sincerity, and *aletheia*—the kind that does the important work of social justice. The kind that reveals that life as black and as multiracial need not necessarily be a miserable affair. The kind that carried the *ethos* of personhood, and with it the imperative of caring for and about the world and the people in it as whole human beings. Where Leo took a circuitous route to becoming "white," Harper's protagonists took a circuitous route to becoming "black" that allowed them, eventually, to acknowledge their multiracial backgrounds and work for social equality among all Americans. Harper realized that in her writing she could create a model for a world in which passing could pass away, a world in which someday it might be possible to cross borders without one space or place considered better or worse than another. Leo, on the other hand, had a very different dream that forced him to abdicate Harper's imperative and go in the opposite direction. As Harper's protagonists pass in order to eradicate passing, Leo passed to eradicate people of color. Thus, we must remember that Leo's story should not be romanticized. We must remember that regardless of whether his identity is ultimately located in external appearance or somewhere deep inside as a set of feelings, Leo's ultimate choices were violence, hate, and destruction.

The fourth and final revelation is that the story of passing is not complete without telling the story of Leo. And it is not complete without acknowledging that there are many Leo Feltons, many people whose identities and politics do not appear to make sense from the perspective of mainstream society. Thus, as Leo's Facebook fan page with 0 "likes" reflects, we must acknowledge Leo and his choice, but we do not have to bring ourselves to like him.[98] And yet we must remember that the personal issue of liking or disliking Leo clouds the deeper object lesson he teaches about the roles of persuasion, power, and privilege in the paradox of passing. He teaches us that we reproduce the paradox when passing is framed as a problem of bad individuals who can be rehabilitated as their identities and beliefs are managed (*Password Eight*). He also teaches us that we begin to resolve the paradox when passing is utilized as a means of challenging and restructuring power inequalities and as a means of forcing us to examine our own complicity in structures of privilege (*Passwords Two, Six*).

And so the paradox of passing comes full circle. It proves that there is a desire to escape racial limits and suggests that we cannot imagine living without racial selves. It forces us to question whether today's "beige" version of multiracial identity is a paradigm shift or just a more sophisticated technology of passing. And it provides the opportunity for us to imagine what real racial progress might look like. Progress could be what Leo imagines, a world of total sameness achieved through violent genocide. It could be a world of beige beauties that lacks structural equality. It could also be what Harper imagines, a world where difference is acknowledged and not belittled. Or it could be a world we cannot yet see but one we can feel. A world that remains for now a real fiction.

Passing as Progress?

Every story of passing is both an ending and a beginning. Passing is an ending because it discourages inquiry. It invites us to pass by, to keep moving, and not to look beneath surfaces. Passing tempts us to accept people as they appear to us and, therefore, as we say they are. End of conversation. Continuing the conversation, however, leads us to see passing as a beginning and as an invitation for us to interrogate our innermost selves, our motives, movements, and meanings. We are invited to explore why people pass, what happens to them and to their relationships, how passing operates, and what passing expresses and embodies in our societies and worlds.

And so it has been in this book, for its end is also a new beginning. Its story is simultaneous and successive, demonstrating how passing becomes more fraught, more dangerous, and more sophisticated over time. In other words, this book has mapped out the progress of passing, which should not be confused with social progress. While passing certainly can be traced back to a colonized, segregated and biracial world, it crosses over from that world and into the worlds of gender, sexuality, age, class, caste, ability, religion, technology, language, and citizenship. Passing crosses over by creating spaces—between races, genders, sexualities, generations, classes, abilities, religions, languages, nations—that are as important as the categories themselves. This analysis of passing has sought to bring the hybrid spaces created by passing into dialogue with each other and the hierarchies in which they are contained. In the process it has introduced thirteen passwords to tease out the rhetorical strategies employed and create a vocabulary that can be extended to describe the experiences of those who pass in terms other than and in addition to race.

Clearly Invisible is the story of unconventional identities and ideals at work in a conventional world. All use synecdoche and metonymy. Some use irony, others use appropriation or eloquence as their medium, and others use tragedy or pathology to communicate what happens when distinctions between passers and personae can no longer be detected. Passing begins as form of persuasion based on intersecting personae (passers, dupes, and in-group clairvoyants) and tropes (irony, appropriation, eloquence, tragedy, and pathology). When these personae and tropes intersect, boundaries between male and female, black and white, contemporary and ancestral, biology and symbolic social construction are blurred. Passers, dupes, and in-group clairvoyants alike find themselves entangled among the thickets of passing—boundaries that entrap because they are, quite ambiguously, there and not there. For instance, passing begins by presuming that duality, what W.E.B. Du Bois aptly termed "double consciousness," is human and that attempting to reconcile this duality is also human. Passing is an attempt at reconciliation that ends with a Platonically inspired worldview—that there can be only one whole and acceptable truth of identity, one that can be possessed and produced only by the voice of one race, gender, class, nation, religion, or set of abilities over another or others. Sophistic rhetoric exposes how Plato's worldview continues to persuade us as we search out who and what we are. It persuades us even as Plato's ideal of singular and authentic identity is fractured and converted to the reality of sincere identities—multiple lives, multiple relations with histories and communities, all with no easy resolutions.

In search of resolutions, passing moves from the realm of persuasion to the realm of power. In the case of Ellen and William Craft, passing presents itself as an unexpected if not always satisfying way of seizing control when everything we value can be swept away in an instant. Whether in the setting of enslavement, segregation, or prison, or of political freedom and equality, passing exposes just how high the stakes can get when identities are the keys that open doors of opportunity. So the power of passing is that it is porous. It leaks. Consequently, the power of passing may not necessarily be comforting, although its outcomes (i.e., personal liberty and expression; class mobility) often prove personally worthwhile. That is to say, passing is ironic and increasingly difficult because of intrapersonal, interpersonal, institutional, and structural power struggles passers confront.

One outcome of these struggles is the transformation of power into property. Passing makes this transformation explicit by exposing secrets. One secret is that race is a symbolic social construction whose acceptance as natural both discourages examination and encourages passing. Another secret is that rights are only as strong as the so-called natural racial identities by which they are upheld, and ultimately as strong or weak as the socially constructed legal definitions assigned to those natural identities. We have read how race was institutionalized as property in *Plessy v. Ferguson*, making the way for passers to raise value by means of what we now call identity theft. Yet passing ultimately exposes the inability of law to contain racial property in the face of persuasive and powerful rhetorical performances. Passing unmasks our desire to crystallize racial identities as property because they are something we want to possess even though we somehow know we never can. Upholding and obtaining racial property rights becomes a matter of principle in a world that says some identities are better or worse than others. For instance, in *Iola Leroy, or, Shadows Uplifted*, passing demonstrates how being alienated from one identity helps precipitate our sense of belonging or ownership in another identity. Thus, passing is a manifestation of the sensation of value. It is what happens when we discover we are valued and valuable as members of some communities and not as members of other communities. It is a complex and eloquent expression of social worth within social hierarchy.

Although passing is eloquent, it can also be destructive. In the literary and cinematic versions of *The Human Stain* and in the case of Leo Felton, passing comes to life as tragic story in which authenticity and essence collide with the nebulous terrains of personal and collective identities and sincere values. Perhaps one tragedy is that some passers see passing as the only path to social equality. A larger tragedy is that as in-group clairvoyants we too often fail to see that what affects the passer can affect a nation and that what transforms a passer can transform a nation. So a passer like Coleman Silk is passing because the society in which he lives is also passing as just, free, equal, or moral. Tragically, Coleman cannot experience society as just, free, equal, or moral unless he too is passing. Sometimes passing is not just tragic. Sometimes in passing we hear words of vengeance, sadness, and fear. We hear words of rage and unfairness, jealousy, ignorance, confusion, and disappointment.[1] We find such words dramatized and reinforced when passing is pathologized, as in the case of Leo Felton. Choosing to listen to passers' angry words rather than dismissing them as insane will ultimately make the difference and can help us address the many paradoxes of passing.

Listening to passers reveals new ways to understand their experiences. One new way of understanding passers is as society's in-group clairvoyants who do not remain silent or complacent about the idyllic personae society projects and values. From this perspective, as society's in-group clairvoyants, passers tell stories that show us how we all are duped as society's injustices are concealed and revealed in an attempt to embody democratic and progressive ideals. The passers' stories told herein share this as a common critical theme: If society stops passing, as moral, just, free, or equal, for instance, then the need many potential passers express for projecting more "acceptable" personae and "valuable" identities would end. The stories also demonstrate that when passers identify themselves sincerely, they can reveal society's injustices and inequalities, dupes' and in-group clairvoyants' prejudices and preferences, and inspire new worldviews that value individuals and communities as much as institutions. Failing to acknowledge how passers' stories emphasize reflexive relationships among individuals, collectives, and institutions means that the things said in passing are destined to remain sealed off and shut inside our respective closets and inside the larger closets of society. Failing to acknowledge things said in passing also means that all passers are destined to remain prisoners in solitary confinement because society says they have committed some crime of identity theft. Sadly, when we fail to acknowledge all that is said in passing, we fail to get to know ourselves better. In contrast, acknowledging the rhetorical relationships that make passing possible allows for the possibilities of exiting closets and finding similarities among personal motivations, movements, and meanings, as well as among public and political resolutions and reconciliations.

Resolutions and reconciliations can begin in the realms of communication and culture, where identities and categories of identification can be reconstructed to encourage audiences' self-conscious scrutiny of their own social locations. Such images, like those presented in this book, would tell the whole story of passing and not just a part. The whole story is told best with delicacy, acknowledging feelings of fear, shame, anger, recrimination, and remorse without forgetting to acknowledge profound possibilities for recognitions, resolutions, and reconciliations. The whole story of passing tells us that when we avoid self-conscious scrutiny we allow social hierarchies to pass as normal or, more troublingly, as nonexistent, and we render them no less powerful. The whole story of passing helps us understand why today's neoconservative postracial language—which takes the forms of "Racial Privacy Initiatives" and defenses against charges of racism based on objectifying multiracial identities as biological booster shots—seems self-contradictory in the face of policies that strengthen hierarchy and allow only a few to gain advantage over many. And the whole story of passing helps us see that neoliberal rhetoric often conflates class inequity with racial and gender inequities in order to avoid the discomfort of acknowledging the differential effects of structural racism and sexism. Talking about inequity in this way conceals how racial hierarchies are the products of very specific economic and labor processes by which one group has consolidated and maintained power at the expense of other groups.

In either case it seems that the more democratic our rhetoric sounds, the less democratic our identities feel and become. That inconsistency is the problem of passing, which, it seems, is also the problem of the twenty-first century. Our desperation to declare that we have progressed beyond passing, simply because we fail to acknowledge passers and the things they say, means that we continue to cultivate an environment in which passing will remain the most sincere strategy for success. The unfortunate result of this problem is a form of cultural neglect through which we abandon opportunities to engage in the important work of reconciliation that can lead to social change. We fail to see that every act of passing presents an opportunity for reconciliation, expresses a desire for social change, and calls for the freedom to be who we are.

And that is where we now find ourselves, where we find the things said in passing, and where we find an ending and a beginning—believing that the motivation to conceal or reveal parts of ourselves as the wholes of who we are is no longer deceptive but honest. Our ending-beginning can take the form of rejection or reception, but not of ignorance. Our ending-beginning can be avoided or approached, but it cannot withstand apathy. Our ending-beginning is an intersection where theory meets practice, where institutions meet individuals, and where we face all parts of the old roots of hierarchies and oppressions. Only then can we put an end to the process of "judging people by the color of their skin" and begin to make the dream of accepting each other based on "the content of our character" a reality. *Clearly Invisible* is the story of how we arrived at this ending-beginning and is proof that we have not gotten here alone. It is also proof that, together, we can generate sincere rhetorical encounters that inspire and allow us to assert ourselves as whole people who do not experience the need to assimilate to dominant norms. For it is only when we assert ourselves as whole people that we can acknowledge the evolution of passing, find a way to lay it to rest, compose its epitaph, and, finally, progress from passing to passed.

Passwords for Passing

1. Passing engages the classical debate between Plato and the Sophists and challenges the binary of *episteme* (objective Truth) versus *doxa* (common sense) through *aletheia* (rhetorical and racial sincerity).
2. Passing is the invention and interaction of rhetorical personae—the passer's acceptable persona, the dupe, and the in-group clairvoyant or fourth persona.
3. Passing is biracial. It begins as a dynamic rhetorical process of expression in which passers identify as monoracial (as either black or white) and not as multiracial (as black and white).
4. Biracial passing begins where synecdoche meets metonymy. Passers use synecdoche to project acceptable personae as either black or white. Dupes and fourth personae interpret passers' representations as metonymy.
5. Biracial passing ends as an "intersectional" process through which tropes, personae, and texts combine to mark social place (institutional categories) and discursive space (passers within institutional categories).

6. Passing is agonistic (operating inside and outside of rhetorical and cultural conventions) and transformative (using irony-synecdoche-metonymy to transform dupes into in-group clairvoyants).

7. Passing reveals whose identities are valued as property, how much they are worth, and what defensive dupes will do to protect them.

8. Passers are treated historically as individual bad persons and not as part of a larger society that treats people unequally based on who they are and appear to be.

9. When one is passing as black, dupes' conceptions are immaterial or at the very most devalued. Utmost value is placed on the passer and in-group clairvoyant, embodied by the passer's ability to justify the seemingly counterintuitive choice to pass as black.

10. Passing is an ongoing and eloquent drama of becoming more racially and rhetorically sincere.

11. A tragic formula exists for passing as entertainment. Audiences must be able to identify passers as passers; identify dupes and potential dupes; identify themselves as in-group clairvoyants and share the secret with other in-group clairvoyants; pity passers' unfortunate circumstances and actions as a function of who they believe passers are; and derive pleasure from their own sympathetic responses to passers' suffering and outing.

12. In the twenty-first century, passing solidifies racial difference, plays on multiracial identities as a new racial formation, and makes racial hierarchy seem so natural that it goes unquestioned.

13. Because of our nation's history of slavery, segregation, and interment (*episteme*), racism is conflated with physical separation on the basis of biological race (*doxa*). Therefore, racial progress is conflated with racial mixing via interracial heterosexual relations. Passing is seen as an affront to racial progress rather than as a sign that racial progress has not been made.

Notes

1   Nathan Irvin Huggins, *Revelations: American History, American Myths* (Oxford: Oxford University Press, 1995), 245. See also Paul R. Spickard. *Mixed Blood* (Madison: University of Wisconsin Press, 1989), 312. Spickard uses the heading "Passing Is Passé."

2   *Oxford English Dictionary Online*, s.v. "passing," http://voyager2.lbcc .edu:2065/cgi/entry/50172474?query_type=word&queryword=passing& first=1&max_to_show=10&sort_type=alpha&result_place=1&search _id=wWNL-wrKOQI-2861&hilite=50172474. The definition I have quoted is the eighth definition for the word "passing" in the *Oxford English Dictionary* and the fortieth definition for the word in Webster's.

3   Notable novels include James Fenimore Cooper's *The Last of the Mohicans* (1826), Gustave de Beaumont's *Marie* (1835), Alexandre Dumas's *Georges* (1843), William Wells Brown's *Clotel* (1853), Frances E. W. Harper's *Iola Leroy, or, Shadows Uplifte*d (1892), Charles Chesnutt's *The House behind the Cedars* (1900), and Frank Yerby's *The Foxes of Harrow* (1946). A host of narratives were also produced during the Harlem Renaissance, the most notable and critiqued of which include Jean Toomer's *Cane* (1923), Walter White's *Flight* (1926), Jessie Fauset's *Plum Bun* (1928), and Nella Larsen's *Passing* (1929).

4   Examples include *Gentleman's Agreement* (1947), *Pinky* (1949), *Lost Boundaries* (1949), *Show-Boat* (1951), two versions of *Imitation of Life* (1934 and 1959). In 1959 *Sapphire*, a British film about a young murdered woman who passed as white, was released. It also bears mentioning that passing films reemerged in the 1980s and continue to be made, including

161

Illusions (1982), *Devil in a Blue Dress* (1995), and *The Human Stain* (2003).

5   Ulli K. Ryder, " 'As Shelters against the Cold': Women Writers of the Black Arts and Chicano Movements, 1965–1978" (Ph.D. diss., University of Southern California, 2008). Ryder also points out the irony that the 1960s and 1970s, the heyday of the Black Power and Chicano movements, also saw a rise in mixed-race labeled births that coincided with Civil Rights legislation outlawing discrimination based on race, color, and national origin.

6   Sharon Jayson, "Interracial Marriage, More Accepted, Still Growing," *USA Today*, November 7, 2011, http://yourlife.usatoday.com/sex-relationships/marriage/story/2011-11-07/Interracial-marriage-More-accepted-still-growing/51115322/1, accessed November 8, 2011. Jayson writes, "It's no surprise that greater numbers today are 'marrying out,' meaning outside of their race. The percentage was 14.6% in 2008, up from 6.7% in 1980, according to a new analysis of Census data by researchers at Ohio State University and Cornell University. The data include only married couples, not the growing segment of unmarried cohabiters; experts expect the intermarriage trend to continue as some of those mixed-race couples head to the altar. An estimated 4.5 million married couples in the USA are interracial, according to 2011 Census data released last week from the Current Population Survey. A USA TODAY/Gallup poll released in September [2011] found that 86% of Americans approve of black-white marriages, compared with 48% in 1991. Among ages 18–37, 97% approved."

7   In an editorial I wrote for *Truthdig*, I pointed out that it is critical to remember that though the taboo against interracial relations eased with the *Loving v. Virginia* decision (because it made marriage equality a federal rights rather than a states' rights issue), that decision is not responsible for today's increasing Two or More Races (TOMR), or multiracial, population in the United States. "Mixed Race Beauty Gets a Mainstream Makeover," http://www.truthdig.com/report/item/mixed_race_beauty_gets_a_mainstream_makeover_20110307/, accessed March 7, 2011. Nor is Susan Eckert's argument true that "the multiracial identity was only truly born in the U.S. with the passing of Statistical Directive 15" on the 2000 U.S. Census. Rather, multiracial populations have been in existence since the days of exploration, colonialism, and enslavement, when Europeans mingled with Native populations and imported African populations, often by force, to North, Central, and South America. And, as will be argued in this book, unique expressions of identity emerged as a result of this mixing prior to the year 2000. Accordingly, the rise that statistics are tracking now per the U.S. 2000 and 2010 censuses reflects people's increasing ability, knowledge, willingness, perceived advantages, and comfort in describing themselves as multiracial in a society whose white majority is shrinking. This growing trend is certainly laudable and may even be a sign of personal and social progress, but it does not (yet) reflect broad-based changes in today's public policy or structural and institutional expressions of racism. It might be more accurate to say that the present surge in TOMR identification is a sign that we are moving away from the old "tragic mulatto" stereotype. This stereotype—applied

mostly to women—says that multiracials desire to be white and that they loathe the nonwhite part(s) of themselves. Note that what is still missing from the conversation is how even this unfortunate stereotype privileges mixes that include whiteness and marginalizes others (i.e., Asian Black; Native American Black).

8   Everett V. Stonequist, *The Marginal Man: A Study in Personality and Culture Conflict* (New York: Russell & Russell, 1937).

9   W. S. Carlos Poston, "The Biracial Identity Development Model: A Needed Addition," *Journal of Counseling and Development* 69, no. 2 (1990): 152–55.

10 This growing roster includes foundational texts such as Maria P. P. Root's anthology *Racially Mixed People in America* (Thousand Oaks, Calif.: Sage, 1992) and Naomi Zack's anthology *American Mixed Race: The Culture of Microdiversity* (Lanham, Md.: Rowman & Littlefield, 1995), which was followed quickly by Root's second anthology, *The Multiracial Experience: Racial Borders as the New Frontier* (Philadelphia: Temple University Press, 1996). These anthologies share a focus on the liminality, alienation, and complex cultural legacies of passing on multiracial identities. Zack's work stands apart from Root's insofar as it incorporates autobiographical and artistic work. And Root's second anthology continues the trajectory of establishing multiracial identity as socially and symbolically resistant "identity movement," complete with "A Bill of Rights for Racially Mixed People" to identify however they choose regardless of social networks, geography, or reflected appraisals. As discussed in the chapters that follow, this "Bill of Rights" sounds a lot like the right to pass. See Maria P. P. Root, "A Bill of Rights for Racially Mixed People," in *Root, The Multiracial Experience*, 3–14. Among other provisions, the Bill asserts the right of "mixed race" people to "identify . . . differently than strangers expect [them] to identify; to identify . . . differently than how . . . parents identify [them]; to identify . . . differently than . . . brothers and sisters; "and "to identify . . . differently in different situations." This critical mixed-race studies explosion includes many titles that address passing, including Lise Funderburg, *Black, White, Other* (New York: William Morrow, 1994); Carol Camper, ed., *Miscegenation Blues: Voices of Mixed Race Women* (Toronto: Sister Vision Press, 1994); Paul C. Rosenblatt, Terri A. Karis, and Richard D. Powell, *Multiracial Couples: Black and White Voices* (Thousand Oaks, Calif.: Sage, 1995); Robyn Weigman, *American Anatomies: Theorizing Race and Gender* (Durham: Duke University Press, 1995); Joel Williamson, *New People: Miscegenation and Mulattoes in the United States* (Baton Rouge: Louisiana State University Press, 1995); Ruth Colker, *Hybrid: Bisexuals, Multiracials, and Other Misfits under American Law* (New York: New York University Press, 1996); Elaine Ginsberg, ed., *Passing and the Fictions of Identity* (Durham: Duke University Press, 1996); Katya Gibel Azoulay, *Black, Jewish, and Interracial: It's Not the Color of Your Skin, but the Race of Your Kin, and Other Myths of Identity* (Durham: Duke University Press, 1997); Jon Michael Spencer and Richard E. Van der Ross, *The New Colored People* (New York: New York University Press, 1997); Rainier Spencer, *Spurious Issues: Race and Multiracial Identity Politics in the United*

States (Boulder: Westview Press, 1999); Gary Nash, *Forbidden Love: The Secret History of Mixed Race Identity* (New York: Henry Holt, 1999); Kathleen Odell Korgen, *From Black to Biracial: Transforming Racial Identity among Americans* (Westport, Conn.: Praeger, 1998); Bea Wehrly, Kelley R. Kenney, and Mark E. Kenney, *Counseling Multiracial Families* (Thousand Oaks, Calif.: Sage, 1999); Pearl Fuyo Gaskins, ed., *What Are You? Voices of Mixed Race Young People* (New York: Henry Holt, 1999); Marion Kilson, *Claiming Place: Biracial Young Adults of the Post–Civil Rights Era* (Westport, Conn.: Greenwood, 2000); Gayle Wald, *Crossing the Line: Racial Passing in Twentieth-Century U.S. Literature and Culture* (Durham: Duke University Press, 2000); Nina Boyd Krebs, *Edgewalkers: Defusing Cultural Boundaries on the New Global Frontier* (Far Hills, N.J.: New Horizon Press, 2000); Paul Gilroy, *Against Race: Imagining Political Culture beyond the Color Line* (Cambridge, Mass.: Harvard University Press, 2000); Ursula M. Brown, *The Interracial Experience: Growing Up Black/White Racially Mixed in the United States* (Westport, Conn.: Praeger, 2001); Kendra R. Wallace, *Relative/Outsider: The Art and Politics of Identity among Mixed Heritage Students* (Westport, Conn.: Greenwood, 2001); David Parker and Miri Song, eds., *Rethinking "Mixed Race"* (London: Pluto Press, 2001); Jonathan Brennan, ed., *Mixed Race Literature* (Stanford: Stanford University Press, 2002); Leon E. Wynter, *American Skin: Pop Culture, Big Business, and the End of White America* (New York: Crown, 2002); Suzanne Bost, *Mulattas and Mestizas: Representing Mixed Identities in the Americas, 1850–2000* (Athens: University of Georgia Press, 2003); Kevin R. Johnson, ed., *Mixed Race America and the Law: A Reader* (New York: New York University Press, 2003); Jayne O. Ifekwunigwe, ed., *Mixed Race Studies: A Reader* (London: Routledge, 2004); G. Reginald Daniel and Paul Spickard, eds., *Racial Thinking in the United States: Uncompleted Independence* (Notre Dame: Notre Dame University Press, 2004); Kelly Ann Rockquemore and Tracy Laszloffy, *Raising Biracial Children* (Lanham, Md.: Altamira Press, 2005); Alexander Courtney, *Hollywood Fantasies of Miscegenation: Spectacular Narratives of Gender and Race, 1903–1967* (Princeton: Princeton University Press, 2005); David Wells Engstrom and Lissette M. Piedra, eds., *Our Diverse Society: Race, Ethnicity, and Class—Implications for 21st Century America* (Washington, D.C.: NASW Press, 2006); Gina Miranda Samuels, "Beyond the Rainbow: Multiraciality in the 21st Century," in Engstrom and Piedra, *Our Diverse Society*, 37–66; Kimberly McClain DaCosta, *Making Multiracials: State, Family, and Market in the Redrawing of the Color Line* (Stanford: Stanford University Press, 2006); David L. Brunsma, ed. *Mixed Messages: Multiracial Identities in the "Color-Blind" Era* (Boulder: Lynne Rienner, 2006); Kim M. Williams, *Mark One or More: Civil Rights in the Multiracial Era* (Ann Arbor: University of Michigan Press, 2006); Kenji Yoshino, *Covering: The Hidden Assault on Our Civil Rights* (New York: Random House, 2007); Mary Beltrán and Camilla Fojas, eds., *Mixed Race Hollywood* (New York: New York University Press, 2009); Susan Sánchez-Casal and Amie A. Macdonald, *Identity in Education* (New York: Palgrave Macmillan, 2009); Stephanie Rose Bird, *Light, Right, and Damned Near White: Biracial and*

Triracial Culture in America (Westport, Conn.: Praeger, 2009); Sultanna Choudry, *Multifaceted Identity of Interethnic Young People: Chameleon Identities* (Farnham, U.K.: Ashgate, 2010); Kip Fulbeck, *Mixed: Portraits of Multiracial Kids* (San Francisco: Chronicle Books, 2010); Shirley Boteler Mock, *Dreaming with the Ancestors: Black Seminole Women in Texas and Mexico* (Norman: University of Oklahoma Press, 2010); Kenji Yoshino, *A Thousand Times More Fair: What Shakespeare's Plays Teach Us about Justice* (New York: HarperCollins, 2011); Nadine Ehlers, *Racial Imperatives: Discipline, Performativity, and Struggles against Subjection* (Indianapolis: Indiana University Press, 2011).

11 Multiracial nonfiction that treated the topic of passing took hold of the *New York Times* Best-Seller List and did not let go in what Danzy Senna calls "The Mulatto Millennium." Some of the most notable titles include Barack H. Obama's bestselling reissue of his 1995 autobiography, *Dreams from My Father: A Story of Race and Inheritance* (New York: Three Rivers Press, 2004); Lisa Jones's collection of autobiographical essays entitled *Bulletproof Diva: Tales of Race, Sex, and Hair* (New York: Random House, 1994); James McBride's autobiography, *The Color of Water: A Black Man's Tribute to His White Mother* (New York: Riverhead Books, 1997); Rebecca Walker's *Black, White, and Jewish: Autobiography of a Shifting Self* (New York: Riverhead Books, 2002); Angela Nissel's *Mixed: My Life in Black and White* (New York: Villard Books, 2006); Elliott Lewis's *Fade: My Journeys in Multiracial America* (New York: Carroll and Graf, 2006); Obama's *The Audacity of Hope* (New York: Random House, 2006); Bliss Broyard's *One Drop: My Father's Hidden Life—A Story of Race and Family Secrets* (New York: Little, Brown, 2007); and Soledad O'Brien's *The Next Big Story: My Journey through the Land of Possibilities* (New York: Penguin, 2010). Though it is not yet a bestseller, Michael Sidney Fosberg's independently published memoir *Incognito* (Chicago: Incognito, 2011) also deserves mention here.

12 Susan Salny, "Black? White? Asian? More Young Americans Choose All of the Above," *New York Times*, January 29, 2011.

13 Anita Kathy Foeman and Teresa A. Nance, "From Miscegenation to Multiculturalism: Perceptions and Stages of Interracial Relationship Development," *Journal of Black Studies* 29, no. 4 (1999): 540–57; Foeman and Nance, "On Being Biracial in the United States," in *Readings in Intercultural Communication: Experiences and Contexts*, ed. Judith N. Martin, Thomas K. Nakayama, and Lisa A. Flores (New York: McGraw-Hill, 2001), 35–43.

14 These include Multiracial Americans of Southern California, I-Pride, Hapa Issues Forum, Project RACE, the MAVIN Foundation, the Association of MultiEthnic Americans, Inc., and the Biracial Family Network. Part of these organizations' push for the 2000 census to include a separate multiracial option included a Multiracial Solidarity March in Washington, D.C., sponsored by the Biracial Family Network on July 20, 1996. For more on the definition of identity work, see David Snow and Leon Anderson, "Identity Work among the Homeless: The Verbal Construction and Avowal of Personal Identities," *American Journal of Sociology* 92, no. 6 (1987): 1336–71. For more on the growing divide

between academic and popular discourses on the subjects of passing and multiracial identities, see Francis Wardle, "Push Back: Academics Are the Enemies of the Multiracial Movement," CSBCHome.org Blog Archive for the Center for the Study of Biracial Children, April 2, 2009, http://www .csbchome.org/.

15 Mary E. Campbell and Jennifer Eggerling-Boeck, "'What About the Children?': The Psychological and Social Well-Being of Multiracial Adolescents," *Sociological Quarterly* 47, no. 1 (2006): 147–73.

16 Julie Suzuki-Crumly and Lauri L. Hyers, "The Relationship among Ethnic Identity, Psychological Well-Being, and Intergroup Competence: An investigation of Two Biracial Groups," *Cultural Diversity and Ethnic Minority Psychology* 10, no. 2 (2004): 138.

17 Though the literature in sociology, communication, social work, and critical mixed race studies suggests that multiracials do not appear to be any more or less deficient, deviant, or confused than their monoracial counterparts, contrary reports emerge periodically in news media. As an example of the hybrid degenerate (i.e., multiracials acquire the worst traits of all groups with which they are associated) variety take the following *Los Angeles Times* article, which covers a survey released on November 7, 2011 in the Archives of General Psychiatry. "Between 2005 and 2007, researchers plumbed the drug and alcohol use patterns of 72,561 adolescents between age 12 and 17. They conducted computer-assisted interviews with adolescents about their use in the past 12 months of alcohol and a wide range of illicit drugs, including marijuana, cocaine and opioid painkillers taken for non-medical reasons." Results indicate that multiracial youths were "more likely than any other group to exhibit signs of problematic drug and alcohol use." Melissa Healy, "White and Mixed-race Youths Rank High in Alcohol, Substance Abuse," *Los Angeles Times*, November 7, 2011, http://www.latimes.com/health/boostershots/ la-heb-drug-alcohol-adolescents-20111107,0,2331740.story, accessed November 8, 2011. As an example of the hybrid vigor (i.e., multiracials inherit the best traits of all groups with which they identify) variety take the report from *Time* magazine, which asserted that multiracials are better off psychologically than their monoracial counterparts. John Cloud, "Are Mixed-Race Children Better Adjusted?," *Time*, February 21, 2009, http://www.time.com/time/health/article/0,8599,1880467,00.html. For a thorough and thoughtful treatment of multiracial representation in news media, see Catherine R. Squires, *Dispatches From the Color Line: The Press and Multiracial America* (Albany: SUNY Press, 2007).

18 Patricia J. Williams. "Not-Black by Default," *The Nation*, April 22, 2010, http://www.thenation.com/print/article/not-black-default, accessed August 18, 2010.

19 Mica Pollack, *Colormute: Race Talk Dilemmas in an American School* (Princeton: Princeton University Press, 2005); Peter Kuryla, "Barack Obama and the American Island of the Colour Blind," *Patterns of Prejudice* 45, nos. 1–2 (2011): 119–32.

20 Gerard A. Hauser, *Introduction to Rhetorical Theory* (Long Grove, Ill.: Waveland Press, 2002).

21 G. Reginald Daniel, "Passers and Pluralists: Subverting the Racial Divide," in Root, *Racially Mixed People in America*, 91–107.

22 This shift in self-identification and yearning for new narratives of racial identification is reflected best in the results for the U.S. 2010 census. Based on recently released data, the number of multiracial Americans jumped roughly 32 percent since 2000, to over 9 million (accounting for approximately 2.9 percent of the total U.S. population).

23 For instance, Joel Williamson argues that the desire to count multiracial identities is an old phenomenon. "Mulatto" became an official census category in 1850, and "mulattoes" were counted and studied obsessively for decades until *Plessy v. Ferguson* reinstitutionalized monoracial identification standards. For more see Joel Williamson, *New People: Miscegenation and Mulattoes in the United States* (Baton Rouge: Louisiana State University Press, 1995).

24 Most scholars across the disciplines agree that there is no biological justification for assigning individuals to distinct racial groups. Support for this assertion can be found in physical anthropology, sociology, literature, rhetoric, ethnic studies, and, most recently, in human genetics. For more see Ashley Montagu, *The Concept of Race* (New York: Free Press, 1965); Barbara Fields, "Ideology and Race in American History," in *Region, Race and Reconstruction: Essays in Honor of C. Vann Woodward*, ed. J. Kousser and J. McPherson (New York: Oxford University Press); Michael Omi and Howard Winant, *Racial Formation in the United States* (New York: Routledge, 1994); Henry Louis Gates Jr., *"Race," Writing, and Difference* (Chicago: University of Chicago Press, 1986); Stuart Hall, "Gramsci's Relevance for the Study of Race and Ethnicity," in *Stuart Hall: Critical Dialogues in Cultural Studies*, ed. D. Morley and K. H. Chen (London: Routledge, 1996); Paul Gilroy, *Against Race: Imagining Political Culture beyond the Color Line* (Cambridge, Mass.: Harvard University Press, 2000); Joseph L. Graves, *The Emperor's New Clothes: Biological Theories of Race at the Millennium* (New Brunswick: Rutgers University Press, 2001).

25 In the pages that follow, I have chosen not to do this except in cases where the words are actual quotations, such as when authors used terms in other historical eras that are not used commonly today (for instance, "Negro," "octoroon," "colored," "mulatto," and so on).

26 DaCosta, *Making Multiracials*.

27 Melissa Harris-Perry, "Black by Choice," *The Nation*, April 15, 2010, http://www.thenation.com/article/black-choice; Carina Ray, "Why Do You Call Yourself Black and African?," blog entry, The Zeleza Post: Informed News and Commentary on the Pan African World, July 4, 2009, http://www.zeleza.com/blogging/global-affairs/why-do-you-call-yourself-black-and-african; Jared Sexton, *Amalgamation Schemes: Antiblackness and the Critique of Multiracialism* (Minneapolis: University of Minnesota Press, 2008); Michele Elam, *The Souls of Mixed Folk: Race, Politics, and Aesthetics in the New Millennium* (Stanford: Stanford University Press, 2011).

28 Maria P. P. Root, introduction to Root, *The Multiracial Experience*, xi.

29 Sinead Moynihan, *Passing into the Present: Contemporary American Fiction of Racial and Gender Passing* (Manchester: Manchester University Press, 2010).

30 Root, introduction to *Root, The Multiracial Experience*, ix–x. "Biracial" is also the term of choice for discussing passing because its use "moves us away from requiring equal 'fractions of blood' to recognize the prevalence of racial blending throughout American history."

31 The topic is further narrowed to passing as it pertains to white or black racial identification in the United States. This is not because the identification processes and experiences of Asian Americans, Native Americans, Hispanic Americans, Arab Americans, and Jewish Americans are irrelevant but, rather, because the area of academic specialization must be restricted for the sake of economy. Additionally, sociohistorical constraints on passers' initial self-concepts as black, white, or multiracial must be acknowledged. Therefore, the level of analysis is constrained to the theoretical realm, acknowledging that biracial passing represents a particular rhetorical choice based on historical facts and ingrained social values and practices. I recognize that additional research that takes a comparative approach to multiracial identities is needed for a more complete theory of passing and its impact on multiracial identities today. It is my hope that the analysis generated herein can be extended and utilized in conducting such investigations and examining the rhetorical construction of nonwhite multiracial identities (i.e., Filipino-African American) as well as a range of multiethnic and multireligious identities. For more on this, see Miri Song, *Choosing Ethnic Identity* (Malden, Mass.: Blackwell, 2003).

32 Bost, *Mulattas and Mestizas.*

33 This is extremely important because much of the research on passing and its effects on multiracial identification remains atheoretical and limited in its approach to locating motives for and mechanics of identification (the motion of bodies in a frame of reference). Important aspects that affect identification, such as physical, social, and communicative comparisons, should also be addressed. Thus, the book concludes by summarizing the analyses conducted and suggesting areas for further research in the domain of passing as a transformative practice that can allow for better connections between rhetoric and the formation of multiracial identities today.

CHAPTER ONE

1 The Race Awareness Project, Cambridge Diversity Consulting, accessed September 7, 2010, http://www.cambridgediversity.com/rap.html.

2 Race Awareness Project. After each guess is made, the user is presented with a historical or cultural factoid related to identity. According to its developers (the Cambridge Diversity Project), "Guess My Race" is meant to support a constructivist view of race and introduce users "to a critical thinking perspective on culture and hegemony more broadly."

3 Charles Scruggs, "Jean Toomer and Kenneth Burke and the Persistence of the Past," *American Literary History* 13, no. 1 (2001): 41–66.

4 Over time, passing has been defined in a variety of scenarios and practiced for a host of purposes. There is a body of literature that discusses

these purposes, which include, but are not limited to, escape from slavery, dignified and humane treatment, geographical and social mobility, housing and employment opportunities, self-reinvention, investigative reporting, interracial romance, racial uplift, the pleasure in withholding information from the group with which one attempts to affiliate, and acceptance within that group. The body of literature, as it pertains to racial and ethnic passing, includes James Weldon Johnson, *Autobiography of an Ex–Coloured Man* (New York: Vintage Books, 1912); Philip Roth, *The Human Stain* (New York: Knopf, 2000); Walter White, *A Man Called White: The Autobiography of Walter White* (Athens: University of Georgia Press, 1948); A. C. Carlson, "'You Know It When You See It': The Rhetorical Hierarchy of Race and Gender in *Rhinelander v. Rhinelander,*" *Quarterly Journal of Speech* (1999): 111–28; Rachel F. Moran, *Interracial Intimacy: The Regulation of Race and Romance* (Chicago: University of Chicago Press, 2001); Jessie Redmon Fauset, *There Is Confusion* (New York: Beacon Press, 1924); Langston Hughes, *The Ways of White Folks* (New York: Alfred A. Knopf, 1933); James M. O'Toole, *Passing: Race, Religion, and the Healy Family, 1820–1920* (Amherst: University of Massachusetts Press, 1996); Werner Sollors, *Neither Black Nor White Yet Both* (Cambridge, Mass.: Harvard University Press, 1997); Mat Johnson (with art by Warren Pleece and lettering by Clem Robins), *Incognegro* (New York: Vertigo/DC Comics, 2008); Zelie Asava, "Multiculturalism and Morphing in I'm Not There," *Wide Screen* (2010): 1–15.

For instance, in a brilliant *Saturday Night Live* parody called "White Like Me," comedian Eddie Murphy engages passing as an information-gathering process. Here, as in the famous exposé "Black Like Me," passing becomes a way to experience different life outcomes a society has to offer for individuals as black and white, most of which are institutional and economic in nature. From Murphy's depiction we learn that passing requires anonymity, knowledge of black and white cultural stereotypes, a shared belief in race as an essential human characteristic, deep social and structural inequality between racial groups, and cosmetic technology. Not to mention a sense of humor and a willingness to be surprised and edified by what is revealed.

More conventional readings of passing focus on its more serious aspects and demonstrate its frequency and importance to white and black racial communities alike. Langston Hughes, in an essay written during the heyday of passing (1880s–1930s), writes of how a passer tells his black mother that he feels "like a dog" because he has disappeared into the white race even though he now feels "free!" ("Passing," in Hughes, *Ways of White Folks*). This rendition of passing is "continuous," involving a complete break with racial and social networks into which one was born. While "Passing" rightly depicts continuous passing as an attempt to bring order to a racial identity that is out of order, it falls short of noting that the passer's distorted sense of what order is stems from the structural dysfunction of racism. Therefore, in this description passing can be considered an individual's tragic adaptation to life, "a traumatic accommodation with traumatic losses of its own." In line with this tragic conception continuous passing has also been defined as a form of social climbing, "a deception that enables a person to adopt certain roles/identities from which he would be barred by prevailing social standards in the absence of his misleading conduct." Others define it as an individual's decision to assert a privileged identity over a non privileged identity, a matter of concealment. In either case passing is depicted as an apparatus for the operation and reproduction of hegemonic racial images of whiteness. Even when reconceptualized for the digital age passing is likened to "identity tourism." And when examined in terms of representation in prominent Hollywood films passing is treated as a violation of the "truth bias" in terms of falsification, equivocation, and outright denial. For more see Werner Sollors, *Neither Black Nor White Yet Both*, 247–48; Hughes, "Passing," 51, 54; G. Reginald Daniel, "Passers and Pluralists: Subverting the Racial Divide," in *Racially Mixed People in America*, ed. Maria P. P. Root (Newbury Park, Calif.: Sage, 1992), 91–107; Kimberlyn Leary, "Passing, Posing, and Keeping It Real," *Constellations* 6 (1999): 88, doi: 10.1111/1467–8675.00122; Randall Kennedy, "Racial Passing," *Ohio State Law Journal* 62 (2001), http://moritzlaw.osu.edu/lawjournal/issues/volume62/number3/kennedy.pdf, accessed June 5, 2006; Catherine R. Squires and Daniel C. Brouwer, "In/Discernible Bodies: The Politics of Passing in Dominant and Marginal Media," *Critical Studies in Media Communication* 19, no. 3 (2002): 283–311; Harryette Mullen, "Optic White: Blackness and the Production of Whiteness," *Diacritics* 24 (1994): 71–89; Lisa Nakamura, *Cybertypes: Race, Ethnicity, and Identity on the Internet* (London: Routledge, 2002); Brooke Kroger, *Passing: When People Can't Be Who They Are* (New York: Public Affairs, 2003).

5   It is also important to note that Jacques Derrida cautions against a simple restaging of the battle between the Sophists and Plato because our culture is significantly different from the Greek situations depicted in the Platonic dialogues. Nevertheless, the way in which we think about identity (and racial identity) is rooted in Platonic thought. For this reason the classical debate is relevant to my discussion of passing from a rhetorical perspective. For more on Derrida's concern about the cultural relevance of this debate, see Jacques Derrida, *Dissemination*, trans. Barbara Johnson (Chicago: University of Chicago Press, 1991); Gary A. Olson, "Jacques Derrida on Rhetoric and Composition: A Conversation," *Journal of Advanced Composition* 10, no. 1 (1990): 1–21.

6   Richard E. Vatz, "The Mythical Status of Situational Rhetoric: Implications for Rhetorical Critics' Relevance in the Public Arena," *Review of Communication* 9, no. 1 (2009): 1. Vatz writes, "In Plato's day, whether one sided with Plato or the Sophists was not an idle matter, of importance only to the intellectuals of the day. It was, instead, a matter of 'life and death' with respect to how one might interpret reality and enact values in the world."

7   By "Sophists," I mean those generally perceived as the main players in this group of classical rhetoric teachers who were independent of Plato—specifically Protagoras, Gorgias, Prodicus, Antiphone, Hippias, Critias, and Thrasymachus. When I use the term "sophistic rhetoric," I do not mean to ignore the fact that the Sophists often differed in their rhetorical

perspectives. Rather, my intent is to emphasize the common features that permitted Plato and other scholars to regard them as a group.

8   John Poulakos, "Toward a Sophistic Definition of Rhetoric," *Philosophy and Rhetoric* 16, no. 1 (1983): 35–48.

9   Plato, *Theaetetus*, trans. M. J. Levett, in *The Complete Works of Plato*, ed. John M. Cooper (Indianapolis: Hackett, 1997), 157–234.

10 Plato, *Phaedo*, trans. G. M. A. Grube, in *The Complete Works of Plato*, 49–100.

11 Plato offers up a long list of pejorative adjectives for rhetoric through-out all the dialogues, including idolatry, semblance, imitation (mimesis), information without knowledge, dissembling deception, false art, long-winded flattering speech.

12 Plato, *Phaedrus* 272d, trans. Alexander Nehamas and Paul Woodruff, in *The Complete Works of Plato*, 549. Plato writes, "for the fact is . . . that one who intends to be an able rhetorician has no need to know the truth . . . they only care about what is convincing."

13 Plato, *Gorgias*, trans. Donald J. Zeyl, in *The Complete Works of Plato*, 238–75. Plato writes, "there is no need for rhetoric to know the facts at all, for it has hit upon a means of persuasion that enables it to appear in the eyes of the ignorant to know more than those who really know." Plato regarded knowledge as a cognitive state of the soul concerned with that which is unchanging and necessary, the Ideas or Forms. Plato contrasts knowledge (*episteme*) with belief (*doxa*), the cognitive state concerned with sensible things. For Plato, the contrast between *episteme* and *doxa* is essential for defining rhetoric as passing. Plato claims that *doxa* was often manipulated by Sophists to persuade the people, while Sophists saw it as a tool for the formation of arguments by using common opinions and experiences.

14 George A. Kennedy, *A New History of Classical Rhetoric* (Princeton: Princeton University Press, 1994), 39. Kennedy writes, "Plato's view of rhetoric here is that it cannot be divided from its substance: a speech must be about something and it is that something that matters most."

15 Considering rhetoric as passing can shed light upon Plato's limited account of the personae, their statuses in social hierarchy, and the goals and ethics of their rhetoric.

16 Nakayama and Krizek, "Whiteness."

17 James C. Scott, *Domination and the Arts of Resistance: Hidden Transcripts* (New Haven: Yale University Press, 1990), 36. Scott writes that rhetoric is one of many "adaptations to inequalities of power." That is why rhetoric is "often depicted as natural characteristics of the subordinate group, a move that has, in turn, the great advantage of underlining the innate inferiority of its members when it comes to logic, truth, honesty, and reason and thereby justifying their continued domination by their betters."

18 Scott Consigny, "Edward Schiappa's Reading of the Sophists," *Rhetoric Review* 14, no. 2 (1996): 253–69.

19 Kenneth Burke, *A Rhetoric of Motives* (Berkeley: University of California Press, 1969).

20 Stanley Fish, *Doing What Comes Naturally: Change, Rhetoric, and the*

Practice of Theory in Literary and Legal Studies (Durham: Duke University Press, 1989), 478–81. Fish writes that truth "assumes a different shape in the light of differing local urgencies and . . . convictions."

21 Poulakos, "Toward a Sophistic Definition of Rhetoric." For a more detailed discussion of sophistic rhetoric as a use of discourse to encode and decode specific cultural practices, see also John Poulakos, *Sophistical Rhetoric in Classical Greece* (Columbia: University of South Carolina Press, 1995). In this text Poulakos links sophistry to ontological perspectives of "Nomadism" by Deleuze and of the "Bricoleur" by Certeau. Additional noteworthy treatments of a sophistic worldview are W. K. C. Guthrie, *The Sophists* (Cambridge: Cambridge University Press, 1971); G. R. Stanton, "Sophists and Philosophers: Problems of Classification," *American Journal of Philology* 94, no. 4 (1973): 350–64; Rosamond Sprague, *The Older Sophists* (Columbia: University of South Carolina Press, 1972); Samuel Ijsseling, *Rhetoric and Philosophy in Conflict* (The Hague: Martinus Nijhoff, 1976); Jane Sutton, "Rereading Sophistical Arguments: A Political Intervention," *Argumentation* 5, no. 2 (1991): 141–57; Harold Barrett, *Sophists: Rhetoric, Democracy and Plato's Idea of Sophistry* (Novato: Chandler & Sharp, 1987); Brian Vickers, *In Defence of Rhetoric* (Oxford: Clarendon, 1988); Susan J. Jarratt, *Rereading the Sophists: Classical Rhetoric Refigured* (Carbondale: Southern Illinois University Press, 1991); James Fredal, "Why Shouldn't the Sophists Charge Fees?," *Rhetoric Society Quarterly* 38, no. 2 (2008): 148–70.

22 Poulakos, "Toward a Sophistic Definition of Rhetoric," 37.

23 In this apagogy, Gorgias identifies four possible causes for Helen's acts: (1) it was a divine plan; (2) Paris took her by force; (3) Paris seduced her; (4) Helen fell in love with Paris. In any case Gorgias asserts that the "truth" of a person's actions is a function of the kinds of language and visual imagery to which they are exposed.

24 Ekaterina V. Haskins, *Logos and Power in Isocrates and Aristotle* (Columbia: University of South Carolina Press, 2004), 15.

25 Kennedy, *A New History of Classical Rhetoric*, 20.

26 C. Jan Swearingen, *Rhetoric and Irony: Western Literacy and Western Lies* (Oxford: Oxford University Press, 1991): 56.

27 Plato, *Sophist* 223b, trans. Nicholas P. White, in *The Complete Works of Plato*, 243.

28 Hal Berghel, "Identity Theft, Social Security Numbers, and the Web," *Communications of the ACM* 43, no. 2 (2000): 17–21. Berghel traces the history of identity theft and defines it as the appropriation of personally identifying information without permission to commit fraud or other crimes. Identity thieves may acquire property, obtain a credit card, or establish a telephone account in someone else's name, and victims may not discover the theft until, in the case of the credit card, a review of the credit report or a credit card statement reveals unauthorized and unrecognized charges. While some identity theft victims resolve their problems with relative ease, others undergo a costly and protracted process of repairing their reputations and credit records. Consumers victimized by identity theft often lose out on employment opportunities or are denied

loans for education, housing, or cars because of negative information on
their credit reports. In rare cases, victims may even be arrested for crimes
they did not commit. In chapter 3, I will discuss the connections between
identity theft, multiracial identities, passing, and public policy in *Plessy
v. Ferguson*. For additional discussion of identity theft, see U.S. Federal
Trade Commission, About Identity Theft, January 2011, http://www
.ftc.gov/bcp/edu/microsites/idtheft/consumers/about-identity-theft.html
(May 9, 2011).

29   Elizabeth B. Spelman, *Inessential Woman: Problems of Exclusion in
Feminist Thought* (Boston: Beacon Press, 1988).

30   Fredal, "Why Shouldn't the Sophists Charge Fees?," 167. As Fredal puts
it, when subalterns speak they "demythologize the apparently objective
realm of value, revealing its purely conventional and subjective source in
collective agreement and cultural perception."

31   C. Jan Swearingen says as much when she writes, "Plato and perhaps even
more so Socrates, as depicted in the dialogues, were Sophists themselves
in the sense that they contributed to an expanded conception of wisdom,
encouraged the development of abstract terms, and provided formal definitions of the most expeditious settings, goals, and internal structures
for philosophizing. . . . What, then, distinguishes Plato, and the 'true
philosophy' . . . , from the sophistic abuses which he depicts?" For more
see Swearingen, *Rhetoric and Irony*, 57–58.

My claim here is also based on Robert L. Scott's discussion of rhetoric as an epistemic phenomenon. For a detailed discussion of this phenomenon, see Robert L. Scott, "On Viewing Rhetoric as Epistemic," *Central
States Speech Journal* 18, no. 1 (1967): 9–17; "Non-Discipline as a Remedy for Rhetoric? A Reply to Victor Vitanza," *Rhetoric Review* 6, no. 2
(1988): 233–37; "On Viewing Rhetoric as Epistemic: Ten Years Later,"
Central States Speech Journal 27 (1976): 258–66; "Epistemic Rhetoric
and Criticism: Where Barry Brummett Goes Wrong," *Quarterly Journal of Speech* 76 (1990): 300–303; "The Necessary Pluralism of Any
Future History of Rhetoric," *A Journal of Rhetorical Theory* 12 (1991):
195–209; "Rhetoric Is Epistemic: What Difference Does That Make?,"
in *Defining the New Rhetoric*, ed. Theresa Enos and Stuart C. Brown
(Newbury Park, Calif.: Sage, 1993), 120–36.

32   Christopher Norris, *Derrida* (Cambridge, Mass.: Harvard University
Press, 1987), 163. *Episteme*'s appearance of stability is the ultimate irony
and very useful for highlighting social negotiations occurring along the
color line, a claim I will revisit in chapter 2.

33   Plato, *Protagoras* 216do–217, trans. Stanley Lombardo and Karen Bell, in
The Complete Works of Plato, 753.

34   Plato, *Protagoras* 319a, 328d–e.

35   Amy Robinson was the first to point out that the shadows about which
Plato writes are almost always translated from the Greek with the verb
form "to pass." "Most standard translations of *The Republic* of Plato
either describe the images projected on the walls of the cave as 'passing shadows' or agree that the shadows 'passed' for wisdom in the cave.
Although I. A. Richards's translation does not use the word 'passing,' his

translation retains the logic of passing when he suggests that the enlightened students contemplate what was taken as wisdom in the cave." As I argue herein, when we think of rhetoric as passing we locate the passer's identity in the personae who interpret it. Amy Robinson, "To Pass//In Drag: Strategies of Entrance into the Visible" (Ph.D. diss., University of Pennsylvania, 1993), 118. For more see Plato, *The Republic of Plato*, trans. Francis MacDonald Cornford (Oxford: Oxford University Press, 1941); Plato, *Plato's Republic*, trans. Benjamin Jowett (New York: Vintage Books, 1970); Plato, *The Republic of Plato*, trans. Allan Bloom (New York: Basic Books, 1968); Plato, *Plato's Republic*, trans. I. A. Richards (Cambridge: Cambridge University Press, 1966); Plato, *Republic*, trans. Nicholas P. White, in *The Complete Works of Plato*.

36 Robinson, "To Pass/In Drag," 120–24.

37 Plato, *Sophist* 234c–235. For further discussion of how Plato explains rhetoric as passing, see Robinson, "To Pass//In Drag."

38 Thomas K. Nakayama and Robert L. Krizek, "Whiteness: A Strategic Rhetoric," *Quarterly Journal of Speech* 81 (1995): 291–309. According to Nakayama and Krizek, "Although the geographical location has moved from the place of ancient Greece to contemporary North America, the concept of *episteme*, an assumed fixed center, as the source of all meaning and identification remains intact and unquestioned."

39 Plato, *Theaetetus*, trans. Stanley Lombardo and Karen Bell, in *The Complete Works of Plato*, 157–234. At 152a Plato quotes Protagoras's man-measure principle: "Man as the measure of all things: of the things which are, that they are, and of the things which are not, that they are not." This principle explains the idea of self-determination; it invites citizens to make sense of their identities, to think through their beliefs and see their actions as capable of promoting social change. This principle is also expressed in Greek drama. Some scholars take it as the beginning of existentialism, while other see it as an origin of pragmatism, where truth is considered what works in a given situation. For a thorough discussion of the man-measure principle, see Joseph P. Maguire, "Protagoras—or Plato?" *Phronesis* 18 (1973): 115–38; Laszlo Versenyl, "Protagoras' Man-Measure Fragment," *American Journal of Philology* 83 (1962): 178–84.

40 William K. Guthrie, *The Sophists* (Cambridge: Cambridge University Press, 1971), 193. Guthrie writes that the Sophists "recognize only accidental as opposed to essential being . . . the conditional and relative as opposed to the self-existent." Passers have the power to support and subvert the realm of Platonic *episteme* as they decide how they will sustain their acts of passing. *Episteme* banishes knowledge that is not authorized by Truth. As applied to passing, *episteme* refuses to grant identity to passers as multiracial and assigns them to either a black or a white category. In strict rhetorical terms, passers subvert the realm of *episteme* by operating in and transforming the territory of opinion, *doxa*—made visible in terms of appearances, reputations, and expectations. This is precisely because they see that no Ideal form exists for the speaker-passer to claim or embody. So passers must enact a racial dramaturgy to gain recognition in the social world by emphasizing the aspects of their identities that will produce the identifications they seek.

41 For this reason rhetoric and passing generally are considered to be merely subjective opinion (*doxa*) rather than knowledge (*episteme*) and of limited efficacy. In order to recover the status of rhetoric, as well as the power of rhetoric as passing, we can extend the definition of *doxa* to include "concealment, an act of metamorphosis" which allows for a break from the *episteme/doxa* binary via *aletheia*—"truth (lit. unhiddenness)" or sincerity. Robert Hariman, "Status, Marginality, and Rhetorical Theory," in *Contemporary Rhetorical Theory: A Reader*, ed. John Louis Lucaites, Celeste Michelle Condit, and Sally Caudill (New York: Guilford Press, 1999), 46.

42 Hariman, "Status, Marginality, and Rhetorical Theory," 47.

43 John L. Jackson Jr., *Real Black: Adventures in Racial Sincerity* (Chicago: University of Chicago Press, 2005). Based on Lionel Trilling's work in literary criticism regarding sincerity and authenticity, Jackson questions whether authenticity is the best way to distinguish the true from the false and proposes a new model for thinking about these issues: "racial sincerity." Jackson argues that authenticity caricatures identity as something imposed on people, imprisoning them within stereotypes—objectifying and paralyzing them instead of allowing them to be living, breathing human beings. He maintains that authenticity denies people agency in their search for identity and presents "sincerity" as an alternative for thinking about identity in general and racial identity in particular. Enlisting "Anthroman," his cape-crusading doppelgänger, Jackson records and recounts his encounters in New York City and, in the process, shows us how race is defined and contested, assigned and complicated. See also Lionel Trilling, *Sincerity and Authenticity* (Cambridge, Mass.: Harvard University Press, 1972).

44 Jackson, *Real Black*, 11. Jackson defines racial sincerity as "how people think and feel their identities into palpable everyday existence, especially as such identities operate within a social context that includes so many causal forces beyond their immediate control." Linda Alcoff expands on the idea of sincerity, arguing that identities' sincerities should be visible and are a requirement for a healthy pluralistic democracy. For a full discussion of this visible conception of social identities, see Linda Martín Alcoff, *Visible Identities: Race, Gender and the Self* (Oxford: Oxford University Press, 2006).

45 *Aletheia* calls for identification based on multiple and competing interpretations rather than representations based on exact calculation (i.e., the one-drop rule). Hariman, "Status, Marginality, and Rhetorical Theory," 47.

46 John O'Neill, "Rhetoric, Science, and Philosophy," *Philosophy of the Social Sciences* 28, no. 2 (1998): 205–25.

47 This is because passing does not just reflect or express *doxa* as a false copy of *episteme*, but is a way to move beyond *episteme* to create an acceptable identity out of one that is, for the most part, inappropriate and unacceptable. Passing provides an opportunity to explore what happens when we free ourselves from the constraints of a Platonic conception. It shows passers' ability to work in the realm of what is possible and, through sincerity, concealment, and revelation (*aletheia*), to express race and racial

injustice appropriately given their rhetorical situations. Passing disregards real, stable, and organized identities and embraces ambiguities, embodies contradictions, and employs sincerity, concealment, and sometimes revelation.

48 Plato, *Republic* bk VII, trans. Nicholas P. White, in *The Complete Works of Plato*, 1141. As Plato puts it, rhetoric muddies our view and shows us that identities cannot exist "as separate, but as mixed up together." Plato's depiction of rhetoric as passing suggests that the greatest subjects for establishing and maintaining status, order, and hierarchy are matters of identification and division.

49 Maurice Charland, "Constitutive Rhetoric: The Case of the Peuple Quebecois," *Quarterly Journal of Speech* 73 no. 2 (1987): 133–50.

50 Bradford Vivian, "Sophistic Rhetoric and Rhetorical Nomads," in *Professing Rhetoric: Selected Papers from the 2000 Rhetorical Society of America Conference*, ed. Frederick J. Antczak, Cinda Coggins, and Geoffrey D. Klinger (Mahwah, N.J.: Lawrence Erlbaum Associates, 2002), 193–98. Vivian writes, "the true moment of rhetoric" may be present "between the poles of" Plato and the Sophists because "we don't get to pick one pole or the other, rather a series of rhetorical doubling occurs in which difference and multiplicity abound."

51 These intersections present the fourth persona (critic) with two ways of figuring truths based on *aletheia*: *episteme* and *doxa*. An epistemic conception is an expression of established conventional power infused with definitions, truth, knowledge, and representational clarity. Passers use synecdoche to represent themselves as either black or white and in effect to announce their epistemologically recognizable identities with respect to others. At the same time, passing is also concerned with *doxa*, which represents an escape from the confinement of compulsory racial identification using ambiguity, appropriateness, and indeterminacy. Any act of (bi)racial passing is enacted at the intersection of *episteme* and *doxa* and both reconciles and exploits the tensions between them through *aletheia*.

52 Truth as *aletheia* is about knowing that the version of truth projected is a version of the truth. In other words, passers show their audiences what truth can look like in a particular rhetorical situation—as either a white or a black person. For instance, each case indicates that biracial passing is a method for overcoming the inability to create or observe different outcomes for the same person at the same time. In passers we find individuals who have managed to become independent of the existence of racially marked positions (i.e., as enslaved or freed persons, as white or "colored," etc.). These passers can be considered personifications of aletheia based on their decisions to commit to particular personal, social and political causes.

53 Robinson, "To Pass//In Drag," 17–18.

54 Peter J. Rabinowitz, "'Betraying the Sender'; The Rhetoric and Ethics of Fragile Texts," *Narrative* 2 no. 3 (1994): 202. Rabinowitz articulates a definition of passing consistent with (and preceding) Amy Robinson's model that he calls "rhetorical passing." According to Rabinowitz, "rhetorical passing is not simply a disguise, but a virtuoso tightrope performance, a flirtation with risk by flaunting your disguise in a context in

which you know that it will fool only some people—an act, in other words, that has built into it the exhilarating possibility of exposure and destruction." The anxiety produced by rhetorical passing is why Plato equates and demotes rhetoric as passing.

55 Judith Butler, *Bodies That Matter: On the Discursive Limits of "Sex"* (New York: Routledge, 1993). Butler would call Dan's normative assumption a "hegemonic presumption."

56 This text message means, "I see you. (Wink) Let's meet at the Starbucks across the street in ten minutes."

57 Robinson, "To Pass//In Drag," 17–18.

58 Lawrence Otis Graham, *Our Kind of People: Inside America's Black Upper Class* (New York: HarperCollins, 2000). In the chapter entitled "Passing for White: When the 'Brown Paper Bag Test' Isn't Enough," Graham outlines twenty rules for successful passing, including avoiding nonpassing African Americans for fear of identification as black by association.

59 According to rhetorical theorist Kenneth Burke, identification, and not persuasion, is at the heart of rhetoric. Persuasion is the byproduct of effective identification, a process through which we align our interests with one another and become "consubstantial." When we are consubstantial with one another, we can be said to be in a state of shared substance. But Burke also points out that consubstantiality does not preclude division or each person's own development of a unique identity. For more see Burke, *A Rhetoric of Motives*.

60 Adrian Piper, "Passing for White, Passing for Black," *Transition* 58 (1992): 14. Piper writes that in-group clairvoyants keep the secret because of "vicarious enjoyment of watching one of [their] own infiltrate and achieve in a context largely defined by institutionalized attempts to exclude [them] from it."

61 Charles E. Morris III, "Pink Herring and The Fourth Persona: J. Edgar Hoover's Sex Crime Panic," in *Readings in Rhetorical Criticism*, 3rd ed., ed. Carl R. Burgchardt (State College, Pa.: Strata, 2005), 667.

62 Morris, "Pink Herring."

63 Morris, "Pink Herring."

64 According to Judith Butler, when the fourth persona/in-group clairvoyant outs a passer, she engages in an act of "queering." "Queering is what upsets and exposes passing; it is the act by which the racially and sexually repressive surface of conversation is exploded, by race, by sexuality, by the insistence on color." Butler, *Bodies That Matter*, 177.

65 Luc Boltanski and Graham Burschell, *Distant Suffering: Morality, Media and Politics* (Cambridge: Cambridge University Press, 1999), 30.

66 Nikki Khanna and Cathryn Johnson, "Passing as Black: Racial Identity Work among Biracial Americans," *Social Psychology Quarterly* 73 (2010): 380–97. Though Khanna and Johnson's is the first sustained analysis of passing as black, it is important to note that other scholars have either used the term or described the concept of passing as black. See also, e.g., Piper, "Passing for White, Passing for Black"; Daniel, "Passers and Pluralists"; F. James Davis, *Who Is Black? One Nation's Definition*

(University Park: Pennsylvania State University Press, 1991), Virginia R. Domínguez, *White by Definition: Social Classification in Creole Louisiana* (New Brunswick, N.J.: Rutgers University Press, 1986).

67 Passing confirms that skin and skin color are symbols used to organize a racially categorized society. A passer can choose one identity or another depending on situation and sociopolitical commitment. Passing rears its head even in the most unlikely places: for example, the stripping industry. According to sociologist Siobhan Brooks, passing is a racial performance through which clients imagine strippers "to be the race of their choice, and even can ignore the fact that she is [in this case] Latina, instead seeing her as a White blonde." When this is the case, passing affirms claims about symbolic demarcations based on skin color that show and hide various attributes, making it unstable evidence for distinguishing among individuals. Andrea Dworkin explains, "The skin is a line of demarcation, a periphery, the fence, the form, the shape, the first clue to identity in a society (for instance, color in a racist society), and, in purely physical terms, the formal precondition for being human. It is a thin veil of matter separating the outside from the inside. It is what one sees and what one covers up; it shows and it conceals; it hides what is inside." The idea that skin both "shows" and "conceals" because of the meanings and powers we assign to it is supported by the existence of passing. Siobhan Brooks, *Unequal Desires: Race and Erotic Capital in the Stripping Industry* (Albany: SUNY Press, 2008), 90. Andrea Dworkin, *Intercourse* (New York: Free Press, 1987), 22.

68 Walter Benn Michaels, "No Drop Rule," *Critical Inquiry* 20 (1994): 765. Michaels "insist[s] that racial designations are purely social and cultural perceptions."

69 Karen A. Foss and Kathy L. Domenici, "Haunting Argentina: Synecdoche in the Protests of the Mothers of the Plaza de Mayo," *Quarterly Journal of Speech* 87, no. 3 (2001): 242.

70 Foss and Domenici, "Haunting Argentina," 242.

71 Kenneth Burke, *A Grammar of Motives* (Berkeley: University of California Press, 1969), 60. As Burke puts it, the representative anecdote is "a summation, containing implicitly what the system that is developed from it contains explicitly" (emphasis in original). A representative anecdote must be specific enough "in that it is broadly a reduction of the subject matter." See also Foss and Domenici, "Haunting Argentina," 237–58.

72 In terms of passing, synecdoche privileges a critical perspective based on taking "the particular for the general, species for genus, product for producer, trade name for general product, general for particular, genus for species, and place for one-time event." S. Davis, "Synecdoche," in *Encyclopedia of Rhetoric and Composition*, ed. Theresa Enos (New York: Garland Press, 1996), 712–13. For more on the worldviews that synecdoche helps the critic to understand theoretically, see Ernest G. Bormann, "Fantasy and Rhetorical Vision: The Rhetorical Criticism of Social Reality," *Quarterly Journal of Speech* 58, no. 4 (1972): 396–407.

73 Burke, *A Grammar of Motives*, 507–8.

74 Foss and Domenici, "Haunting Argentina," 237–58.

75 Bridgette Nerlich and David D. Clarke, "Synecdoche as Cognitive and

Communication Strategy," in *Historical Semantics and Cognition*, ed. Andreas Blank and Peter Koch (Berlin/New York: Mouton de Gruyter, 1999), 210. The authors state that synecdoche "reflects and exploits order in our categories . . . it exploits semantic relations, and . . . it brings order into texts and into social relations."

76 Burke, *A Grammar of Motives*, 509. Burke writes that "representation (synecdoche) stresses a relationship or connectedness between two sides of an equation, a connectedness that, like a road, extends in either direction."

77 Burke, *A Grammar of Motives*, 507–8.

78 Foss and Domenici, "Haunting Argentina," 237–58.

79 Burke, *A Grammar of Motives*, 508–9.

80 Also known as the "one-drop rule," hypodescent classifies any person with any trace of black ancestry as black, and classifies any person as white if he or she has no trace of black (or other non-white) ancestry. Blood fraction standards for black classification varied by state: 1/8 (e.g., Missouri), 1/16 (e.g., Alabama), or 1/32 (e.g., Louisiana). According to Naomi Zack, U.S. history reveals that "there has never been a recognized category of mixed black and white race. Individuals with both black and white forebears have always been considered black, both legally and socially, in the contexts of both white and black society." Case in point: Booker T. Washington. Washington, a proponent of racial accommodation, acknowledged but did not identify himself based on the white part of his ancestry. He identified as "Negro." Racial identification based on hypodescent leads to what Kenneth Burke called a "paradox of purity," wherein race assumes such power that it becomes essential—the category from which all of an individual's characteristics and motivations are derived. This means we generally believe that knowing someone's race also means knowing that person's sexual identity, personal interests, and preferences. Of course, it is not possible to know another simply by knowing her race, but Americans have used and continue to use these kinds of racial assumptions to navigate social interactions. I will return to the rhetorical power of these assumptions as they pertain to motives for passing in chapters that follow. For now it is sufficient to mention their effects: solidifying the color line; empowering the one-drop rule's definition and recognition of identity on the basis of partial ancestry; pathologizing multiracial identities; and, ultimately, serving the interests of white supremacy. For a full discussion of the effects of hypodescent on multiracial individuals in the twenty-first century, see Arnold K. Ho, Jim Sidanius, Daniel T. Levin, and Mahzarin R. Banaji, "Evidence for Hypodescent and Racial Hierarchy in the Categorization and Perception of Biracial Individuals," *Journal of Personality and Social Psychology* 94 (2010): 1–15.

81 Burke, *A Grammar of Motives*, 508. Burke calls this "the perfect paradigm or prototype for all future uses." Contemporary scholars have elaborated on Burke's concept. "For Burke, this prototype or 'noblest synecdoche' is, in fact, the case in which the whole can represent the part, and the part simultaneously represents the whole" (Foss and Domenici, "Haunting Argentina," 242).

82 Burke, *A Grammar of Motives*, 509. Burke elaborates, "I would want to deliberately 'coach' the concept of the synecdochic by extending it to cover all such relations and their reversals as: before for after; implicit for explicit; temporal sequence for logical sequence; name for narrative; disease for cure; hero for villain; active for passive."

83 We have already noted the convertible relationship between *episteme* and *doxa* as they create the preconditions of passing based on a Platonic model of identity. In Plato's model, passing hinges on the ingrained standard of racial difference, which assumes that the appearance of blackness and whiteness always stays within the enduring borders of white and black identity.

84 Rita Keresztesi, *Strangers at Home* (Lincoln: University of Nebraska Press, 2005), 35. For Keresztesi, this kind of passing plays on the subversive character of racial mimicry as Homi Bhabha describes it, which is as a "metonymy of presence." This play is not harmless. It causes much suffering for the passer and audiences alike that deal with the stress of ambiguous identities whose "recurring experiences are those of exile, relocation and displacement; that is being permanent strangers at home and in the world." Homi K. Bhabha, *The Location of Culture* (Oxford: Routledge, 1994), 88–89, which is as a "metonymy of presence."

85 Eve Kosofsky Sedgwick and Adam Frank, introduction to *Shame and Its Sisters: A Silvan Tomkins Reader*, ed. Eve Kosofsky Sedgwick and Adam Frank (Durham, N.C.: Duke University Press, 1995), 5. Kosofsky Sedgwick describes passing as "kinda subversive, kinda hegemonic."

86 Glenn Stanfield Holland, *Divine Irony* (Cranbury, N.J.: Associated University Presses, 2000), 37.

87 Burke, *A Grammar of Motives*, 517.

88 Burke, *A Grammar of Motives*, 512. Burke refers to this holistic point of view as a "perspective of perspectives."

89 Simon Goldhill, "The Language of Tragedy: Rhetoric and Communication," in *The Cambridge Companion to Greek Tragedy*, ed. P. E. Easterling (Cambridge: Cambridge University Press, 2008), 132.

90 Rachel F. Moran, "Love with a Proper Stranger: What Anti-Miscegenation Laws Can Tell Us about the Meaning of Race, Sex, and Marriage," *Hofstra Law Review* 32 (2004): 1663–79. Moran and others intimate that same-sex interracial couples engaged in their own brand of passing, as they were able to present acceptable public personae as partners in a platonic relationship. I would argue that the failure to fully explore this additional layer of passing (because it does not produce offspring and does produce additional social anxieties) is one reason why intersections with LGBTQ identities are under-articulated in neoconservative quarters of the multiracial movement.

91 Rainier Spencer, *Reproducing Race: The Paradox of Generation Mix* (Boulder: Lynne Rienner, 2010), 36.

92 Kenneth Burke, *Attitudes toward History* (Berkeley: University of California Press, 1984).

93 The tragic flaw(s) with which multiracials are born, what I call the "Tragedy of With," stem(s) from latent heterosexism in today's multiracial discourse. Because multiracial discourse has focused historically on positive

or negative characteristics of offspring from heterosexual relationships, those multiracial individuals and families who do not identify as heterosexual are marginalized. The "Tragedy of With" is often conflated with the social tragedy into which multiracials are born, what I call the "Tragedy Into." The "Tragedy Into" stems from a larger social and historical context of enslavement, Jim Crow, racism, and hierarchical distinction among homogenized racial groups. The "Tragedy Into" disallows multiracial wholeness and multiplicity of wholenesses. In the "Tragedy Into," which turns out to be an example of the logical fallacy of the false dilemma, one is either white or black: membership in one of these groups excludes membership in the other. The false dilemma ultimately demands that multiracials demand recognition as a unique and distinct group, and explains why such demands are interpreted as passing as postracial. As I will argue throughout this book, a closer reading of passing suggests that its relation to multiracial discourse and identities constitutes a well-intentioned yet problematic attempt to deal with the tragic history of racism into which we are all born.

94 Frank Costigliola, "The Nuclear Family: Tropes of Gender and Pathology in the Western Alliance," *Diplomatic History* 21, no. 2 (2002): 163. Costigliola explains that tropes of pathology "tap the deepest emotions . . . and map onto abstract concepts a sense of order that derives from our physical or personal experiences." See also Sander L. Gilman, *Difference and Pathology: Stereotypes of Sexuality, Race, and Madness* (Ithaca: Cornell University Press, 1985), 129–30. Gilman writes about "how easily racial stereotypes have been linked with images of pathology, especially psychopathology. In this case the need to create the sense of difference between the self and the 'Other' builds upon the xenophobia inherent in all groups. That which defines one's group is 'good.' Everything else is frighteningly 'bad.' The cohesiveness of any group depends on a mutually defined sense of identity, usually articulated in categories that reflect the group's history." Ultimately, the "Other is therefore both ill and infectious, both damaged and damaging." In chapter 6 we will chart how this rhetoric of pathology was employed by news media reports to associate the Jewish-black white supremacist Leo Felton with narratives of mental illness.

95 Spencer, *Reproducing Race*, 36.

96 Robinson, "To Pass//In Drag," 190.

97 Edward W. Said, *The World, the Text, and the Critic* (Cambridge, Mass.: Harvard University Press, 1983), 226. Said writes that appropriation as movement forces critics to consider "what kinds of movements are possible, what is gained or lost by virtue of movement, and what constraints of time and place are made known."

98 Robinson, "To Pass//In Drag."

99 Earlene Stetson, "The Mulatto Motif in Black Fiction" (Ph.D. diss., SUNY Buffalo, 1976), 156.

100 Arthur Schopenhauer, *The World as Will and Idea*, vol. 2, trans. E. F. Payne (Mineola, N.Y.: Dover, 1966), 305. Schopenhauer describes eloquence as "the faculty of awakening in others our view of a thing, or our opinion about it, of kindling in them our feeling concerning it, and thus putting them in sympathy with us."

101 Sally A. Freeman, Stephen W. Littlejohn, and W. Barnett Pearce, "Communication and Moral Conflict," *Western Journal of Communication* 56 (1992): 311–29.

102 Kenneth Cmiel, *Democratic Eloquence: The Fight over Popular Speech in Nineteenth-Century America* (Berkeley: University of California Press, 1990), 24. Cmiel describes eloquence as "far more than the ability to handle words deftly; it invoke[s] larger concerns about audience, personality, and social order."

103 Costigliola, "The Nuclear Family," 162–83.

104 Darrel Enck-Wanzer, "Trashing the System: Social Movement, Intersectional Rhetoric, and Collective Agency in the Young Lords Organization's Garbage Offensive," *Quarterly Journal of Speech* 92, no. 2 (2006): 176. Enck-Wanzer reminds us that "intersect" signals "intersection," requiring us to see beyond how tropes, texts, and personae function on their own, and begin seeing how tropes-texts-personae combine in passing to form a rhetoric that employs multiple forms and draws from diverse perspectives.

105 Like Enck-Wanzer, by "intersectional rhetoric" I mean a kind of "rhetoric that places multiple rhetorical forms (in this case, speech, embodiment, and image) on relatively equal footing, is not leader-centered, and draws from a number of diverse discursive political or rhetorical conventions" ("Trashing the System," 177). Passing is interpreted through this lens of intersectional rhetoric as an attempt by passers to lay bare the internal inconsistencies of a bipolar black-white mutually exclusive racial hierarchy and establish a sense of agency. Tropes also intersect in passing. Irony speaks to the arbitrary and closed-ended natures of racial representation and categorization. Tragedy becomes a way to pathologize passers and, later, foreclose multiracial identities. Appropriation highlights the symbolic substance and social properties that accompany privileged racial identifications. Eloquence stresses the need for resolving moral conflicts through dialogue initiation. For more on intersectional rhetoric as it relates to social movements and social change, see Enck-Wanzer, "Trashing the System." For a full discussion of intersectionality as a critical praxis, see Kimberlé Crenshaw, "Mapping the Margins: Intersectionality, Identity Politics, and Violence against Women of Color," *Stanford Law Review* 43 (1991): 1241–65.

106 Historical and legal cases reveal that symbolic disclosure of passing (crossing over to one side of the color line and telling people about it) is followed by either material denial of rights or tentative acquisition of rights that can be snatched away. Literary cases demonstrate the ways in which passers deploy rhetorical principles to reproduce and change the symbolic relationships that influence their interpersonal interactions, ethics, and morality. These historical, legal and literary cases also comprise a timeline from the earliest to the latest benchmark representations of passing. Case studies have been selected according to certain criteria. First, each case entails an act of passing that is multidirectional and synecdochic from the passer's perspective (involves passing as white and/or as black in distinct episodes) and is sustained at one or more intersections (race, gender, class, ability). Second, in each case the passer utilizes synecdoche to putatively conform to but transform the standards

of *episteme* in conjunction with any of the rhetorical principles identified by Plato as being crucial to rhetorical passing: appropriation, eloquence, irony, or tragedy used as expressions of *doxa* and aletheia. Third, each case acknowledges the life chances for the passer on either side of the color line, thereby clearly demarcating what happened before and after. In this way each case puts passers' and audiences' personae and interpretations in dialogue. Fourth, cases were chosen because of their social significance. The Crafts had an impact because they went on tour and sold their story to raise funds for the abolitionist movement. *Plessy v. Ferguson* set the precedent for legalized segregation and future court action. *Iola Leroy* was the first novel written by an African American woman that dealt with the theme of passing in the Reconstruction era. *The Human Stain* is the first mainstream representation of passing in the twenty-first century (in literature and film) and presents several defining moments in the life of a passer who chooses a white ethnic identity as a way to change life chances. Leo Felton is the first white supremacist revealed to be a biracial passer in the twenty-first century. My first level of analysis focuses on rhetorical intersections, tying synecdoche to at least one other trope in each case study (as detailed in *Passwords Three* and *Four*). My second level of analysis builds on the first by analyzing each case from the passer's perspective over time as well as from the perspective of each diverse persona or audience (as in *Passwords One* and *Two*). My third level of analysis explores the intersections of racial identification in each case (as in *Password Five*).

CHAPTER TWO

1   Ellen Craft and William Craft, *Running a Thousand Miles for Freedom* (1860; repr., Athens: University of Georgia Press, 1999), 20–21.

2   William Still, *The Underground Railroad* (1872; repr., New York: Arno Press, 1987), 49–51. Henry "Box" Brown was a slave on a Virginia tobacco farm who persuaded a local white carpenter sympathetic to the abolitionist cause to build a box that would carry him safely from slavery in freedom. He brought water and biscuits with him for the journey. In addition to traveling in cramped quarters, Brown could not speak or else he would give himself away. When he arrived safely in Philadelphia and emerged from the box, his first reaction was to sing. African American artist Glenn Ligon's 2011 exhibition entitled *America,* contains a series of box works that are a tribute to Brown's voice and experience and to freedom from enslavement.

3   Ellen M. Weinauer, "'A Most Respectable Looking Gentleman': Passing, Possession, and Transgression in *Running a Thousand Miles for Freedom*," in *Passing and the Fictions of Identity*, ed. E. K. Ginsberg (Durham: Duke University Press, 1996), 38.

4   Craft, *Running*, 3.

5   Craft, *Running*, 3.

6   Craft, *Running*, 3.

7   Craft, *Running*, 3.

8   There has been much scholarly analysis and discussion of *Running*. Some of the most notable contributions include Larry Gara, "The Professional

Fugitive in the Abolition Moment," *Wisconsin Magazine of History* 48, no. 3 (1965): 196–204; Florence B. Freedman, *Two Tickets for Freedom: The True Story of Ellen and William Craft, Fugitive Slaves* (New York: Peter Bedrick Books, 1971); Richard J. M. Blackett, "The Odyssey of William and Ellen Craft," in *Beating against the Barriers: Biographical Essays in Nineteenth-Century Afro-American History* (Baton Rouge: Louisiana State University Press, 1986), 87–137; Marjorie Garber, "Passing to Freedom: The Art of the Crafts," in *Vested Interests: Cross-Dressing and Cultural Anxiety* (New York: Routledge, 1992), 282–85; Barbara McCaskill, "'Yours Very Truly': Ellen Craft—the Fugitive as Text and Artifact," *African American Review* 28, no. 4 (1994): 509–29; Dorothy Sterling, "Ellen Craft: The Valiant Journey," in *Black Foremothers: Three Lives*, 2nd ed. (Old Westbury, N.Y.: Feminist Press, 1988), 3–59; Lindon Barrett, "Handwriting: Legibility and the White Body in *Running a Thousand Miles to Freedom*," *American Literature* 69, no. 2 (1997): 315–36; Barbara McCaskill, "'Trust No Man!' But What about a Woman? Ellen Craft and a Genealogical Model for Teaching Douglass' *Narrative*," in *Approaches to Teaching the Narrative of the Life of Frederick Douglass*, ed. James C. Hall (New York: Modern Language Association, 1999), 95–101; Valli Kalei Kanuha, "The Social Process of Passing to Manage Stigma: Acts of Internalized Oppression of Acts of Resistance," *Journal of Sociology and Social Welfare* 26 (1999): 27–46; Tobin Anthony Siebers, "Disability as Masquerade," *Literature and Medicine* 23 (2004): 3; Daneen Wardrop, "Ellen Craft and the Case of Salome Muller in *Running a Thousand Miles for Freedom*," *Women's Studies* 33, no. 7 (2004): 961–84; Ellen Samuels, "'A Complication of Complaints': Untangling Disability, Race and Gender in William and Ellen Craft's *Running a Thousand Miles for Freedom*," *MELUS* 31, no. 3 (2006): 15–47; John Ernest, "Representing Chaos: William Craft's *Running a Thousand Miles for Freedom*," *PMLA* 121, no. 2 (2006): 469–83.

9   Steven Mailloux, *Rhetorical Power* (Ithaca: Cornell University Press, 1989).

10 Michel Foucault, *Power*, ed. James D. Faubion (New York: New Press, 2001).

11 Mailloux, *Rhetorical Power*, 60.

12 James C. Scott, *Weapons of the Weak* (New Haven: Yale University Press, 1985).

13 Barbara Welke, *Recasting American Liberty: Gender, Race, Law, and the Railroad Revolution, 1865–1920* (Cambridge: Cambridge University Press, 2001). Though Welke's book focuses on the Reconstruction Era through the early twentieth century, she takes time to trace the origins of racial and gendered spatial logics aboard railroads to the era of enslavement.

14 Welke, *Recasting American Liberty*, 25.

15 Samuels, "A Complication of Complaints," 6.

16 *Oxford English Dictionary Online*, s.v. "poultice."

17 Craft, *Running*, 18.

18 Siebers, "Disability as Masquerade"; Siebers, "Disability in Theory: From Social Constructionism to the New Realism of the Body," in *The*

Disability Studies Reader, 2nd ed., ed. Lennard J. Davis (New York: Routledge, 2006), 173–84.

19 Barrett, "Handwriting," 327.

20 Craft, *Running*, 8.

21 Craft, *Running*, 31.

22 Craft, *Running*, 42.

23 Craft, *Running*, 42. Ellen's "longer way around" into "one of the best" carriages is contrasted sharply with William's forced passage in "the negro car." From this comparison we infer that black slaves like William were unwelcome.

24 Still, *The Underground Railroad*, 266.

25 Brown later adapted the Crafts' story for his 1853 novel *Clotel, or The President's Daughter*. Brown was largely involved in arranging the Crafts' speaking engagements throughout the United States. Ellen's and William's experiences also inspired abolitionist and feminist Lydia Maria Child to dramatize and retell the tale in her 1858 play *The Stars and Stripes: A Melodrama*.

26 Prior to their first speaking engagement in early 1849, William Wells Brown published excerpts from their story in William Lloyd Garrison's famous abolitionist newsletter, the *Liberator*. Lloyd Garrison founded the *Liberator* in 1831 in order to advocate the cause of abolition. In it he published letters from famous abolitionists and former slaves. Though it had fewer than four hundred subscribers subscriptions in its second year, the publication gained subscribers and influence over the next three decades. Garrison published the last issue (number 1820) after the Civil War, on December 29, 1865. For more information, see Henry Mayer, *All on Fire: William Lloyd Garrison and the Abolition of Slavery* (New York: St. Martin's Press, 1998). On January 12, 1849, Garrison provided the following account of the Crafts' escape in the *Liberator*. "One of the most interesting cases of the escape of fugitives from American slavery that have ever come before the American people, has just occurred, under the following circumstances:—William and Ellen Craft, man and wife, lived with different masters in the State of Georgia. Ellen is so near white that she can pass without suspicion for a white woman. Her husband is much darker. He is a mechanic, and by working nights and Sundays, he laid up money enough to bring himself and his wife out of slavery. Their plan was without precedent; and though novel, was the means of getting them their freedom. Ellen dressed in man's clothing, and passed as the *master*, while her husband passed as the *servant*. In this way they travelled from Georgia to Philadelphia. They are now out of the reach of the blood-hounds of the South. On their journey, they put up at the best hotels where they stopped. Neither of them can read or write. And Ellen, knowing that she would be called upon to write her name at the hotels, &c., tied her right hand up as though it was lame, which proved of some service to her, as she was called upon several times at hotels to 'register' her name. In Charleston, S.C., they put up at the hotel which Gov. M'Duffie and John C. Calhoun generally make their home, yet these distinguished advocates of the 'peculiar institution' say that the slaves cannot take care of themselves. They arrived in Philadelphia, in four days from the time they started. Their

history, especially that of their escape, is replete with interest. They will be at the meeting of the Massachusetts Anti-Slavery Society, in Boston, in the latter part of this month, where I know the history of their escape will be listened to with great interest. They are very intelligent. They are young, Ellen 22, and Wm. 24 years of age. Ellen is truly a heroine. Yours, truly, WM. W. BROWN.

"P.S. They are now hid away within 25 miles of Philadelphia, where they will remain until the 6th when they will leave me for New England. Will you please say in the Liberator that I will lecture, in connexion with them, as follows:—

"At Norwich, Conn., Thursday evening, Jan. 18.

"At Worcester, Mass., Friday evening, 19.

"At Pawtucket, Mass., Saturday evening, 20.

"At New Bedford, Mass., Sunday afternoon and evening, 28." "William Wells Brown Describes the Crafts' Escape," *Liberator*, January 12, 1849, Documenting the American South, University Library, University of North Carolina, http://docsouth.unc.edu/neh/craft/support1.html.

An added benefit of this media attention is that it did away with the need for embedded authentication of their credibility and tests of narrative probability for their autobiography, processes most other narratives of the enslaved were forced to undergo.

27 William Lloyd Garrison, "The Crafts in New Bedford," *Liberator*, February 16, 1849, http://www.theliberatorfiles.com/crafts-in-new-bedford/, accessed March 29, 2011.

28 Sociological research suggests that questions about Ellen's racial identity and appearance could also result from fear of contagion and latent racism. Thus, audiences may believe that the negative attributes of stereotypical blackness can "spoil" the positive attributes of the dominant group. Racism also plays a role. In addition research reveals that "racism plays a role in the categorization of racially ambiguous individuals, with those high in racism more likely to take longer to categorize such individuals." Arnold K. Ho, Jim Sidanius, Daniel T. Levin, and Mahzarin R. Banaji, "Evidence for Hypodescent and Racial Hierarchy in the Categorization and Perception of Biracial Individuals," *Journal of Personality and Social Psychology* 94 (2010): 13.

For white audiences this could also explain why passers are more readily perceived as people of color than as white. For nonwhite audiences this could result in a desire to preserve an ethnic minority culture and/or for racial solidarity and political mobilization. For more see Jim Blascovich, Natalie A. Wyer, Laura A. Swart, and Jeffrey L. Kibler, "Racism and Racial Categorization," *Journal of Personality and Social Psychology* 72 (1997): 1364–72; Paul Rozin and Edward Royzman, "Negativity Bias, Negativity Dominance, and Contagion," *Personality and Social Psychology Review* 5 (2001): 296–320; C. B. Hickman, "The Devil and the One Drop Rule: Racial Categories, African Americans, and the U.S. Census," *Michigan Law Review* 95 (1997): 1161–1265; *Boston Liberator*, September 5, 1851.

29 Mary Doniger, *The Woman Who Pretended to Be Who She Was: Myths of Self-Imitation* (Oxford: Oxford University Press, 2004), 102.

30 These questions led to other questions. Which metonymic representation was more correct? Was there a higher threshold for perceiving Ellen as white than as black? Would white audience members perceive Ellen as relatively more white than black audience members? Would anyone perceive Ellen as both white and black? These kinds of questions forced audiences to confront a number of issues upon which their social existences were based: namely, social categories by which they lived such as race and how race impacted gender roles, class distinctions, and what constituted disability. Thus, as Michele Elam points out, the important thing about passing is that it highlights social anxieties about multiracial subjectivities and cultural practices of representation. Michele Elam, *The Souls of Mixed Folk: Race, Politics, and Aesthetics in the New Millennium* (Stanford: Stanford University Press, 2011).

31 In the decade before their book's publication, when they were forced to flee to the United Kingdom because of the Fugitive Slave Act of 1850, Ellen and William told their story publicly to myriads of international antislavery groups and learned how to read and write. The Crafts joined forces with William Wells Brown and an international abolitionist tour whose success depended on their experience, presence, and eloquence in the form of performances and presentations that could bridge gaps between nations, cultures, races, and classes. Blackett describes the informational-persuasive presentations and the question-and-answer sessions which followed. Richard J. M. Blackett, "The Odyssey of William and Ellen Craft," in *Beating Against the Barriers: Biographical Essays in Nineteenth-Century Afro-American History* (Baton Rouge: Louisiana State University Press, 1986), 87–137. According to Blackett, reports from the *Liberator* provide evidence of the rhetorical power of the Crafts' presentations, recounting how audiences not only witnessed their passing but were compelled to experience its effects. Of Ellen's appearance one *Liberator* reporter observes that it was nearly impossible to imagine Ellen as a woman of black ancestry. This reporter was not the only party interested in whether the negatively perceived attributes of blackness and stereotypes about multiracials as degenerates could destroy the positively perceived attributes of whiteness. Josephine Brown, in her report, documents the lack of spoilage in Ellen's phenotype, describing her as "white as most persons of the clear Anglo-Saxon origin. Her features were prominent, hair straight, eyes of a light hazel color, and no one . . . would suppose that a drop of African blood coursed through her veins." For more see Josephine Brown, "Biography of an American Bondsman, 1856," in *Two Biographies by African American Women*, ed. Henry Louis Gates Jr. (Oxford: Oxford University Press, 1991), 76.

32 Charles J. Heglar, *Rethinking the Slave Narrative: Slave Marriage and the Narratives of Henry Bibb and William and Ellen Craft* (Westport: Greenwood Press, 2001), 79–108.

33 Craft, *Running*, iii.

34 The enslaved were denied the right to literacy for a host of reasons. Most important to my analysis of the Crafts' case is that they were prohibited from learning how to read and write because it was feared that they would then write passes for themselves and other slaves to abet escape.

This practice is discussed in Frederick Douglass and Harriet Ann Jacobs, *Narrative of the Life of Frederick Douglass, an American Slave*, and *Incidents in the Life of a Slave Girl*, introduction by Kwame Anthony Appiah (New York: Random House, 2000), 84.

35 Craft, *Running*, 36.

36 Craft, *Running*, 2. Historians have confirmed how the "peculiar institution" of slavery created many individuals like Ellen Craft, the progeny of slave holders and the enslaved. For an in-depth discussion of coerced interracial intimacies and their effects, see Edward Ball, *Slaves in the Family* (New York: Ballantine, 1998).

37 According to Annette Gordon-Reed, the *partus sequitur ventrem* doctrine is a response to the 1655 court case involving Elizabeth Key, a multiracial woman who won her freedom by suing the colony of Virginia on the basis of her paternal white and English ancestry. For a full discussion, see Annette Gordon-Reed, *The Hemingses of Monticello: An American Family* (New York: W.W. Norton, 2008), 37–56.

38 Daniel Sharfstein, *The Invisible Line: Three American Families and the Secret Journey from Black to White* (New York: Penguin Press, 2011). In chapter 1 Sharfstein explains both sides of the doctrine. On one hand, the *partus sequitur ventrem* doctrine legalized the widespread rape of black female slaves and created generations of multiracial, racially ambiguous slaves like Ellen Craft. On the other hand, the doctrine "formed the basis for the first communities of free people of color. English servant women had children with African men in numbers that continually alarmed . . . lawmakers. In certain courts, practically the only record that slavery existed consisted of cases of 'mulatto bastards' born to English women. In the seventeenth century, thousands of mixed-race people were born into freedom."

39 Craft, *Running*, 8.

40 "Almost white" slaves were seen as more intelligent and capable than pure blacks. For a full discussion of distinctions made between "mulattoes" and the rest of the enslaved population, see Leroy Gardner, *Black/White Race Mixing* (St. Paul, Minn.: Paragon House, 2000).

41 Diana R. Paulin, "Acting out Miscegenation," in *African American Performance and Theater History: A Critical Reader*, ed. Harry Elam and David Krasner (Oxford: Oxford University Press, 2001), 257. Paulin discusses the 1882 play *The White Slave*, particularly in support of her argument that "the numerous behavioral standards established for elite white women (refinement, chastity, submission to patriarchs)" were at odds with "the roles assigned to slaves (licentious, hard laboring, primitive)." Thus, "black women, whether or not they performed gentility successfully or even looked white, were still considered part of an inferior class" (257). Consequently, we should not assume that Ellen Craft's "white" appearance negated her position as a fugitive African American slave. For more on multiracial identities, miscegenation, slavery, and performance, see Diana R. Paulin, "Performing Miscegenation: Rescuing *The White Slave* from the Threat of Interracial Desire," *Journal of Dramatic Theory and Criticism* 13 (1998): 71–86.

42 Lerone Bennett Jr., *Before the Mayflower: A History of Black America*, 8th ed. (New York: Penguin Books, 2007). In addition, some such actual and imagined instances of white enslavement in the United States are described in Bourne's *Picture of Slavery* (1834), Stowe's *Uncle Tom's Cabin* (1852), the Crafts' *Running a Thousand Miles for Freedom* (1860), and Harper's *Iola Leroy* (1893).

43 Craft, *Running*, 4.

44 The Crafts imply this in their text when they mention the many young white men and women who are enslaved unjustly. The Crafts pay special attention to the case of Salome Müller (also known as Sally Miller), a white woman enslaved "by mistake." For a full discussion of this case's rhetorical significance and its historical and contemporary effects, see Marouf Hasian Jr., "Performative Law and the Maintenance of Interracial Social Boundaries: Assuaging Antebellum Fears of 'White Slavery' and the case of Sally Miller/ Salome Müller," *Text and Performance Quarterly* 23 (2003): 55–86.

45 Ellen's biracial passing shocked duped audiences and upset the material and symbolic bases of race and racial identification based on the color line. To enhance cognitive dissonance and provide dupes with an opportunity to identify with the enslaved, William continued by telling the story of Salome Müller, a white woman who spent twenty-five years as a Southern slave due to a case of mistaken identity. Moving audiences to an in-group clairvoyant perspective, he also reminded audiences that Ellen was not unique, but one of many multiracial or white-looking slaves. The Crafts used this narrative tactic because they understood the powers of irony when combined with synecdoche-metonymy in promoting their abolitionist cause (*Password Four*). When duped audiences located the transition from Ellen to Mr. Johnson and back through concealment and revelation, they questioned the notion that appearance correlates with a verifiable identity. This catalyzed the development of a more nebulous conception of identity that is not necessarily self-fulfilling, thus challenging the *episteme/doxa* binary (*Passwords One, Five*). For if Craft could be enslaved, then racial categorizations lose their meanings.

46 Craft, *Running*, 30.

47 Craft, *Running*, 31.

48 Craft, *Running*, 32.

49 Craft, *Running*, 33.

50 On pp. 8–10 of *Running*, William describes his interaction with the slave auctioneer, who refused to allow him to bid his biological family farewell. On pp. 11–17 William describes interactions and conversations between slaves and masters to demonstrate the dominant strategies that often overpowered slaves' subversive and resistant tactics. On pp. 29–30 we read of Mr. Johnson and Mr. Cray's interaction aboard the train. On pp. 31–33 Mr. Johnson explains that he does not want to sell William to a "rough slave dealer." On pp. 33–34 Mr. Johnson hears from an officer who counsels him not to "spoil" William by acknowledging his humanity. On pp. 35–36 William speaks with other slaves about the power of his master's kindness and generosity. On pp. 36–39 Mr. Johnson confronts

the steamer captain, who asks him to certify his and William's passage. On p. 39 Mr. Johnson escapes politely from conversation with two ladies who are smitten with him. On pp. 39–43 Mr. Johnson tells an elderly lady that William is his slave and not her "missing boy" named Ned and hears a debate about the religious foundations for enslavement. On pp. 44–47 an officer confronts Mr. Johnson and William, saying it is against his personal policy to allow slaves to travel any further North. On p. 48 Mr. Johnson asks another white man to help him locate William. The man refuses. On pp. 48–49 a guard shakes William violently and declares that he is needed by Mr. Johnson. On pp. 49–50 William talks to a freed black man, who gives him tips on how to escape from Mr. Johnson once the train arrives in Philadelphia. On p. 50 Ellen expresses her profound relief that the pair made it to freedom.

51 Michael Hyde, *The Life-Giving Gift of Acknowledgment* (West Lafayette, Ind.: Purdue University Press, 2006), 142. Hyde writes, "By responding to another's call for acknowledgment, we secure and strengthen the ontological structure of the caress that forms the fundamental ethical and rhetorical relationship between the self and the other."

52 Craft, *Running*, 43.

53 Justin D. Edwards, *Gothic Passages: Racial Ambiguity and the American Gothic* (Iowa City: University of Iowa Press, 2003), 42–43.

54 Valerie Smith, *Not Just Race, Not Just Gender* (London: Routledge, 1998), 36.

55 Craft, *Running*, 45–46.

56 Craft, *Running*, 46. This exchange is also cited by Uri McMillan, "Ellen Craft's Radical Techniques of Subversion," *E-misférica* 5, no. 2 (2008), accessed March 29, 2011, http://hemi.nyu.edu/hemi/en/e-misferica-52/mcmillan.

57 Craft, *Running*, 29.

58 McMillan, "Ellen Craft's Radical Techniques."

59 McMillan, "Ellen Craft's Radical Techniques."

60 In *Running*, the Crafts use irony as both empowerment and a form of critical literacy, exploiting the broadened subversive horizons that passing offers for race, class, gender, and ability. As it pertains to passing, irony asks audiences to become critics, to take on the in-group clairvoyant, and to rely on their abilities to locate logical inconsistencies and fallacies, admit that things can be other than as they appear, and recognize personae—Ellen (passer), Mr. Johnson (acceptable persona), William (in-group clairvoyant), white passengers and officials, enslaved and free blacks (dupes), readers-audiences (dupes-in-transition and in-group clairvoyants). This perspective enables and sustains multiple readings of what passing means, which capture and protract moments in which ideologies of race, class, and ability are poised in mutually informing yet unresolved symbolic tension with gender. As aforementioned, there is no ambiguous language, no pronoun confusion when it comes to Ellen's gender identity. There was little if any confusion after passing either.

61 Katharina Barbe, *Irony in Context* (Amsterdam: John Benjamins, 1995), 16.

62 Barbe, *Irony in Context*, 16.

63　Michael Leff and Ebony A. Utley, "Instrumental and Constitutive Rhetoric in Martin Luther King Jr.'s 'Letter from Birmingham Jail,'" *Rhetoric and Public Affairs* 7, no. 1 (2004): 48. According to Leff and Utley, a text like *Running* can show readers "how to adopt personae that will make them more effective agents for change and about the means for implementing this agency."

64　Kenneth Burke, *A Grammar of Motives* (Berkeley: University of California Press, 1969), 514. As Burke puts it, "true irony" is "based upon a sense of fundamental kinship with the enemy as one *needs* him, is *indebted* to him, is not merely outside him as an observer but contains him *within*, being consubstantial with him."

65　Eva Saks, "Representing Miscegenation Law," in *Interracialism: Black-White Intermarriage in American History, Literature, and Law,* ed. Werner Sollors (New York: Oxford University Press, 2000), 73.

66　Craft, *Running,* 41–42.

67　U.S. State Department, "Trafficking in Persons Report 2011," June 27, 2011, http://www.state.gov/g/tip/rls/tiprpt/2011/, accessed July 9, 2011.

68　U.S. State Department, "Trafficking in Persons Report 2011."

69　International Justice Mission, "Forced Labor Slavery," December 31, 2010, http://www.ijm.org/sites/default/files/resources/Factsheet-Forced-Labor-Slavery.pdf, accessed July 9, 2011.

70　Nicholas D. Kristof and Sheryl WuDunn, *Half the Sky: Turning Oppression into Opportunity for Women Worldwide* (New York: Random House, 2009).

71　Abigail Pesta, "Diary of an Escaped Sex Slave," *Marie Claire*, October 9, 2009, accessed July 9, 2011, http://www.marieclaire.com/world-reports/news/international/diary-escaped-sex-slave.

72　International Justice Mission, "Forced Labor Slavery."

73　Jenny Nordberg, "Afghan Boys Are Prized, So Girls Live the Part," *New York Times,* September 20, 2010, http://www.nytimes.com/2010/09/21/world/asia/21gender.html, accessed July 9, 2011.

74　Nancy Lindisfarne, "Gender, Shame, and Culture: An Anthropological Perspective," in *Shame: Interpersonal Behavior, Psychopathology, and Culture,* ed. Paul Gilbert and Bernice Andrews (Oxford: Oxford University Press, 1998), 246.

75　Lindisfarne, "Gender, Shame, and Culture," 248. According to Lindisfarne, "Descriptions of systems of honor and shame are disarmingly consistent in their focus on competition between dominant men and the passive subordination of women."

76　Matt (aka Mattilda) Bernstein Sycamore, *Nobody Passes: Rejecting the Rules of Gender and Conformity* (Emoryville, Calif.: Seal Press, 2006).

77　Sadiqua Hamdan, email to author, November 22, 2011.

78　Laura Gottesdiener, "The Cross-Dressing Girls of Afghanistan," *Ms Magazine,* October 7, 2010, http://msmagazine.com/blog/blog/2010/10/07/the-cross-dressing-girls-of-afghanistan/, accessed July 10, 2011.

79　CNN World, "No 'Boys' and 'Girls' at Gender-Netural School in Sweden," *CNN World,* June 26, 2011, http://globalpublicsquare.blogs.cnn.com/2011/06/26/no-boys-and-girls-at-gender-neutral-preschool-in-sweden/, accessed July 17, 2011.

80 Ulli K. Ryder, "Gender Neutral or Wishful Thinking," The Feminist Wire, May 30, 2011, http://thefeministwire.com/2011/05/gender-neutral -or-wishful-thinking/, accessed July 10, 2011.

81 Tom Leonard, "The Baby Who Is Neither Boy nor Girl: As Gender Experiment Provokes Outrage, What About the Poor Child's Future?," Mail Online, May 28, 2011, http://www.dailymail.co.uk/news/arti- cle-1391772/Storm-Stocker-As-gender-experiment-provokes-outrage -poor-childs-future.html, accessed July 10, 2011.

CHAPTER THREE

1 In a strategy reminiscent of the Crafts', Plessy appropriated the traditional definition of passing. Plessy's new meaning of passing—as property— allowed him to find a sense of control over his social situation and exploit the agency provided by his racially ambiguous appearance to assert that control using civil disobedience.

2 Keith Weldon Medley, *We as Freedmen: Plessy v. Ferguson* (Gretna, La.: Pelican, 2003), 89. Section 2 of Louisiana's Separate Car Act (1890) stated that "the officers of passenger trains shall have power and are hereby required to assign each passenger to the coach or compartment used for the race to which such passenger belongs; any person insisting on going into a coach or compartment to which by race he does not belong, shall be liable to a fine of Twenty Five Dollars or in lieu thereof to imprisonment for a period of not more [than] twenty days in the Parish Prison."

3 Medley, *We as Freedmen*, 140.

4 Also known as the "chicken or the egg" question, circular cause and con- sequence is a circumstance of causality in which the consequence of a phenomenon is also its cause.

5 While discrimination and segregation were practiced in the United States prior to 1890, only three states had approved similar legislation prior to the Louisiana statute. After the 1896 Supreme Court ruling in *Plessy v. Ferguson*, North Carolina, Virginia, Arkansas, South Carolina, Tennes- see, Mississippi, Maryland, Florida, and Oklahoma soon adopted similar provisions. By 1920, nearly every southern state had enacted Jim and Jane Crow legislation that required "separate but equal" facilities for black and white people. For a complete account, see C. Vann Woodward, *The Strange Career of Jim Crow* (Oxford: Oxford University Press, 1955); Lerone Bennett Jr., *Before the Mayflower: A History of Black America* (Chicago: Johnson, 2007).

6 Robert Bines, "Plessy and Ferguson: Descendants of a Divisive Supreme Court Decision Unite," *Washington Post*, June 5, 2011. It should be noted that 119 years after Plessy's pass, descendants of the plaintiff (Plessy) and defendant (Ferguson) joined forces "to start a new civil rights organiza- tion that would bear their famous names[;] they sealed the deal in a fitting local spot: Café Reconcile."

7 In this regard I am indebted to existing research on and criticism of the case. Derrick A. Bell Jr., *Race, Racism, and American Law* (Boston: Lit- tle, Brown, 1980); Barton J. Bernstein, "Case Law in *Plessy v. Ferguson*," *Journal of Negro History* 47, no. 3 (1962): 192–98; David W. Bishop,

"Plessy v. Ferguson: A Reinterpretation," *Journal of Negro History* 62, no. 2 (1977): 125–33; Mark Elliott, "Race, Color Blindness, and the Democratic Public: Albion W. Tourgée's Radical Principles in *Plessy v. Ferguson*," *Journal of Southern History* 67, no. 2 (2000): 287–330; Theodore L. Gross, *Albion W. Tourgée* (New York: Twayne, 1963); Loren Miller, *The Petitioners: The Story of the Supreme Court of the United States and the Negro* (New York: Random House, 1966); Paul Oberst, "The Strange Career of *Plessy v. Ferguson*," 15 *Ariz. L. Rev.* 389 (1973): 433–41; Otto H. Olsen, *The Thin Disguise: Plessy v. Ferguson, a Documentary Presentation* (New York: Humanities Press, 1967); Otto H. Olsen, *The Carpetbagger's Crusade: A Life of Albion Winegar Tourgée* (Baltimore: Johns Hopkins Press, 1965); Richard Kluger, *Simple Justice: The History of Brown v. Board of Education and Black America's Struggle for Equality* (New York: Vintage Books, 1975); Amy Robinson, "To Pass//In Drag: Strategies of Entrance into the Visible" (Ph.D. diss., University of Pennsylvania, 1993); Eric Sundquist, "Mark Twain and Homer Plessy," *Representations* 21 (1998): 102–28; Brook Thomas, *"Plessy v. Ferguson* and the Literary Imagination," *Cardozo Studies in Law and Literature* 91 (1997): 45–65; C. Vann Woodward, *American Counterpoint: Slavery and Racism in the North-South Dialogue* (Boston: Little, Brown, 1964).

8   "Fourteenth Amendment Equal Protection Clause," *Legal Information Center*, last modified September 25, 2008, http://public.getlegal.com/legal-info-center/14th-amendment-equal-protection-clause. According to the Legal Information Center, "The Equal Protection Clause of the 14th Amendment prohibits states from denying any person within its jurisdiction the equal protection of the law. In other words, the laws of a state must treat an individual in the same manner as other people in similar conditions and circumstances. A violation would occur, for example, if a state prohibited an individual from entering into an employment contract because he or she was a member of a particular race. The clause is not intended to provide equality among individuals or classes but only equal application of the law. The result of a law, therefore, is not relevant so long as there is no discrimination in its application. By denying states the ability to discriminate, the Equal Protection Clause is crucial to the protection of civil rights."

9   *Scott v. Sanford*, 60 U.S. 393 (1856). In 1857, the United States Supreme Court ruled in *Dred Scott v. Sanford* that "A free negro of the African race, whose ancestors were brought to this country and sold as slaves, is not a 'citizen' within the meaning of the Constitution of the United States." The court concurrently declared the 1820 Missouri Compromise unconstitutional, thus permitting slavery in all of the country's territories. The Court explained away the language in the Declaration of Independence that includes the phrase "all men are created equal," arguing that "it is too clear for dispute, that the enslaved African race were not intended to be included, and formed no part of the people who framed and adopted this declaration, for if the language, as understood in that day, would embrace them, the conduct of the distinguished men who framed the Declaration of Independence would have been utterly and flagrantly inconsistent with the principles they asserted."

10 Kenneth C. Davis, *Don't Know Much about History* (New York: HarperCollins, 2003). According to Davis, in the case of *Santa Clara County v. Southern Pacific Railroad Company*, 118 U.S. 394 (1886), the U.S. Supreme Court decided that a private corporation is a person and entitled to the legal rights and protections the Constitution affords to any person. The doctrine of corporate personhood, which subsequently became a cornerstone of corporate law, was introduced into this 1886 decision without argument. Over a century later the conception of corporate personhood was extended by the U.S. Supreme Court in *Citizens United v. Federal Election Commission*, 588 U.S. 50 (2010). The Court ruled that limits on so-called independent expenditures by corporations violate the First Amendment right to free speech. This decision effectively gives corporations the same First Amendment rights as persons. Unsurprisingly, these rulings were decided on related, but not necessarily acknowledged, principles. As we will see in this chapter, the rulings share a conception of identity that constitutes personhood based on property, ownership, appropriation, and a right to privacy.

11 Medley, *We as Freedmen*, 146. Quoting from the *Crusader*, Medley provides the following account: "Homer A. Plessy boarded the East Louisiana Railroad, at the foot of Press Street, for Covington. He held a first-class ticket and naturally took his seat in a first-class coach. As the train was moving out of the station, the conductor came up and asked if he was a white man. Plessy, who is as white as the average white Southerner, replied that he was a colored man. Then, said the conductor, 'you must go in the coach reserved for colored people.' Plessy replied that he had a first-class ticket and would remain in the first-class coach. The conductor insisted that he retire to the Jim Crow coach. Plessy determinedly told him that he was an American citizen and proposed to enjoy his rights as such and to ride for the value of his money. The conductor, seeing his own powers of persuasion unavailing, invoked the aid of the police. Captain C. C. Cain . . . told Plessy that if he was a colored man, he would have to go to the colored coach. Plessy again refused. . . . Plessy said he would go to jail first before relinquishing his right as a citizen."

12 Wayne Anderson, *Plessy v. Ferguson: Legalizing Segregation* (New York: Rosen, 2004), 48.

13 Emily Finch, "What a Tangled Web We Weave: Identity Theft and the Internet," in *Dot.cons: Crime, Deviance, and Identity on the Internet*, ed. Yvonne Jewkes (Cullompton: Willan, 2002), 86–104.

14 "Defensive dupe" is a term I invented to describe a persona that is too invested in and empowered by racial hierarchy to take on an in-group clairvoyant perspective. A defensive dupe is immune to the transformative qualities of passing outlined in *Password Six*.

15 *Oxford English Dictionary Online*, s.v. "appropriation."

16 Ruth Colker, *Hybrid: Bisexuals, Multiracials, and Other Misfits under American Law* (New York: New York University Press, 1996).

17 Joan M. Martin, "Plaçage and the Louisiana Gens de Couleur Libre: How Race and Sex Defined the Lifestyles of Free Women of Color," in *Creole: The History and Legacy of Louisiana's Free People of Color*, ed. Sybil Kein (Baton Rouge: Louisiana State University Press, 2000), 57–70. On

pages 57 and 58 Martin defines the practice: "*Plaçage* was the practice that existed in Louisiana (and other French and Spanish slaveholding territories) whereby women of color—the option of legal marriage denied them—entered into long-standing, formalized relationships with white European men. This practice was so common that laws were written to prevent it. The laws had no impact, nor did the futile public indignation. The controversy began with the inception of *plaçage* in the colony, and rages even today . . . members of this elite group (male and female) seemed to be granted privileges nearly always denied their darker brothers."

18 Marouf Hasian Jr., "Critical Legal Theorizing, Rhetorical Intersectionalities and the Multiple Transgressions of the 'Tragic Mullata,' Anastasie Desarzant," *Women's Studies in Communication* 27 (2004): 119–48. Louisiana's antebellum libraries provided ample evidence of this tripartite system with collections that documented the racial and social privileges of Creoles as "octoroons, quadroons, etc."

19 For a general discussion of passing in the postbellum South, see Joel Williamson, *New People: Miscegenation and Mulattoes in the United States* (Baton Rouge: Louisiana State University Press, 1995). For a detailed account of the undoing of the three-tiered racial system, see Shirley Elizabeth Thompson, *Exiles at Home: The Struggle to Become American in Creole New Orleans* (Cambridge, Mass.: Harvard University Press, 2009).

20 Joseph Logsdon and Caryn Cosse Bell, "The Americanization of Black New Orleans, 1850–1900," in *Creole New Orleans: Race and Americanization*, ed. Arnold R. Hirsch and Joseph Logsdon (Baton Rouge: Louisiana State University Press, 1992), 201–320.

21 For a detailed discussion of the unique cultural features of New Orleans's Creole community, see Gwendolyn Midlo Hall, "The Formation of Afro-Creole Culture," in Hirsch and Logdson, *Creole New Orleans*, 58–90.

22 This group was also known as the Citizens' Committee to Test the Constitutionality of the Separate Car Law.

23 On February 24, 1892, the Comité put its first plan in motion. Their passer was Daniel F. Desdunes, a man described as an "octoroon," of seven-eighths European and one-eighth African heritage. Desdunes held a first-class ticket and boarded a train heading from Louisiana to Alabama. Desdunes did not get very far because a detective, hired by the Comité, promptly arrested him for violating the Act. Desdunes was tried shortly thereafter and acquitted. This acquittal was not considered a victory because Desdunes's case did not broach the issue of racist biracial classification as the root of legalized segregation. The reason Desdunes was acquitted was that the provisions in the Louisiana law regarding interstate travel were not compatible with federal legislation. For a full account, see Medley, *We as Freedmen*, 158–59.

24 Woodward, *American Counterpoint*, 221. Hypodescent is the rule that made any person with a "drop" of African blood black, and therefore not entitled to whiteness or its privileges.

25 Harvey Fireside, *Separate and Unequal: Homer Plessy and the Supreme Court Decision That Legalized Racism* (New York: Carroll & Graf, 2004).

26 *Plessy v. Ferguson*, 163 U.S. 537 (1896).

27 Medley, *We as Freedmen*, 139–45.

28 I use the term "colored" rather than "black" or "African American" in this chapter because it is the historical term used in all the documents and research pertaining to the case as well as the term commonly used at the time of the pass and at the trials. The significance of "colored" is that it is meant as a plural or inclusive term for all those whose racial identities were anything other than white. The term, like "Negro," "black," and later "African American," was deployed in binary opposition to the exclusive category of "white-only."

29 Albion W. Tourgée, Brief for Plaintiff in Error [Homer Plessy], in *Landmark Briefs and Arguments of the Supreme Court of the United States: Constitutional Law*, ed. Philip B. Kurland and Gerhard Casper, vol. 13 (Washington, D.C.: University Publications of America, 1975), 27, 55–56.

30 Amy Robinson, "To Pass//In Drag: Strategies of Entrance into the Visible."

31 Elliott, "Race, Color Blindness, and the Democratic Public."

32 Tourgée, Brief, 19. According to Thomas, "*Plessy v. Ferguson* and the Literary Imagination," Tourgée invented this argument in a novel he wrote about a multiracial individual who could pass as white. Tourgée, *Pactolus Prime* (New York: Cassel, 1890).

33 Cheryl I. Harris, "Whiteness as Property," *Harvard Law Review* 106, no. 8 (1993): 1706–91.

34 In this way Plessy's case can also be considered as one in a long line of racial determination trials in U.S. legal history. For a thoughtful and thorough discussion of racial identity trials, see Ariela Julie Gross, *What Blood Won't Tell: A History of Race on Trial in America* (Cambridge, Mass.: Harvard University Press, 2008).

35 Harris, "Whiteness as Property."

36 Mark Poster, "The Secret Self: The Case of Identity Theft," *Cultural Studies* 21, no. 1 (2007): 118–40.

37 Mark Golub, "Plessy as 'Passing': Judicial Responses to Ambiguously Raced Bodies in *Plessy v. Ferguson*," *Law and Society Review* 39, no. 3 (2005): 563–600.

38 *Plessy*, 163 U.S. at 544, 551.

39 *Plessy*, 163 U.S. at 552; Golub, "Plessy as 'Passing,'" 590. According to Golub, "In each of the cases that Justice Brown cited as evidence that the problem of racial ambiguity can be easily resolved by state law, a closer reading suggests just the opposite to be true. In none of the cases was a petitioner's contestation of racial classification simply dismissed. In three of the cases, convictions were overturned or remanded for a new trial (*State v. Chavers*, 50 N.C. 11 [1857]; *Gray v. State*, 4 Ohio 354 [1831]; and *Jones v. Commonwealth*, 80 Virginia 538 [1885]), and in one case a state law was ruled unconstitutional (*Monroe v. Collins*, 17 Ohio St. 665 [1867]). In none of the cases was a blood-quantum rule sufficient to settle an individual's racial status, which ultimately comes to depend on the contingent factors of social performance, presentation, and reception. Justice Brown's attempt to rein in the racially destabilizing implications of passing in Tourgée's argument cannot in the end be considered a success. Rather

than 'resolving' racial ambiguity through legal fiat, the cases demonstrate the extent to which racial categories are produced and maintained through the constitutive power of the law."

40 *Plessy*, 163 U.S. at 549.

41 Thomas K. Nakayama and Robert L. Krizek, "Whiteness: A Strategic Rhetoric," *Quarterly Journal of Speech* 81 (1995): 293.

42 Nakayama and Krizek, "Whiteness," 300.

43 *Plessy*, 163 U.S. at 550–51.

44 Amy Robinson, "Forms of Appearance of Value: Homer Plessy and the Politics of Privacy," in *Performance and Cultural Politics*, ed. Elin Diamond (New York: Routledge, 1996), 237–61. Robinson is the first to link *Plessy v. Ferguson* to the trope of appropriation.

45 Various legal guarantees actually create zones of privacy. The First Amendment creates the "freedom to association and privacy in one's associations." The Fourth Amendment affirms the "right of the people to be secure in their persons, houses, papers and effects against unreasonable searches and seizures." The Fifth Amendment allows for a personal zone of privacy in its Self-Incrimination Clause. The Ninth Amendment provides "the enumeration in the Constitution, of certain rights, shall not be construed to deny or disparage others restrained by the people." Thus, *Plessy v. Ferguson* concerns a relationship lying within a zone of privacy protected by several constitutional guarantees.

46 John Locke, *The Second Treatise of Civil Government* (Rockville, Md.: Wildside Press, 2008), 19. He writes that "every man has a property in his own person; this nobody has any right to but himself." The state serves to publicly protect private ends. Within this paradigm, privacy derives from property rights and the right to ownership of one's own person. Locke grounds the basis of property in that with which one mixes one's labor. Each person has a right to "his own person" and to extend that right through labor. For a thorough review and persuasive reversal of this argument, see Judith Wagner DeCew, *In Pursuit of Privacy: Law, Ethics, and the Rise of Technology* (Ithaca: Cornell University Press, 1997).

47 Robinson, "Forms of Appearance of Value," 237–61. Robinson argues that *Plessy v. Ferguson* constructs a zone of privacy to protect the property that is "natural" (racial) identity. If natural (racial) identity—what we are—is a form of property, it follows that identity is no longer an internal self-concept but is our social value. Effectively, Locke's equation for "natural rights" of citizenship becomes legal precedent, and racial identity becomes a commodity. Like any other commodity, racial identity becomes visible only through the value it is accorded in society. To be clearly invisible is to occupy the most valued position of all.

48 Bell, *Race, Racism, and American Law*, 207.

49 Bryan A. Garner, ed., *Black's Law Dictionary*, abridged 9th ed. (St. Paul: Thomson Reuters, 2010), 93.

50 Despite Plessy's existence, which Tourgée cited as proof that at least some whites consented to social equality and passed whiteness on to Plessy, the Court maintained that he acquired whiteness without permission. Therefore, his actions were illegal.

51 Robinson, "Forms of Appearance of Value," 237–61.
52 John Fiske, *Media Matters: Race and Gender in U.S. Politics* (Minneapolis: University of Minnesota Press, 1994).
53 *Plessy*, 163 U.S. at 559. Since Harlan wrote these words color-blindness has been understood in two ways: the idea that we should live in a society where people are treated equally regardless of racial background or skin color, or the belief that we are now living in a society where race no longer shapes life chances.
54 James W. Gordon, "Did First Justice Harlan Have a Black Brother?," *Western New England Law Review* 15, no. 2 (1993): 159–238.
55 *Plessy*.
56 Neil Gotanda, "A Critique of 'Our Constitution Is Color-Blind,'" in *Critical Race Theory: The Key Writings That Formed the Movement*, ed. Kimberlé Crenshaw, Neil Gotanda, and Garry Peller (New York: New Press, 1995), 257–75.
57 Linda Przybyszewski, *The Republic According to John Marshall Harlan* (Chapel Hill: University of North Carolina Press, 1999).
58 *Plessy*.
59 Andrew Gyory, *Closing the Gate: Race, Politics and Chinese Exclusion* (Chapel Hill: University of North Carolina Press, 1998). Gyory discusses the Court's ruling in *Chew Heong v. United States*, 112 U.S. 536.
60 Gabriel J. Chin, "The Plessy Myth: Justice Harlan and the Chinese Cases," *Iowa Law Review* 82 (1996): 151–82.
61 Golub, "Plessy as 'Passing.'"
62 Patricia Williams, *The Alchemy of Race and Rights* (Cambridge, Mass.: Harvard University Press, 1991).
63 Sally Ackerman, "The White Supremacist Status Quo: How the American Legal System Perpetuates Racism as Seen through the Lens of Property Law," *Hamline Journal of Public Law and Policy* 21 (1999): 142–60. Ackerman explains how Plessy's belief could have been argued according to the Fifth Amendment's Takings Clause. "Because Mr. Plessy 'passed' for white, he was able to 'trespass' on the privileged space reserved for whites. . . . Arguably, Mr. Plessy's property interest in his white appearance was 'taken' from him by the state when it began to identify 'whiteness' by blood rather than appearance. American property law defines a 'taking' as a government action 'directly interfering with or substantially disturbing the owner's use and enjoyment of [his] property.' Mr. Plessy, therefore, might have argued that his eviction from the train reflected an unlawful taking because it directly interfered with and substantially disturbed his use and enjoyment of the rights and benefits that accompanied his visible whiteness." Ackerman's interpretation provides a provocative spin on the relation between passing and identity theft by suggesting that the Court stole Plessy's identity. However, Plessy's case was not argued in this manner because its objective was to destabilize dominant racial categories so that their appropriation would be impossible. Plessy's self-outing overcame the risk of potentially reifying racial categories because it exposed the fissures in systems of identification based on appearance as biological and natural. For that reason the Court controlled Plessy's passing by comparing it to

identity theft, thereby protecting the symbolic norms used to invent and maintain racial division as natural and necessary.

64 "FTC Issues Final Rules on FACTA Identity Theft Definitions, Active Duty Alert Duration, and Appropriate Proof of Identity," last modified October 29, 2004, http://www.ftc.gov/opa/2004/10/facataidtheft.shtm.

65 Kurt M. Saunders and Bruce Zucker, "Counteracting Identity Fraud in the Information Age: The Identity Theft and Assumption Deterrence Act," *Cornell Journal of Law and Public Policy* 8 (1999): 661–75.

66 Heather M. Howard, "The Negligent Enablement of Imposter Fraud: A Common-Sense Common Law Claim," *Duke Law Journal* 54 (2005): 1263–94.

67 Saunders and Zucker, "Counteracting Identity Fraud."

68 Section 3 of this act defines identity theft, making all "transfers or uses, without lawful authority, [of] a means of identification of another person with the intent to commit, or to aid or abet, any unlawful activity . . . a violation of Federal law, . . . constitut[ing] a felony under any applicable State or local law." This law was extended on May 10, 2005, when President George W. Bush approved the REAL ID Act, a comprehensive measure to establish new identification requirements across the United States. The legislation "mandates federal identification standards and requires state DMVs, which have become the targets of identity thieves, to collect sensitive personal information." Identity Theft and Assumption Deterrence Act, October 30, 1998, H.R. 4151. The legislation was amended in 2004 with the Identity Theft Penalty Enhancement Act. For additional information on identity theft and its original legislation, see Katherine Slosarik, "Identity Theft: An Overview of the Problem," *Criminal Justice Studies* 15, no. 4 (2002): 329–43.

69 G. Reginald Daniel, *More than Black? Multiracial Identity and the New Racial Order* (Philadelphia: Temple University Press, 2002). Daniels refers to full-time passing as "continuous" passing. He refers to part-time passing as "discontinuous" passing.

70 Finch, "What a Tangled Web We Weave," 90.

71 Anxieties about full-time passing, identity, and property were dramatized in the FX series *The Riches*. The series is about a gypsy family who steals a large amount of money from a rival clan. While escaping, the family is involved in a car accident that kills a very wealthy family, the Riches. In hope of pursuing a "better life," the gypsy family passes as the Riches. They steal the Riches' identities in an affluent gated community in Louisiana and struggle to adjust to their new personae while attempting to avoid exposure by in-group clairvoyants from both their gypsy past and the Riches' past.

72 Finch, "What a Tangled Web We Weave," 90.

73 Finch, "What a Tangled Web We Weave," 90.

74 U.S. Congress, Identity Theft and Assumption Deterrence Act of 1998, 18 U.S.C. 1028 (a) (7), as amended. http://www.law.cornell.edu/uscode/html/uscode18/usc_sec_18_00001028----000-.html, accessed January 31, 2011.

75 Sandra K. Hoffman and Tracy C. McGinley, *Identity Theft: A Reference Handbook* (Santa Barbara: ABC-CLIO, 2010).

76 Finch, "What a Tangled Web We Weave."
77 Sheila R. Cherry, "Al-Qaeda May Be Stealing Your ID," *Insight on the News,* August 26, 2002, http://findarticles.com/p/articles/mi_m1571/is_31_18/ai_90990420/pg_2/?tag=content;col1.
78 For instance, bureau officials claim that some credit card holders make charges on their accounts and later report them as identity thefts. Thus, credit bureaus themselves are innocent victims. This argument can be likened to the defensive dupe perspective represented by the Court in *Plessy v. Ferguson.* The Court saw no hand of its own in creating the situation in which Plessy passed. Rather, the Court cast itself as the innocent victim of Plessy's passing and treated the case as an identity theft, even though Plessy's attorneys argued that no identity theft had in fact taken place. Plessy's attorneys argued that because Plessy was (part) white he was therefore entitled to the rights, privileges and benefits of whiteness.
79 Ruth La Ferla, "Generation E.A.: Ethnically Ambiguous," *New York Times,* December 28, 2003, Style Section.
80 Homi K. Bhabha, "Culture's in Between," in *Multicultural States: Rethinking Difference and Identity,* ed. David Bennett (London: Routledge, 1998), 31.
81 Ramnath K. Chellappa and Raymond G. Sin, "Personalization versus Privacy: An Empirical Examination of the Online Consumer's Dilemma," *Information Technology and Management* 6, nos. 2–3 (2005): 181–202.
82 Ward Connerly, *Creating Equal: My Fight against Race Preferences* (New York: Encounter Books, 2000).
83 "California Proposition 54 Initiative Text," Leadership Conference, accessed April 13, 2011, http://www.civilrights.org/equal-opportunity/proposition-54/initiative_text.html. As a follow-up to Connerly's Proposition 209 campaign, which ended affirmative action programs in the state of California, Proposition 54 aimed to ban California from collecting racial data in all but a few exempted areas. California's Proposition 54 was placed on the October 7, 2003, state ballot as a constitutional amendment to allow the State of California to live up to the nation's "color-blind" core as detailed in Justice Harlan's dissent in *Plessy v. Ferguson.* Proposition 54's proponents sought the help of conservative politicians and businesspeople, including Newt Gingrich; John Moores, owner of the San Diego Padres major league baseball team; media mogul Rupert Murdoch; retired brewery mogul Joseph Coors; Jerry Hume, president of a San Francisco food-processing company; John Uhlmann, a Kansas City businessman; and Harlan Crow, a Dallas-based investor. In addition, the proposition was supported by the advocacy efforts of several multiracial organizations. The initiative was defeated in 2003 (63 percent–36 percent). For a thorough description of growing neoconservative political interests in multiracial identities and legal constructions of privacy, see Kim M. Williams, *Mark One or More* (Ann Arbor: University of Michigan Press, 2006).
84 Lisa A. Flores, Drema G. Moon, and Thomas K. Nakayama, "Dynamic Rhetorics of Race: California's Racial Privacy Initiative and the Shifting Grounds of Racial Politics," *Communication and Critical/Cultural Studies* 3, no. 3 (2006): 181–201.

85 Peggy Pascoe, "Miscegenation Law, Court Cases, and Ideologies of 'Race' in Twentieth-Century America," *Journal of American History* 83, no. 1 (1996): 44–69.

86 Elissa Gootman, "Proposal Adds Options for Students to Specify Race," *New York Times*, August 9, 2006. Gootman's article cites research conducted by the Harvard Civil Rights project (now housed at UCLA), directed by Gary Orfeld, which reveals that increasing populations of self-identifying multiracials and individuals who opt out of racial categorization all together cripple efforts to track race and discrimination on school campuses.

87 Peggy Gargis, "Alabama Sets Nation's Toughest Immigration Law," *Reuters*, http://www.reuters.com/article/2011/06/09/us-immigration-alabama-idUSTRE7584C920110609.

88 Jose Antonio Vargas, "My Life as an Undocumented Immigrant," *New York Times*, June 22, 2011.

89 danah boyd, "Networked Privacy," Personal Democracy Forum, New York, June 6, 2011. In this talk boyd discusses today's battles over privacy as overly focused on individual harm. She suggests that societies take a step beyond individual-centered notions of privacy and consider focusing on collective notions of social and data privacy to ensure justice in an increasingly interactive and digital world.

90 Scott Thurm and Yukari Iwatni Kane, "Your Apps Are Watching You," *Wall Street Journal*, December 17, 2010. According to the article, Rovio Mobile Ltd., the developer of Angry Birds, says "it transmits user data to a game platform and analytics service to better understand what users want and to improve the product. User allowed the app to transmit a user-name/password for the Crystal game network to Crystal; allowed app to see location; and allowed app to search contacts for friends."

91 Rovio Entertainment Limited, "Angry Birds," http://www.rovio.com/en/our-work/games/view/1/angry-birds/reviews/.

92 Ryan Kuo, "What's Next for Angry Birds?," *Wall Street Journal*, March 1, 2011, http://blogs.wsj.com/speakeasy/2011/03/01/whats-next-for-angry-birds/, accessed November 8, 2011.

93 Kuo, "What's Next for Angry Birds?"

94 Matt Ridley, "Tracing Those Angry Birds to the Dawn of Man," *Wall Street Journal*, January 15, 2011, http://online.wsj.com/article/SB100014240527487037797045760742225432742688.html.

95 Brian Stetler, "Upending Anonymity, These Days the Web Unmasks Everyone," *New York Times*, June 20, 2011, http://www.nytimes.com/2011/06/21/us/21anonymity.html?_r=1&nl=todaysheadlines&emc=tha23.

96 588 U.S. Sections 2(a–b). The U.S. Supreme Court's landmark decision in *Citizens United v. Federal Election Commission* held that corporate funding of independent political broadcasts in candidate elections cannot be limited because of the First Amendment. "Although the First Amendment provides that 'Congress shall make no law . . . abridging the freedom of speech,' §441b's prohibition on corporate independent expenditures is an outright ban on speech, backed by criminal sanctions. It is a ban notwithstanding the fact that a PAC created by a corporation can still

speak, for a PAC is a separate association from the corporation. Because speech is an essential mechanism of democracy—it is the means to hold officials accountable to the people—political speech must prevail against laws that would suppress it by design or inadvertence . . . (b) The Court has recognized that the First Amendment applies to corporations." http://www.supremecourt.gov/opinions/09pdf/08-205.pdf.

97 Eli Pariser, *The Filter Bubble: What the Internet Is Hiding from You* (New York: Penguin Press, 2011).

98 dana boyd, "Networked Privacy."

99 Amy Goodman, "WikiLeaks, Wimbledon and War," *Democracy Now,* July 6, 2011, http://www.democracynow.org/blog/2011/7/6/wikileaks _wimbledon_and_war.

WikiLeaks was officially launched in 2007 to receive leaked infor- mation from whistle-blowers, using the latest technology to protect the anonymity of the sources. "The organization gained global recognition with the successive publication of massive troves of classified documents from the U.S. government relating to the wars in Iraq and Afghanistan, and thousands of cables from the U.S. embassies around the world." In October 2011, Wikileaks announced that it would temporarily suspend its operations because it ran out of funding.

100 Anonymous, "Everything Anonymous," last modified June 28, 2011, http://www.anonnews.org/?p=press&a=item&i=787. Anonymous, an organization that withholds the identities of its own members, attacks corporations it believes violate consumer privacy, abuse the judicial system to censor information about how products work, and prevent consumers from exercising full ownership rights over products/property they have purchased. According to its website, Anonymous has hacked Gawker, Amazon, Mastercard, HBGary, Sony, the city of Orlando, Florida, and NATO.

LulzSec, another anonymous hacktivist group, is named for a deriva- tive of LOL (laugh out loud) combined with security. Its mascot is a car- toon of a man with a handlebar mustache, wearing a top hat and tie and holding a glass of wine. LulzSec is reported to have brought the CIA's, the Senate's, Canada's Conservative Party's, Sony's, and Nintendo's websites down. In addition, the group hacked Rupert Murdoch's News Corp's sys- tem and defaced a PBS website after the network broadcasted a documen- tary criticizing WikiLeaks founder Julian Assange. CBS News, "Hackers Report Taking Down CIA Website," *CBS News Techtalk,* June 15, 2011, http://www.cbsnews.com/8301-501465_162-20071392-501465.html #ixzz1PSs9J5qk.

101 Noam Cohen, "WikiLeaks, Facebook and the Perils of Oversharing," *New York Times,* December 5, 2010, http://www.nytimes.com/2010/12/06/ business/media/06link.html?pagewanted=1&_r=2.

102 Andrew S. Ross, "Rupert Murdoch Scandal Raises Questions in U.S.," *San Francisco Chronicle,* July 15, 2011. WikiLeaks is not the only organi- zation whose journalistic integrity is under fire. Recently, the UK's *Guard- ian* newspaper published allegations that the country's leading weekly tabloid, the *News of the World,* hired a private investigator to access and delete messages from a murdered teenager's voicemail. The questionable

ethical practices appear to have traveled across the Atlantic, as the FBI launched an investigation into whether Rupert Murdoch's News Corp. attempted to hack the phones of 9/11 victims in the United States as well.

103 Patrick Seybold, "Settlement in George Hotz Case," PlayStation Blog, last modified April 11, 2011, http://blog.us.playstation.com/2011/04/11/settlement-in-george-hotz-case/?utm_source=twitter&utm_medium =social&utm_campaign=george_hotz_041111. George "Geohot" Hotz, an American hacker known for being the first to jailbreak the iPhone, is a perfect example of a twenty-first-century high-tech version of Plessy's pass. Geohot's intervention allowed the iPhone to be used with wireless carriers other than AT&T, a freedom that was contrary to AT&T and Apple's intentions. More recently, Geohot is alleged to have hacked Sony's PlayStation 3 and was sued by Sony Computer Entertainment America LLC. The case was settled with Geohot consenting to a permanent injunction. Sony's attorney said that "we want our consumers to be able to enjoy our devices and products in a safe and fun environment and we want to protect the hard work of the talented engineers, artists, musicians and game designers who make PlayStation games and support the PlayStation Network." Geohot argued that his hacking is a form of social protest similar to Plessy's staged pass, and that when a consumer buys an iPhone or a PlayStation 3 it becomes the consumer's property and should be used and enjoyed however the consumer wishes. When consumers' ability to use and enjoy their property is limited by what corporations deem appropriate, Geohot argued, consumers' own privacy and property rights are violated. Geohot claims his hacking is in the interests of exposing weaknesses and insecurities in communication technology and reappropriating consumers' property rights.

104 danah boyd, "Networked Privacy."

105 Robinson, "Forms of Appearance of Value," 23.

CHAPTER FOUR

1 Wolfgang Iser, "The Reality of Fiction: A Functionalist Approach to Literature," *New Literary History* 7 no. 1, (1975): 7–38. On page 7 Iser writes, "If fiction and reality are to be linked, it must be in terms not of opposition but of communication, for the one is not the mere opposite of the other—fiction is a means of telling us something about reality."

2 Frances E. W. Harper, *Iola Leroy, or, Shadows Uplifted* (New York: Oxford University Press, 1988).

3 Harper, *Iola Leroy*, 245.

4 Henry Louis Gates Jr., foreword to Harper, *Iola Leroy*, vii–xxii.

5 Gabrielle P. Foreman, "'Reading Aright': White Slavery, Black Referents, and the Strategy of Histotextuality in *Iola Leroy*," *Yale Journal of Criticism* 10, no. 2 (1997): 327–54.

6 By presenting blackness as one way to be multiracial in the wake of the Civil War Harper also introduces the possibility that, for future generations, being multiracial could be one way to be black. For more on the latter, see Eugene Robinson, *Disintegration: The Splintering of Black America* (New York: Random House, 2010).

7   Aristotle, *Nicomachean Ethics*, trans. David Ross (New York: Oxford University Press, 1988).

8   Nikki Khanna and Cathryn Johnson, "Passing as Black: Racial Identity Work among Biracial Americans," *Social Psychology Quarterly* 73 (2010): 380–97.

9   Harper's *Iola Leroy*, set after the Civil War with flashbacks to incendiary incidents of passing, is composed of multiple settings and outcomes for passers. In this way, the text depicts passing ideologically as the culmination and catalyst for a series of events with specific outcomes. Moreover, situating the novel at differing points in space and time implies a nonlinear coherence related to the process of passing itself. Specifically, a nonlinear coherence allows Harper to acknowledge the very real presences of racial oppression and interracial interaction before, during, and after the Civil War's tumult and also to allow for the possibility of action and change.

10 Harper, *Iola Leroy*, 66.

11 Harper, *Iola Leroy*, 79.

12 Julie Cary Nerad, "Slippery Language and False Dilemmas: The Passing Novels of Child, Howells, and Harper," *American Literature* 75, no. 4 (2003): 831.

13 Harper, *Iola Leroy*, 106.

14 Harper, *Iola Leroy*, 105.

15 Harper, *Iola Leroy*, 105.

16 Richard L. Wright, "The Word at Work: Ideological and Epistemological Dynamics of African American Rhetoric," in *Understanding African American Rhetoric: Classical Origins to Contemporary Innovations*, ed. Ronald L. Jackson II and Elaine B. Richardson (New York: Routledge, 2003), 95.

17 Khanna and Johnson, "Passing as Black."

18 Harper, *Iola Leroy*, 320.

19 After being held by an evil slave master, Iola is rescued by a friend and former slave, Tom Anderson, and becomes a nurse in the army.

20 Patricia S. E. Darlington and Becky Michele Mulvaney, "Gender, Rhetoric, and Power: Toward a Model of Reciprocal Empowerment," *Women's Studies in Communication* 25 (2002): 159.

21 Harper, *Iola Leroy*, 317.

22 Harper, *Iola Leroy*, 57.

23 Harper, *Iola Leroy*, 112, 230.

24 Harper, *Iola Leroy*, 117.

25 Harper, *Iola Leroy*, 272–73.

26 Michelle Bimbaum, *Race, Work and Desire in American Literature, 1860–1930* (Cambridge: Cambridge University Press, 2003), 68. Bimbaum writes, "The proposal is of course lighthearted, but even after she has accepted his proposal, Iola continues to call him "doctor," just as she calls her earlier suitor, Gresham, "doctor," after he, too . . . confesses love."

27 Bimbaum, *Race, Work and Desire*, 68–70.

28 Over a century after Harper dramatized Iola's romantic experiences as expressions of her racial self-identification, sociological and psychological

research within the field of critical mixed-race studies would make Harper's claims concrete. See Frances Winddance Twine, "Heterosexual Alliances: The Romantic Management of Racial Identity," in *The Multiracial Experience: Racial Borders as the New Frontier*, ed. Maria P. P. Root (Thousand Oaks, Calif.: Sage, 1996), 291–304.

29   Harper, *Iola Leroy*, 120–21.

30   Harper, *Iola Leroy*, 125.

31   Geoffrey Sandborn, "Mother's Milk: Frances Harper and the Circulation of Blood," *ELH* 72, no. 3 (2005): 695.

32   *Oxford English Dictionary Online*, s.v. "eloquence."

33   Marcus Tullius Cicero, *De oratore*, 2nd ed., trans. E. N. P. Moore (London: Methuen, 1904), III.xiv.55.

34   Cicero, *De oratore* III.xiv.55.

35   Harper, *Iola Leroy*, 273.

36   Mary Louise Roberts, "True Womanhood Revisited," *Journal of Women's History* 14, no. 1 (2002): 150–55.

37   Harper, *Iola Leroy*, 118.

38   Giambattista Vico, *The Autobiography of Giambattista Vico* (Ithaca: Cornell University Press, 1944).

39   Hugh Blair, *Lectures on Rhetoric and Belles Lettres* (Philadelphia: Porter & Coates, 1873), 273.

40   Blair, *Lectures on Rhetoric and Belles Lettres*, 264.

41   Jackson, *Real Black*, 15.

42   W. Barnett Pearce and Stephen W. Littlejohn, *Moral Conflict* (Thousand Oaks, Calif.: Sage, 1997). In this text the authors explore forms of eloquence appropriate to transcendent discourse. "To be eloquent is to represent the highest form of expression within a frame of rules adopted by a moral community. Within a moral community, eloquent speech elicits attention, respect, and compliance. Between moral communities, however, it can create frustration, hatred, anger, and even violence" (157). To exercise transcendent eloquence the rhetor must be able to identify with multiple communities, assess the validity of their competing perspectives and lifestyles, identify with each of them, and create a new more inclusive vocabulary to promote mutual respect and understanding.

43   Harper, *Iola Leroy*, 243.

44   Harper, *Iola Leroy*, 247–48.

45   Harper, *Iola Leroy*, 249.

46   Harper, *Iola Leroy*, 250.

47   Harper, *Iola Leroy*, 251.

48   Barack Obama, *The Audacity of Hope: Thoughts on Reclaiming the American Dream* (New York: Random House, 2006).

49   Harper, *Iola Leroy*, 253.

50   Harper, *Iola Leroy*, 253.

51   Harper, *Iola Leroy*, 254.

52   Harper, *Iola Leroy*, 260.

53   Harper, *Iola Leroy*, 260.

54   Vorris L. Nunley, "From the Harbor to Da Academic Hood: Hush Harbors and an African American Rhetorical Tradition," in *African American Rhetorics: Interdisciplinary Perspectives*, ed. Ronald Jackson and

Elaine Richardson (Carbondale: Southern Illinois University Press, 2004), 221–41.

55 Gayle Rubin, "'Thinking Sex': Notes for a Radical Theory of the Politics of Sexuality," in *Pleasure and Danger: Exploring Female Sexuality*, ed. Carole S. Vance (London: Routledge, 1984), 267–319.

56 Jenifer L. Bratter and Rosalind B. King, "'But Will It Last?': Marital Instability among Interracial and Same-Race Couples," *Family Relations* 57, no. 2 (2008): 160–71. The authors suggest that black/white interracial couples experience negative reactions from strangers and diminished support from family and friends. Further, they find that stigmas attached to interracial interaction are strongly gendered as well as racially specific. Specifically, white women are perceived as a threat to black women's marriage opportunities and white women experience more psychological distress in interracial relationships.

57 Robert K. Merton, "Intermarriage and the Social Structure: Fact and Theory," *Psychiatry* 4 (1941): 361–74; Ian Haney Lopez, *White by Law: The Legal Construction of Race* (New York: New York University Press, 1996); Martha Elizabeth Hodes, ed., *Sex, Love, Race: Crossing Boundaries in North American History* (New York: New York University Press, 1999); Rachel F. Moran, *Interracial Intimacy: The Regulation of Race and Romance* (Chicago: University of Chicago Press, 2001); Peter Wallenstein, "Reconstruction, Segregation, and Miscegenation: Interracial Marriage and the Law in the Lower South, 1865–1900," *American Nineteenth Century History* 6, no. 1 (2005): 57–76; Katherine Ellinghaus, "The Pocahontas Exception: Indigenous 'Absorption' and Racial Integrity in the United States, 1880s–1920s," in *Rethinking Colonial Histories: New and Alternative Approaches*, ed. Penelope Edmonds and Samuel Furphy (Melbourne: RMIT, 2006), 123–36; Peggy Pascoe, *What Comes Naturally: Miscegenation Law and the Making of Race in America* (Oxford: Oxford University Press, 2009).

58 Susan Salny, "Race Remixed: Black? White? Asian? More Young Americans Choose All of the Above," *New York Times*, January 29, 2011, http://www.nytimes.com/2011/01/30/us/30mixed.html?pagewanted =2&_r=1&hp.

59 Harper, *Iola Leroy*, 238–39.

60 Because of the fictional and historical constraints on this narrative, it is impossible to claim definitively to what degree the siblings were willing and able to embrace multiracial identities. But at the very least Harper opens the door to that as a viable choice with positive outcomes for individuals and communities so long as they acknowledge the whole and not the part (i.e., blackness in addition to other parts of their racial identities).

CHAPTER FIVE

1 Philip Roth, *The Human Stain* (New York: Knopf, 2000), 6.

2 When I refer to Coleman as white and Jewish I mean to reference a larger history of European descended Jewish immigrants who, like the Irish, "became" white in the U.S. through a particular process of racial and ethnic assimilation. As I discuss later in this chapter, for some immigrants

part of the process of assimilation involved blackface minstrelsy. I recognize that not all Jewish immigrants engaged in this discriminatory performance practice. I also recognize that there is a Jewish diaspora, and, consequently, that not all Jewish people in the United States, Israel or elsewhere identify as white. For thorough scholarly discussions of Jewish diasporic and Jewish American identity development, see the following texts: Michael Rogin, *Blackface, White Noise: Jewish Immigrants in the Hollywood Melting Pot* (Berkeley: University of California Press, 1996); Eric Goldstein, *The Price of Whiteness: Jews, Race, and American Identity* (Princeton: Princeton University Press, 2006); Schlomo Sand, *The Invention of the Jewish People* (London: Verso, 2010).

3   Coleman is banished by Athena College, just as the ancient goddess Athena banished the crow that brought her bad tidings in the Greek myth of "Athena and Erichthonius." "In most versions of the story Erichthonius [a half snake, half human] was conceived during an encounter between Athena and Hephaestus . . . [when] Hephaestus finally discharged his semen onto her thigh. Athena wiped her leg clean with a piece of wool, which she then threw onto the ground. Divine intercourse is always procreative, and Hephaestus's seed, wrapped in wool (the product of female labor), on touching the earth . . . caused the conception of the baby Erichthonius." C. Scott Littleton, *Gods, Goddesses and Mythology Volume 4* (White Plains, N.Y.: Marshall Cavendish, 2005), 485. One thoughtful movie reviewer named "Curt" saw a deeper relationship between *The Human Stain* and this myth as it pertains to the crow as a tragic figure. "Athena hid the monster-child Erichthonius. . . . When Erichthonius is eventually revealed to the world, three women kill themselves. A crow brings this news to Athena, and for being the bearer of bad tidings, she turned crows from white to black. *The Human Stain* gives us a new twist on the story. Athena (the college) is the refuge of the self-created 'monster' (Coleman) until Bill Clinton, in his lust, spills his seed on Monica Lewinsky's dress, thus creating a climate of Political Correctness so severe that it forces Coleman out of his hiding place" (http://themoviespoiler.com/Spoilers/humanstain.html). In such a "climate," and despite his best intentions, Coleman (the passing crow) is transformed from white to black throughout *The Human Stain*.

4   David Hume, "Dissertation III: Of Tragedy," in *Four Dissertations* (London: A. Millar, 1757), 184–200.

5   Lorrie Moore, "The Wrath of Athena," *New York Times,* May 7, 2000, http://www.nytimes.com/books/00/05/07/reviews/000507.07mooret .html.

6   A. D. Powell, *"Passing" for Who You Really Are: Essays in Support of Multiracial Whiteness* (Palm Coast: Backintyme, 2005), 3.

7   Rachel Gelder, "Passing and Failing: Reflections on the Limitations of Showing the Passer in *The Human Stain,*" *Women and Performance Quarterly* 15, no. 1 (2005): 293–312. I borrow the terminology of "passing and failing" from Gelder.

8   Not since Carl Franklin's *Devil in a Blue Dress* (1995) has a major studio tried to tackle passing and its many struggles. The author is aware of a

screenplay written by Heidi W. Durrow and Fanshen Cox entitled *Passing*, which is an update of Nella Larsen's classic novel, currently under consideration by a major motion picture studio.

9   Peter Travers, review of *"The Human Stain," Rolling Stone*, September 25, 2003, http://www.rollingstone.com/movies/reviews/the-human-stain-20030925.

10 However, some critics did not find Miller believable as a younger version of Anthony Hopkins either, or, more significantly, as an authentic member of a black family. They were unable to see how he could pass as black and only found Miller's performance authentic once his character began to pass as white. Film critic Roger Ebert challenges this critique when he asks audiences to consider that there is often more difference within racial groups than there is between them, in part because of the long history of racial passing. These critiques are part of an online debate over Wentworth Miller's racial status and whether he can be considered black enough to be cast as an African American in television and film roles. The catalyzing post is titled "Sorry Wenty Pal, You're Not Black and You'll Never Be Black." For full commentary, see http://www.imdb.com/name/nm0589505/board/flat/177479029.

11 Nick Paumgarten, "Central Casting: The Race Card," *New Yorker*, December 10, 2003. Like many other critics, Paumgarten ignores world history and racial formation in the UK. The Welsh are a minority in Britain, and thus not quite English (and thus not quite "white"). For a brief but thorough discussion of the sociological and linguistic origins of the Welsh in the British Empire, see Margaret Deuchar, "Minority Language Survival in Northwest Wales: An Introduction," in *ISB4: Proceedings of the 4th International Symposium on Bilingualism*, ed. James Cohen, Kara T. McAlister, Kellie Rolstad, and Jeff MacSwan (Somerville, Mass.: Cascadilla Press, 2005), 621–25.

12 Aesop, "The Crow and the Raven," in *Aesop's Fables*, trans. V. S. Vernon Jones, ed. George Stade (New York: Fine Creative Media, 2003), 226. "A crow became very jealous of a raven, because the latter was . . . held in great respect by men. She was very anxious to get the same sort of reputation herself; and one day, seeing some travelers approaching, she flew onto a branch of a tree at the roadside and cawed as loud as she could. The travelers were in some dismay at the sound . . . till one of them . . . said to his companions, 'It's all right, my friends . . . it's only a crow and that means nothing. Those who pretend to be something they are not, only make themselves ridiculous.'"

13 Roth, *The Human Stain*, 242.

14 Jeffrey Rubin-Dorsky, "Philip Roth and American Jewish Identity: The Question of Authenticity," *American Literary History* 13, no. 1 (2001): 79–107.

15 Amy Robinson, "It Takes One to Know One: Passing and Communities of Common Interest," *Critical Inquiry* 20, no. 4 (1994): 716. Robinson discusses reading as a "shift from a politics of substance to a politics of optics" wherein "identity itself no longer possesses the reassuring signs of ontological distinction that we are accustomed to reading."

16 In the example of *The Human Stain* we can see how identities are "enacted and embodied through plot and character" and how they are also constituted through "disembodied statements" as "reviews make explicit claims." For a full discussion of the rhetorical dimensions of mediated identities, see Randall A. Lake, "Argumentation and Self: The Enactment of Identity in Dances with Wolves," *Argumentation and Advocacy* 34 no. 2 (1997): 66–90.

17 Roth, *The Human Stain*, 126.

18 Cutting ties with the family can be interpreted as Coleman's transition from the black to the white sphere of social activity. Sadly, it is through this experience of severing the metaphorical umbilical cord that Coleman inaugurates the space for his individual motivation and purification as his own man. In order to purify himself, he had to erase his past. Coleman becomes his own antagonist and must eradicate his black side if he is to pass as white. This is accomplished partially by cutting ties with his black mother. The novel paints the heartrending moment as matricide. Matricide extends to Coleman's own symbolic suicide and is the impetus for his rebirth. As he goes forward, his prepassing black persona is dead and his Jewish persona is born. He proceeds to use and enjoy his white reputation along with his professional reputation as a professor of classics, the epitome of a white-centered curriculum. Coleman's elder brother Walter summarizes the situation powerfully when he describes Coleman as whiter than white people. I discuss this scene thoroughly in Marcia Alesan Dawkins, "In Search of a 'Singular I': A Structurational Analysis of Passing," *Ethnic Studies Review* 28, no. 2 (2005): 1–16.

19 Many critics speculate that Coleman's story and character are inspired by the life of Anatole Broyard, though Roth and Benton say they are not. What is discussed with less frequency is that Coleman can also be considered a multigenerational multiracial person who was born into and identifies (initially) with an African American family. He is the only racially ambiguous (white-looking) member of his family.

20 Roth, *The Human Stain*, 108.

21 Roth, *The Human Stain*, 108.

22 Amy Hungerford, "Philip Roth, *The Human Stain*" (lecture, Yale University, New Haven, Conn., Spring 2008), http://freevideolectures.com/Course/2460/The-American-Novel-Since-1945/21.

23 Ross Posnock, "Purity and Danger: On Philip Roth," *Raritan* 21, no. 2 (2001): 85–101.

24 Roth, *The Human Stain*, 138.

25 Collective identifications occur when positive terms have been made dialectical and come to be the qualities by which a group of persons is substantively judged (e.g., race, class, sexuality, gender). Positive terms refer to aspects or objects of the visible world. Dialectical terms refer to intangible ideals. These ideals are often attached to positive terms that reflect aspects of the material world and can affect biological processes. The process by which this attachment happens is what Kenneth Burke calls "symbolic action" or language.

26 Roth, *The Human Stain*, 117.

27 Michele Elam, *The Souls of Mixed Folk: Race, Politics, and Aesthetics in the New Millennium* (Stanford: Stanford University Press, 2011), 107–8. Elam writes, "Earlier in the narrative, Silk is called the same epithet [nigger] and the 'impact was devastating'; it is no accident, then that the same expression from Silk's lips—as causally, cruelly rendered—becomes a speech act (re)creating the racial divide and securing his chosen side on it."

28 Roth, *The Human Stain*, 109.

29 Roth, *The Human Stain*, 98–99.

30 Roth, *The Human Stain*, 120. Admittedly, Coleman's choice is ironic. Why take on an identity that will be problematic while disavowing an identity to avoid problems? An obvious answer is that Jewish identity is a physical and cultural buffer zone between blackness and whiteness used to explain away any of Coleman's questionable traits (e.g., less than "Silky" hair—pun intended; an olive-tinged complexion). But a deeper look at Roth's work suggests another answer: the condition that W.E.B. Du Bois referred to as "double consciousness." In *The Human Stain* this historical condition of always looking at oneself through the eyes of others is universalized. In making this condition universal, Roth's text reminds us that ethnic and racial identities are always interdependent and contested. And the enormous cost of Coleman's passing—his effort to avoid double consciousness—is for his pre- and post-passing personae to be stained by what caused it, racism and anti-Semitism.

31 Roth, *The Human Stain*, 139.

32 Susan L. Feagin, "The Pleasures of Tragedy," *American Philosophical Quarterly* 20 no. 1 (1983): 95–104.

33 Hume, "Of Tragedy."

34 Richard von Busack, "Passing Zone: Anthony Hopkins Turns Racial Classifications Upside Down in Film Adaptation of Philip Roth's 'The Human Stain,'" *Metroactive*, October 29, 2003, http://www.metroactive.com/papers/cruz/10.29.03/human-0344.html.

35 Karen M. Bowdre, email to author, April 8, 2010. According to Bowdre, a film scholar from the University of Indiana, Bloomington, the film version of *The Human Stain* is part of a historical privileging of whiteness in film, as characters of mixed race have largely been played by white actors. To cite a few examples, Lena Horne was passed over in favor of Ava Gardner for a role as multiracial singer Julie LaVerne in 1951's *Show Boat* and in favor of Jeanne Crain to play the protagonist in 1949's *Pinky*. More recently, though her performance was approved by Mariane Pearl, Angelina Jolie was criticized for playing the Afro Cuban/Dutch wife of slain reporter Daniel Pearl in the 2007 film *A Mighty Heart*. In contrast, multiracial actors like Halle Berry are honored for their portrayals of black roles as in *Monster's Ball* but are not taken seriously when they express interest in racially ambiguous and/or white roles, as Berry planned to do by playing Tierney Cahill in *Class Act*. Cahill was a white teacher from Reno, Nevada who accepted a challenge from her sixth grade class to run for Congress in 2000. With regard to *The Human Stain*, the choice to cast Hopkins is part business decision. Bowdre says that "Hopkins was probably cast because he is who he is, has a following and perhaps box office clout. The producers/directors, etc. couldn't find—or didn't

look for—a qualified (popular, bankable) mixed race actor to play the part of the older Coleman." However, according to Bowdre, the casting decision is also equal parts colorblind and solipsistic. "On multiple levels it shows how the industry continues to privilege whiteness while being able to think they are progressive because they chose this subject matter." Keeping the above in mind, the point of interest to this chapter is that racial categories (*episteme*) and appearances (*doxa*) more often serve to limit rather than expand actors' opportunities and audiences' interpretations (*Password One*). Thus, multiracial roles, racial passing and media typecasting raise important questions for audiences both onscreen and off screen. One of these questions is whether films should double as racial Rorschach tests.

36 Allyson Hobbs, "The Fictions of Race, Custom, and Law: The Problem of Racial Passing in U.S. Social and Cultural History, 1840–1950" (Ph.D. diss., University of Chicago, 2007), 30.

37 Kimberly Cooper Plaszewski, "*Human Stain*'s Lessons about U.S. Assimilation," *Los Angeles Times,* November 17, 2003, http://articles.latimes.com/2003/nov/17/entertainment/et-counterpunch17.

38 Michael Wilmington, "Movie Review: 'The Human Stain,'" *Chicago Tribune*, October 30, 2003, http://www.chicagotribune.com/entertainment/movies/mmx-031029movies-review-mw-humanstain,0,7250714.story.

39 Frank Swietek, "Robert Benton on 'The Human Stain,'" Oneguysopinion.com, http://www.oneguysopinion.com/InterviewsResults.php?s_review=human+stain&ID=232.

40 Scott Holleran, "Interview: Robert Benton on 'The Human Stain," Box Office Mojo, November 26, 2003, http://www.boxofficemojo.com/features/?id=1260&p=.htm.

41 Michael Rogin, "Blackface, White Noise: The Jewish Jazz Singer Finds His Voice," *Critical Inquiry* 18, no. 3 (1992): 417–53.

42 James Baldwin, "On Being White and Other Lies," *Essence,* April 1984.

43 Baz Dreisinger, *Near Black: White-to-Black Passing in American Culture* (1843; Amherst: University of Massachusetts Press, 2008).

44 John Leland, "The Perils of Improvising a Racial Self," *New York Times*, November 10, 2003, El, 6. In this article Leland cites Irving Howe, who wrote that many Jewish entertainers performed as minstrels during the Jim Crow era in order to elevate their socioeconomic status in relation to (further devaluing) African Americans' status. For more see Irving Howe, *World of Our Fathers: The Journey of the Eastern European Jews to America and the Life They Found and Made* (New York: New York University Press, 2005).

45 Jeffrey Melnick, *A Right to Sing the Blues: African Americans, Jews, and American Popular Song* (Cambridge, Mass.: Harvard University Press, 1999).

46 Daniel Itzkovitz, "Passing Like Me: Jewish Chameleonism and the Politics of Race," in *Passing and Interpretation in Sexuality, Race, and Religion,* ed. María Carla Sánchez and Linda Schlossberg (New York: New York University Press, 2001), 38–63. Itzkovitz asserts that Jewish identity is constructed culturally in terms of "mimicry" and that this construction is fundamentally disruptive to traditional narratives of racial

and ethnic formation. Inherent in Jewish identity is a performance and a struggle between individual and collective values embedded in American discourses of identity since the days of Ralph Waldo Emerson.

47 See note 8 above.

48 Walter Chaw, "Miller's Crossing: Up-'n'-Comer Wentworth Miller Talks about *The Human Stain*," interview with Wentworth Miller III, http://www.filmfreakcentral.net/notes/wmillerinterview.htm. Miller explains this significance as part of a multiracial identity. He says that "there is the sense of being between communities and you sometimes wonder if you don't have to answer to any group or interest, that you're some sort of racial Lone Ranger, but the flipside of that is that a racial community, functioning at its best, provides not only a sense of identity . . . but a sense of security and support. When I run into trouble, what group will rally to my defense, come to my aid? The answer, and it's scary, might be 'no one.' "

49 Robert Benton (director), *The Human Stain* (2003).

50 Charles Taylor, "Life and Life Only," *Salon.com*, April 24, 2000, http://www1.salon.com/books/feature/2000/04/24/roth/index.html.

51 Sean P. Means, "Short Takes: Movie Reviews in Brief," *Salt Lake Tribune*, November 21, 2003, E6; Marty Mapes, review of *The Human Stain*, *Movie Habit*, http://www.moviehabit.com/reviews/hum_ji03.shtml; John Leland, "The Perils of Improvising a Racial Self," *New York Times*, November 10, 2003, E1, 6.

52 Dreisinger, *Near Black*, 123–25.

53 Hungerford, "Philip Roth, *The Human Stain*."

54 By "certain kinds of racial ambiguity" I mean to make two points. The first is about gender. As will be detailed in chapter 6, consumers of mainstream popular culture appear to have reached a level of comfort with women's racial ambiguity, as it is considered the most beautiful and a part of a pleasurable, entertaining experience. Comfort with (multiracial) women's racial ambiguity as beautiful coincides with cultural traditions that value beauty as women's primary goal. Men's racial ambiguity manifests in their consideration as strong and as problem solvers, coinciding with cultural traditions that value these traits as men's primary goals. The second is about racialization. At present the trend to racial ambiguity appears to be more focused on the rapid inclusion of Hispanics, Asians, and other non-European immigrant groups as well as certain Native American tribes into the mainstream media and marketplace, and not focused on African Americans. This is due to the "one-drop rule" and the accompanying cultural tradition that presumes a person with any trace of black ancestry should be and look black. For a full discussion of the above, see Margaret L. Hunter, *Race, Gender, and the Politics of Skin Tone* (New York: Routledge, 2005); Arnold K. Ho, Jim Sidanius, Daniel T. Levin, and Mahzarin R. Banaji, "Evidence for Hypodescent and Racial Hierarchy in the Categorization and Perception of Biracial Individuals," *Journal of Personality and Social Psychology* 94 (2010): 1–15.

55 Subsequent representations of passing in popular culture can be read as responses to *The Human Stain*'s unanswered call to develop new responses to age-old questions. This is due, in part, to the fact that a

new generation is engaging the classical theme of passing and presenting it to an audience less fettered by the demands of monoracial categorization. Heidi Durrow's critically acclaimed *The Girl Who Fell from the Sky* (Chapel Hill, N.C.: Algonquin Books of Chapel Hill, 2010) is an example. At first glance Durrow's novel seems like an updated take on the same old "tragic mulatto" passing story, complete with a catastrophic event that brings an end to family life, pressure to choose a race or a culture, pressure to choose a romantic partner, and a new family full of characters who are either absent or uncaring. But a deeper look reveals something more. Durrow's protagonist, Rachel, is a young multiracial woman who is anything but tragic. Despite her complex journey through alienation and despair, and the constraints of her upbringing, the blue-eyed Rachel emerges with her own eloquent voice, open to a world of possibilities. Rachel embodies a freer version of the passing crow that can rise above, take flight, and really move on. And, most importantly, shed light on possibilities for being multiracial and not being miserable.

Danzy Senna's collection of short stories *You Are Free* (New York: Riverhead Books, 2011) is another example. The collection focuses on women of various racial and multiracial backgrounds who explore issues of motherhood, class, and self-determination through passing. In one of the vignettes, "What's the Matter with Helga and Dave?," the multiracial white-looking narrator and her multiracial black-looking husband find themselves passing as an interracial couple in Los Angeles. As in her novels, *Caucasia* (New York: Riverhead Books, 1998) and *Symptomatic* (New York: Riverhead Books, 2004), and her memoir, *Where Did You Sleep Last Night? A Personal History* (New York: Farrar, Straus & Giroux, 2009), Senna explores the experiences of multiracial and black women who look white to question notions of racial and multiracial purity. Her writing alternately reveals and conceals issues of interracial intimacy, gender, and heterosexuality within the larger landscape of passing to expose current exigencies—such as reproductive rights and the state of education—from fresh perspectives.

Mat Johnson, like Senna and Durrow, uses passing, racial ambiguity, and multiracial identities to resist whiteness' rhetorical silence and postracial invisibility. In his graphic novel *Incognegro* (with art by Warren Pleece and lettering by Clem Robins) (New York: Vertigo/DC Comics, 2008), about an investigative reporter who passes as white to expose lynchings in the 1930s South, and novel *Pym* (New York: Spiegel & Grau, 2011), about a multiracial ("octoroon") professor of American literature who sets out on a journey to uncover the origins of white supremacy, Johnson reincarnates historical tragedies to usher in contemporary resolutions. By updating classic stories such as Edgar Allan Poe's *The Narrative of Arthur Gordon Pym of Nantucket* (1838) and Walter White's autobiography *A Man Called White* (1948), Johnson argues that resisting racism requires returning to its roots through meta-theoretical dialogue. To do this Johnson uses passing to implicate unspoken and unseen dimensions of race and to open discursive spaces where the power of whiteness is invoked without its explicit vocabulary and images. Only time will tell whether this new generation's updated takes on classical themes

will generate sustainable change to long-standing representational contexts and expectations and thereby avert the tragic formula of passing as
pastime in contemporary popular culture.

56 Phillip Brian Harper, "Passing for What? Racial Masquerade and the
Demands of Upward Mobility," *Callaloo* 21 (1998): 381–97.

57 Eugene Robinson, *Disintegration: The Splintering of Black America*
(New York: Random House, 2010), 10. Robinson argues that emerging
multiracial identities are one expression of blackness that should not be
devalued or ignored by African Americans of prior generations. Instead,
multiracial identities should been seen as serving a critical function that
helps us to develop a new vocabulary that more accurately reflects today's
changing demographics and racial paradigms. Robinson writes, "Wider
DNA testing has shown that nearly one-third of all African Americans
trace the heritage to a white male ancestor—likely a slave owner. So forget
about whether the mixed-race Emergents are 'black enough.' How black
am I? How black can any of us claim to be?" The historical and social
significance of mixed race-African American identities is also discussed
by Lawrence Wright, "One Drop of Blood," *New Yorker*, July 24, 1994,
http://www.afn.org/~dks/race/wright.html.

CHAPTER SIX

1 Thanassis Cambanis, "Juror Scrutiny Reaches New Level; Post-9/11
Anger Seen Fueling Bias," *Boston Globe*, July 12, 2002, B1.

2 Thanassis Cambanis, "No African-Americans on Race-Terror Case Jury,"
Boston Globe, July 13, 2002, B2.

3 John L. Jackson Jr., *Real Black: Adventures in Racial Sincerity* (Chicago:
University of Chicago Press, 2005).

4 Farah Stockman, "Terror Suspect No Racist, Supremacist, Father Says,"
Boston Globe, July 4, 2001, A1.

5 I chose the papers that provided the most coverage. I was interested mostly
in what most coverage said and not what most newspapers said because,
as Van Dijk argues, coverage "manufactures a racial consensus in which
the very latitude of opinions and attitudes is quite strictly constrained.
[Coverage] not only set[s] the agenda for public discussion (what people
should think about), but, more important . . . strongly suggest[s] how the
readers should think and talk about racial/ethnic relations." Teun A. Van
Dijk, *Racism and the Press* (London: Routledge, 1991), 236. The majority of coverage of Felton's case was by the *Boston Globe*. The *Boston
Globe* is a daily newspaper, based in Boston, Massachusetts, that has
consistently been ranked in the forefront of American journalism. *Time*
magazine listed it as one of the ten best U.S. daily newspapers in 1974 and
1984, and the *Globe* tied for sixth in a national survey of top editors who
chose "America's Best Newspapers" in the *Columbia Journalism Review*
in 1999. The *Globe* and the *New York Times*, the largest metropolitan
newspaper in the United States, are both owned by the New York Times
Company. Both papers are owned and staffed primarily by white Americans, have no official orientation toward any particular racial or ethnic
group in editorial policies, and publish news they deem to be of value to

a general audience. ProQuest and Lexis-Nexis search results listed over a thousand articles on Leo Felton whose origins can be traced to the *Boston Globe*. The *Globe* reports that Felton is pathological because he has gone against his antiracist multiracial nature. Moreover, it casts him as somewhat of a lone ranger because we have entered an era in which race, read racism, has lost its sting. For the sake of completeness, a concurrent search for coverage on Leo Felton and his case using the Ethnic News-Watch database yielded less than a hundred articles on Leo Felton and his case. A vast majority of the coverage came from Jewish newspapers, especially the *Jewish Advocate*, a Jewish weekly newspaper serving Greater Boston and the New England area. The *Advocate* is owned and staffed primarily by Jewish Americans and speaks out on behalf of this community. It was established in 1902 and is the oldest continuously circulated English-language Jewish newspaper in the United States. The *Advocate* reports that we do not live in a postracial or postethnic nation and that extremists like Felton are not as marginalized as we would like to believe. Rather, they pose an increasing threat to our racial and ethnic communities, our nation and the world at large.

6 Jenifer L. Bratter and Rosalind B. King, "'But Will It Last?': Marital Instability among Interracial and Same-Race Couples," *Family Relations* 57, no. 2 (2008): 160–71. This study supports previous research that reveals that interracial (or exogamous) couples are more likely to divorce by the tenth year of marriage than homogamous marriages.

7 Paul Tough, "The Black Supremacist," *New York Times*, May 25, 2003.

8 Farah Stockman, "Black, White Past Clouded Felton's Identity," *Boston Globe*, July 17, 2001, A1.

9 Tough, "Black Supremacist."

10 Tough, "Black Supremacist."

11 Stockman, "Black, White Past."

12 Tough, "Black Supremacist."

13 Farah Stockman, "Leo Felton and Me We're Both Children of Black and White Marriages. I Grew Up to Become a Journalist; Leo Felton Became a Neo-Nazi Racist. And I Wanted to Know Why," *Boston Globe*, November 3, 2002, 13.

14 Andrew McDonald, *The Turner Diaries* (New York: Barricade Books, 1996), 34, 207.

15 Ulick Varange, *Imperium: The Philosophy of History and Politics* (Sausalito, Calif.: Noontide Press, 1948).

16 Jeffrey Kaplan, *Encyclopedia of White Power: A Sourcebook on the Radical Racist Right* (Lanham, Md.: Altamira Press, 2000), 42–43.

17 Judith Butler, *Excitable Speech: A Politics of the Performative* (New York: Routledge, 1997).

18 Thanassis Cambanis, "Ex-Wife Testifies against Felton," *Boston Globe*, July 23, 2002, B3.

19 Thanassis Cambanis, "27-Year Sentence Sought for Neo-Nazi; Prosecutors Cite Felton's Lack of Remorse," *Boston Globe*, December 10, 2002, B3.

20 Thanassis Cambanis, "Felton Case Goes to the Jury," *Boston Globe*, July 26, 2002, B3.

44 G. Reginald Daniel, *More than Black? Multiracial Identity and the New Racial Order* (Philadelphia: Temple University Press, 2002), 146. This assumption ignores the reality that interracial romantic relationships still experience higher rates of failure and divorce than same-race relationships. See also Bratter and King, " 'But Will It Last?' "

45 Dorcas D. Bowles, "Bi-racial Identity: Children Born to African-American and White Couples," *Clinical Social Work Journal* 21 (1993): 427.

46 Ruth G. McRoy and Edith Freeman, "Racial-Identity Issues among Mixed Race Children," *Social Work in Education* 8 (1986): 166.

47 Elaine Pinderhughes, "Bi-racial Identity—Asset or Handicap?," in *Racial and Ethnic Identity: Psychological Development and Creative Expression*, ed. Herbert W. Harris, Howard C. Blue, and Ezra E. H. Griffith (New York: Routledge, 1995), 83.

48 Tough, "Black Supremacist."

49 Justin A. Frank, "Excerpt from Obama on the Couch," November 11, 2011, http://www.rollingstone.com/politics/blogs/national-affairs/obama-on-the-couch-inside-the-mind-of-the-president-20111111#ixzz1dn75f5MB. Even president Obama, who has been touted as a post-racial icon since his election in 2008, has not escaped critique and analysis on the basis of multiracial pathology. Dr. Justin A. Frank says as much when he describes the president as "born split" in the first chapter of *Obama on the Couch: Inside the Mind of the President* (New York: Simon & Schuster, 2011). In an excerpt Frank provided for *Rolling Stone* he writes, "Obama's easily observed characteristics—his abilities to link thinking and feeling, to listen to and assimilate the feelings of others, to transform their input into new thoughts, to have a firm grip on internal and material reality, and to consult both his passions and conscience when making decisions—exemplify strong mental health. They also reveal his personal triumph over a turbulent childhood, and we'll explore how many of his positive attributes—such as his brilliant facility with language, his calm in the face of chaos, and his ability to find common ground and build consensus—in fact developed out of coping mechanisms in response to the challenges he faced growing up." Frank continues, Obama "faced particular challenges as the mixed-race, ostensibly black child of a white mother, which inevitably made it harder for mother and son to recognize themselves in each other in the critical early stages of his infancy, despite his mother's apparent strengths at being a committed and effective nurturer. Additionally, growing up in a fatherless home, at least after his namesake left the family well before young Barry was two, posed another significant challenge, further complicated by the fact that Obama Sr.'s departure left his son the only black face in an otherwise white family."

50 Shelley Murphy, "Bomb Suspect Recuperating after Slashing; Jail Says Cuts Self-Inflicted," *Boston Globe*, June 26, 2001, B2; Stockman, "Terror Suspect No Racist"; Shelley Murphy, "White Supremacist Accused of Targeting DC Museum," *Boston Globe*, September 20, 2001, B3; Mehren, "Trial Begins for 2."

51 Rainier Spencer, *Reproducing Race: The Paradox of Generation Mix* (Boulder: Lynne Rienner, 2010).

52 Marcia Alesan Dawkins, "Mixed Messenger: Barack Obama and Post-racial Politics," *Spectator* 30, no. 2 (2010): 9–17.

53 Camille Nelson, "Racial Paradox and Eclipse: Obama as a Balm for What Ails Us," *Denver University Law Review* 86 (2009): 743–83.

54 Jack E. White, Tamala M. Edwards, Elaine Lafferty, Sylvester Monroe, and Victoria Rainert, "Race: I'm Just Who I Am," *Time*, May 5, 1997, http://www.time.com/time/magazine/article/0,9171,986278,00.html.

55 Michael C. Thornton, "Policing the Borderlands: White-and-Black-American Newspaper Perceptions of Multiracial Heritage and the Idea of Race, 1996–2006," *Journal of Social Issues* 65, no. 1 (2009): 105–27. Unfortunately, newspapers also ignored history by reporting this change to the 2000 Census as brand new. The U.S. Census included categories for multiracials until the year 1850. According to the *New Orleans Times-Picayune* and the *New York Times*, "By the census of 1850, the aggregate number of slaves in the United States was 3,204,313. Of this number, 246,656 were of mixed blood, mulattoes. The number of 'unmixed' negro blood was, therefore, 2,487,455. The free black and mulatto population was 434,495, in the following proportions: blacks, 275,400; mulattoes, 159,095." For more, see "Southern Views of the Census," *New York Times*, July 31, 1980; Jill E. Rowe, "Mixing It Up: Early African American Settlements in Northwestern Ohio," *Journal of Black Studies* 39, no. 6 (2009): 924–36.

56 Erin Texeira, "Multiracial Scenes Now Common in TV Ads," Associated Press, February 15, 2005, http://www.msnbc.msn.com/id/6975669/.

57 "2010 Census Data," U.S. Census Bureau, http://2010.census.gov/2010census/data/.

58 Kimberly McClain DaCosta, *Making Multiracials: State, Family, and Market in the Redrawing of the Color Line* (Stanford: Stanford University Press, 2007).

59 Alexis Garrett Stodghill, "New Gerber Babies Reflect Rainbow of Racial Diversity," *Atlanta Post*, June 27, 2011. Stodghill reports that nonwhite beige children now featured in advertisements and on baby food labels represent the new generation of "majority-minority" America, where whites will be outnumbered. Fueled by increases in birthrates among Latino/a immigration and interracial marriages, this new generation is "a piece of cultural capital worth investing in." Demographers predict that "rainbow babies" now in the cradle (who all strangely seem to appear beige in photographs) will be part of an evolving American identity and worldview that represents good news and will ultimately touch public policy in every way. Twelve states and Washington, D.C., are already majority-minority—Hawai'i, California, New Mexico, Texas, Arizona, Nevada, Florida, Maryland, Georgia, New Jersey, New York, and Mississippi. Seven more states are set to join the group in the next decade(s)—Illinois, North Carolina, Virginia, Colorado, Connecticut, South Carolina, and Delaware.

60 Brian Resnick, "The Ever-Changing American 'Race,'" *Atlantic*, July 21, 2011, http://www.theatlantic.com/national/archive/2011/07/the-ever-changing-american-race/242017/.

61 Dave Chappelle makes three points that support my argument about Leo Felton's passing and the mainstream construction of multiracial identities

in this "Frontline" sketch: (1) Color-blindness (i.e., being physically unable to see any color) does not serve the interests of antiracism. Chappelle implies that color-blindness is actually a physical and psychological impairment and not an enlightened state of being. (2) Interracial romantic relationships do not inherently imply an antiracist agenda, as evidenced by Bigsby and his wife's relationship. (3) Racial identity should not be related to physical characteristics like phenotype, ability, or biological ancestry. Racial identity is expressed best via racial and rhetorical sincerity. (4) Passers can be their own dupes and/or in-group clairvoyants. Sometimes everyone knows when the passer is passing, and sometimes no one knows. Not even the passer, especially when the passer comes from a "color-blind" perspective. For a thorough discussion of the blind and black white supremacist "Frontline" sketch in particular, and of Chappelle's work more generally, see Bambi Haggins, *Laughing Mad: The Black Comic Persona in Post-soul America* (Piscataway: Rutgers University Press, 2007).

62 Mary C. Beltrán, "The New Hollywood Racelessness: Only the Fast, Furious (and Multiracial) Will Survive," *Cinema Journal* 44 (2005): 50.

63 Sarah Palin, The Charge of Racism: It's Time to Bury the Divisive Politics of the Past," comment on Facebook, July 13, 2010 (8:58 p.m.), http://www.facebook.com/#!/notes/sarah-palin/the-charge-of-racism-its-time-to-bury-the-divisive-politics-of-the-past/408166998434.

64 Courtney W. Bailey, "Coming Out as Homophobic: Isaiah Washington and the *Grey's Anatomy* Scandal," *Communication and Critical/Cultural Studies* 8, no. 1 (2011): 1–21.

65 Bailey, "Coming Out."

66 *Oxford English Dictionary Online*, s.v. "apophasis." What I have dubbed "I can't be a racist because I am multiracial" defense is actually a type of rhetorical passing that classical rhetoricians call *apophasis*. According to the *Oxford English Dictionary, apophasis* is "a kind of an Irony, whereby we deny that we say or doe that which we especially say or doe." In other words, apophasis happens "when we really say or advise a thing under a feigned show of passing over, or dissuading it."

67 Ulli K. Ryder, "The Sheen Defense: Charlie Sheen and Multiracial Identity," blog, entry, Open Salon, March 12, 2011, http://open.salon.com/blog/ulli_k_ryder/2011/03/12/the_sheen_defense_charlie_sheen_and_multiracial_identity.

68 Louis F. Miron and Jonathan Xavier Inda, "Race as a Kind of Speech Act," *Cultural Studies* 5 (2000): 85–86.

69 Michael Fletcher, "Interracial Marriages Eroding Barriers," December 28, 1998, *Washington Post*, A01.

70 Ruth La Ferla, "Generation E.A.: Ethnically Ambiguous," *New York Times*, December 28, 2003, Style Section.

71 Eli Steele, "Where the Interracials May Take Us," *Los Angeles Times*, September 21, 2010. In this opinion piece the author suggests that today's multiracials really are a new creation. He writes that they "are naturally more diverse than any amount of social engineering in neighborhoods, schools or offices can achieve. They are creations of a high humanism: the

love of their parents, grandparents and great-great grandparents. [They] are the result that social engineering—integration, inclusion and diversity—often fails to achieve." Note the word "naturally" here. This well-intentioned but flawed way of celebrating multiracial identities promotes the fallacy that multiracial people are both *post*racialists and nonracists by nature. What is more, this celebration is based totally on appearances projected by mainstream media, moves racial politics into the realm of personal romance, friendship and feeling, diverts attention from historical and structural aspects of racial injustice, and refers to anti-racist political and legal interventions as artificial acts of "social engineering."

72   News stories such as these owe themselves to the assimilationist "melting pot" myth, a metaphor for a diverse society becoming more homogeneous. As a result, such stories disguise the historicity of multiracial identities in order to stage their originality and history in the present and declare the emergence of a new multiracial population as the mark of racial reconciliation and a *post*racial (read *post*racist) era.

73   Alison Caporimo, "What's Beautiful Now: The *Allure* American Beauty Survey," *Allure*, March 1, 2011, http://www.allure.com/magazine/2011/03/american-beauty-census#slide=1. Interestingly, the readers surveyed selected Angelina Jolie as the icon of mixed race beauty. In light of this it is important to remember that beauty standards and definitions of appearance that mark certain groups as less or more attractive raise normative questions. Such standards and definitions cannot be viewed simply as matters of personal preference. Rather, they draw upon a broader system of attitudes and actions that devalue particular categories of individuals and privilege other categories of individuals. In societies beleaguered by social inequalities, such beauty standards and definitions of appearance (i.e., multiracial women's faces are the most beautiful) are related to sociohistorical injustices and are, therefore, a matter of politics, aesthetics, and rhetorical construction. For more see Marcia Alesan Dawkins, "Mixed Race Beauty Gets a Mainstream Makeover," *Truthdig*, March 7, 2011, http://www.truthdig.com/report/item/mixed_race_beauty_gets_a_mainstream_makeover_20110307/.

74   John Cloud, "Are Mixed-Race Children Better Adjusted?," *Time*, February 21, 2009, http://www.time.com/time/health/article/0,8599,1880467,00.html. What is more, some (spurious) academic research confirms that multiracial youth who identify themselves as multiracial (i.e., with more than one racial group regardless of its comparative status in racial hierarchy) are more socially engaged and better off psychologically. Put simply, those who identify multiracial experience palpable personal advantages (but not political, social, or institutional advantages) over those who do not. What is unexplored in either the *Time* magazine article or the academic study is how these supposed personal advantages compare and/or contrast with any structural and political advantages of multiraciality. See Kevin R. Binning, Miguel M. Unzueta, Yuen J. Huo, and Ludwin E. Molina, "The Interpretation of Multiracial Status and Its Relation to Social Engagement and Psychological Well-Being," *Journal of Social Issues* 65, no. 1 (2009): 35–49.

75 Rainier Spencer, "Beyond Pathology and Cheerleading," 108. Spencer explains that the tropes of cheerleading and pathology continue to "dominate" discussions of multiracial identities despite "the compellingness and intellectual rigor of the growing body of critical multiracial scholarship." Rather than simply lament these dominant tropes Spencer encourages scholars and activists alike to "displace naïve and essentialist appeals to an elitist, exotic, and 'wiser' multiracial identity in favor of a far more nuanced and intellectually demanding analysis."

76 Peggy Orenstein, "Mixed Messenger," *New York Times Magazine,* March 23, 2008. In this article Orenstein gestures toward structural problems to which multiracialism-as-anti-racism may contribute. However, Orenstein ultimately lands squarely in an optimistic, emotional, and interpersonal racial space. Orenstein writes, "I sometimes wonder what will happen in another 50 years. Will my grandchildren feel Jewish? Japanese? Latino? African-American? Will they be pluralists? Pass as Anglo? Refuse categorization? Will Hapa Nation eventually make tracking "race" impossible? Will it unite us? Or will it, as some suggest, further segregate African-Americans from everyone else? The answer to all these questions may be yes. Regardless, watching Senator Obama campaigning with his black wife, his Indonesian-Caucasian half-sister, his Chinese-Canadian brother-in-law and all of their multiculti kids, it seems clear that the binary, black-and-white—not to mention black-or-white—days are already behind us."

77 Gregory Rodriguez, "President Obama: Black and More So," *Los Angeles Times*, April 4, 2011. For instance, President Obama was criticized for identifying monoracially as African American on the 2010 Census. Some multiracial advocates, who insist on the option to identify themselves as they see fit, chastise Obama for identifying as black. Critics charge that the president missed an important opportunity to identify with the more progressive multiracial vision of our nation. Those who support Obama's decision remind us to consider the variable of generation (i.e., that different generations define and identify multiracial identities differently based on their experiences) and to remember the purposes of the Census, which include apportionment of government resources and forecasting the nation's needs based on race (in addition to other important demographic dimensions). For a nuanced discussion of these perspectives, see Michele Elam, "2010 Census: Think Twice, Check Once," *Huffington Post*, March 8, 2010, http://www.huffingtonpost.com/michele-elam/2010 -census-think-twice-c_b_490164.html. Marcia Alesan Dawkins, "2010 Census: Stressed Out of the Box," *Huffington Post*, March 10, 2010, http://www.huffingtonpost.com/marcia-alesan-dawkins/2010-census -stressed-out_b_492791.html.

78 Bailey, "Coming Out." What happened as news media framed Felton's case is similar to Bailey's discussion of what happened after "Isaiah Washington's use of an anti-gay slur to describe his co-star T. R. Knight" from the hit TV series *Grey's Anatomy*.

79 Fanshen Cox, "Black White Supremacist," blog entry, Mixed Chicks Chat Blog, August 16, 2007, http://mixedchickschat.typepad.com/mixed _chicks_chat/2007/08/black-white-sup.html.

80 Cox, "Black White Supremacist."

81 Felton's identity "in here" is an intimate and emotional affair that displaces appearance as the signifier of race. Felton presents us with a version of *aletheia* through which revealing an identity as a white supremacist involves concealing a multiracial identity and background. Identity "in here" is a vast reservoir of power that he can access to empower himself. Identity "in here" is juxtaposed with identity "out there," through which Felton perceives a vast distance between himself and others. Identity, what dupes and in-group clairvoyants think Felton is and what Felton thinks dupes and in-group clairvoyants think he is, remains "out there" and remains difficult to change. Quests for meaning and power can reach their pinnacle in passing, as Felton attempts to fuse identity "out there" and identity "in here" paradoxically—by policing appearances because they are now by his own proof more unreliable as sings of racial identity.

82 Tough, "Black Supremacist."

83 Tough, "Black Supremacist."

84 George Lipsitz, *The Possessive Investment in Whiteness: How White People Profit from Identity Politics* (Philadelphia: Temple University Press, 1998).

85 Tough, "Black Supremacist."

86 Bob Moser, "From the Belly of the Beast: A White-Supremacist Prison Plot Hits the Streets—with an Unusual 'Aryan' at the Helm," *Southern Poverty Law Center Intelligence Report* 108 (2002), http://www.splcenter.org/get-informed/intelligence-report/browse-all-issues/2002/winter/from-the-belly-of-the-beast?page=0,1.

87 Sam Roberts, "Projections Put Whites in Minority in U.S. by 2050," *New York Times*, December 17, 2009, http://www.nytimes.com/2009/12/18/us/18census.html.

88 Moser, "From the Belly of the Beast."

89 Moser, "From the Belly of the Beast."

90 Tough, "Black Supremacist."

91 Tough, "Black Supremacist."

92 Tough, "Black Supremacist."

93 Jackson Jr., *Real Black*.

94 George M. Fredrickson, *White Supremacy: A Comparative Study in American and South African History* (New York: Oxford University Press, 1982).

95 David Alan Grier, *Barack Like Me: The Chocolate-Covered Truth* (New York: Simon & Schuster, 2009).

96 Naomi Pabst, "Blackness/Mixedness: Contestations over Crossing Signs," *Cultural Critique* 54, no. 1 (2003): 178–212.

97 Danzy Senna, "Passing and the Problematic of Multiracial Pride (or, Why One Mixed Girl Still Answers to Black)," in *Black Cultural Traffic: Crossroads in Global Performance and Popular Culture*, ed. Harry J. Elam Jr. and Kennell A. Jackson (Ann Arbor: University of Michigan Press, 2005), 83–87.

98 Leo Felton's Facebook fan page, http://www.facebook.com/pages/Leo-Felton/138840829468394.

CONCLUSION

1   Kate Ransohoff, *Money: Contradictions and Conundrums* (Boston: KRQ Publishing, 2011), 22.

Bibliography

Ackerman, Sally. "The White Supremacist Status Quo: How the Am
    ican Legal System Perpetuates Racism as Seen Through the L
    of Property Law." *Hamline Journal of Public Law and Policy*
    (1999): 142–60.

Aesop. *Aesop's Fables.* Translated by V. S. Vernon Jones. Edited
    George Stade. New York: Fine Creative Media, 2003.

Alcoff, Linda Martín. *Visible Identities: Race, Gender, and the S*
    New York: Oxford University Press, 2006.

Anderson, Wayne. *Plessy v. Ferguson: Legalizing Segregation.* N
    York: Rosen, 2004.

Aristotle. *The Basic Works of Aristotle.* Edited by Richard McKe
    New York: Modern Library, 2001.

———. *Nicomachean Ethics.* Translated by David Ross. New Yo
    Oxford University Press, 1988.

Asava, Zelie. "Multiculturalism and Morphing in *I'm Not Ther*
    Wide Screen 1 (2010): 1–15.

Azoulay, Katya Gibel. *Black, Jewish, and Interracial: It's Not i*
    Color of Your Skin, but the Race of Your Kin, and Other Myths
    Identity. Durham, N.C.: Duke University Press, 1997.

Bailey, Courtney W. "Coming Out as Homophobic: Isaiah Washingt
    and the *Grey's Anatomy* Scandal." *Communication and Critic*
    Cultural Studies 8, no. 1 (2011): 1–21.

Baldwin, James. "On Being White and Other Lies." *Essence.* Ap
    1984.

Ball, Edward. *Slaves in the Family*. New York: Ballantine, 1998.

Barbe, Katharina. *Irony in Context*. Amsterdam: John Benjamins, 1995.

Barrett, Harold. *Sophists: Rhetoric, Democracy and Plato's Idea of Sophistry*. Novato: Chandler & Sharp, 1987.

Barrett, Lindon. "Handwriting: Legibility and the White Body in *Running a Thousand Miles for Freedom*." *American Literature* 69, no. 2 (1997): 315–36.

Beaumont, Gustave de. *Marie, or, Slavery in the United States*. Translated by Barbara Chapman. Baltimore: Johns Hopkins University Press, 1999. Originally published in 1835 (in French).

Bell, Derrick A., Jr. *Race, Racism, and American Law*. Boston: Little, Brown, 1980.

Beltrán, Mary C. "The New Hollywood Racelessness: Only the Fast, Furious (and Multiracial) Will Survive." *Cinema Journal* 44, no. 2 (2005): 50–67.

Beltrán, Mary C., and Camilla Fojas, eds. *Mixed Race Hollywood*. New York: New York University Press, 2009.

Bennett, Lerone, Jr. *Before the Mayflower: A History of the Negro in America, 1619–1964*. 8th ed. Chicago: Johnson, 2007.

Berghel, Hal. "Identity Theft, Social Security Numbers, and the Web." *Communications of the ACM* 43, no. 2 (2000): 17–21.

Bernstein, Barton J. "Case Law in *Plessy v. Ferguson*." *Journal of Negro History* 47, no. 3 (1962): 192–98.

Bhabha, Homi K. "Culture's in Between." In *Multicultural States: Rethinking Difference and Identity*, edited by David Bennett, 29–36. London: Routledge, 1998.

———. *The Location of Culture*. New York: Routledge, 1994.

Bimbaum, Michelle. *Race, Work and Desire in American Literature, 1860–1930*. Cambridge: Cambridge University Press, 2003.

Binning, Kevin R., Miguel M. Unzueta, Yuen J. Huo, and Ludwin E. Molina. "The Interpretation of Multiracial Status and Its Relation to Social Engagement and Psychological Well-Being." *Journal of Social Issues* 65, no. 1 (2009): 35–49.

Bird, Stephanie Rose. *Light, Right, and Damned Near White: Biracial and Triracial Culture in America*. Westport, Conn.: Praeger, 2009.

Bishop, David W. "*Plessy v. Ferguson*: A Reinterpretation." *Journal of Negro History* 62, no. 2 (1977): 125–33.

Blackett, Richard J. M. "The Odyssey of William and Ellen Craft." In *Beating Against the Barriers: Biographical Essays in Nineteenth-Century Afro-American History*, 87–137. Baton Rouge: Louisiana State University Press, 1986.

Blair, Hugh. *Lectures on Rhetoric and Belles Lettres*. Philadelphia: Porter & Coates, 1873.

Blascovich, Jim, Natalie A. Wyer, Laura A. Swart, and Jeffrey L. Kibler. "Racism and Racial Categorization." *Journal of Personality and Social Psychology* 72 (1997): 1364–72.

Boltanski, Luc, and Graham Burschell. *Distant Suffering: Morality, Media and Politics*. Cambridge: Cambridge University Press, 1999.

Bormann, Ernest G. "Fantasy and Rhetorical Vision: The Rhetorical Criticism of Social Reality." *Quarterly Journal of Speech* 58, no. 4 (1972): 396–407.

Bost, Suzanne. *Mulattas and Mestizas: Representing Mixed Identities in the Americas, 1850–2000*. Athens: University of Georgia Press, 2003.

Bowles, Dorcas D. "Bi-racial identity: Children Born to African-American and White Couples." *Clinical Social Work Journal* 21, no. 4 (1993): 417–28.

boyd, danah. "Networked Privacy." Personal Democracy Forum, New York, June 6, 2011. http://www.danah.org/papers/talks/2011/PDF2011.html.

Bratter, Jenifer L., and Rosalind B. King. "'But Will It Last?': Marital Instability among Interracial and Same-Race Couples." *Family Relations* 57, no. 2 (2008): 160–71.

Brennan, Jonathan, ed. *Mixed Race Literature*. Stanford: Stanford University Press, 2002.

Bronicel, Ty. "Interview: Robert Benton." Movies.com. http://movies.go.com/moviesdynamic/story?id=642910.

Brooks, Siobhan. *Unequal Desires: Race and Erotic Capital in the Stripping Industry*. Albany: SUNY Press, 2008.

Brown, Josephine. "Biography of an American Bondsman, 1856." In *Two Biographies by African American Women*, edited by Henry Louis Gates Jr., 3–104. Oxford: Oxford University Press, 1991.

Brown, Ursula M. *The Interracial Experience: Growing Up Black/White Racially Mixed in the United States*. Westport, Conn.: Praeger, 2001.

Brown, William Wells. *Clotel; or The President's Daughter*. Armonk, N.Y.: M. E. Sharpe, 1996.

Broyard, Bliss. *One Drop: My Father's Hidden Life—A Story of Race and Family Secrets*. New York: Little, Brown, 2007.

Brunsma, David L., ed. *Mixed Messages: Multiracial Identities in the "Color-Blind" Era*. Boulder: Lynne Rienner, 2006.

Burke, Kenneth. *Attitudes toward History*. Berkeley: University of California Press, 1984.

————. *A Grammar of Motives*. Berkeley: University of California Press, 1962. Repr. 1969.

Busack, Richard von. "Passing Zone: Anthony Hopkins Turns Racial Classifications Upside Down in Film Adaptation of Philip Roth's 'The Human Stain.'" *Metro Santa Cruz,* October 29, 2003. http://www.metroactive.com/papers/cruz/10.29.03/human-0344.html.

Butler, Judith. *Bodies That Matter: On the Discursive Limits of "Sex."* New York: Routledge, 1993.

————. *Excitable Speech: A Politics of the Performative*. New York: Routledge, 1997.

"California Proposition 54 Initiative Text." The Leadership Conference. http://www.civilrights.org/equal-opportunity/proposition-54/initiative_text.html.

Cambridge Diversity Consulting. The Race Awareness Project. Last modified August 1, 2010. http://www.cambridgediversity.com/rap.html.

Campbell, Mary E., and Jennifer Eggerling-Boeck. "'What about the Children?': The Psychological and Social Well-Being of Multiracial Adolescents." *Sociological Quarterly* 47, no. 1 (2006): 147–73.

Camper, Carol, ed. *Miscegenation Blues: Voices of Mixed Race Women*. Toronto: Sister Vision Press, 1994.

Caporimo, Alison. "What's Beautiful Now: The *Allure* American Beauty Survey." *Allure*, March 1, 2011. http://www.allure.com/magazine/2011/03/american-beauty-census#slide=1.

Carlson, A. Cheree. "'You Know It When You See It': The Rhetorical Hierarchy of Race and Gender in *Rhinelander v. Rhinelander*." *Quarterly Journal of Speech* 85, no. 2 (1999): 111–28.

Charland, Maurice. "Constitutive Rhetoric: The Case of the *Peuple Quebecois*." *Quarterly Journal of Speech* 73, no.2 (1987): 133–50.

Chaw, Walter. "Miller's Crossing: Up-'n'-ComerFilmfreak Central Interviews Actor Wentworth Miller Talks about *The Human Stain*." Interview with Wentworth Miller III. http://www.filmfreakcentral.net/notes/wmillerinterview.htm.

Chellappa, Ramnath K., and Raymond G. Sin. "Personalization versus Privacy: An Empirical Examination of the Online Consumer's Dilemma." *Information Technology and Management* 6, nos. 2–3 (2005): 181–202.

Chesnutt, Charles W. *The House behind the Cedars*. 1900; New York: Penguin, 1993.

Child, Lydia Maria. *Stars and Stripes: A Melodrama*. National Anti-Slavery Standard, 1853. Electronic ed., http://pid.emory.edu/ark:/25593/17bd6.

Chin, Gabriel J. "The Plessy Myth: Justice Harlan and the Chinese Cases." *Iowa Law Review* 82 (1996): 151–82.

Choudry, Sultanna. *Multifaceted Identity of Interethnic Young People: Chameleon Identities.* Farnham: Ashgate, 2010.

Cicero, Marcus Tullius. *De oratore.* 2nd ed. Translated by E. N. P. Moore. London: Methuen, 1904.

Citizens United v. Federal Election Commission, 588 U.S. (2010). http://www.supremecourt.gov/opinions/09pdf/08-205.pdf.

Cloud, John. "Are Mixed-Race Children Better Adjusted?" *Time,* February 21, 2009. http://www.time.com/time/health/article/0,8599,1880467,00.html.

Cmiel, Kenneth. *Democratic Eloquence: The Fight over Popular Speech in Nineteenth-Century America.* Berkeley: University of California Press, 1990.

Colker, Ruth. *Hybrid: Bisexuals, Multiracials, and Other Misfits under American Law.* New York: New York University Press, 1996.

Connerly, Ward. *Creating Equal: My Fight against Race Preferences.* New York: Encounter Books, 2000.

Consigny, Scott. "Edward Schiappa's Reading of the Sophists." *Rhetoric Review* 14, no. 2 (1996): 253–69.

Cooper, James Fenimore. *The Last of the Mohicans.* 1826; New York: Penguin Books, 1986.

Corrigan, Patrick W., Annette Backs Edwards, Amy Green, Sarah Lickey Diwan, and David L. Penn. "Prejudice, Social Distance, and Familiarity with Mental Illness." *Schizophrenia Bulletin* 27, no. 2 (2001): 219–25.

Corrigan, Patrick W., Fred E. Markowitz, and Amy C. Watson. "Structural Levels of Mental Illness Stigma and Discrimination." *Schizophrenia Bulletin* 30, no. 3 (2004): 481–91.

Costigliola, Frank. "The Nuclear Family: Tropes of Gender and Pathology in the Western Alliance." *Diplomatic History* 21, no. 2 (1997): 163–83.

Courtney, Alexander. *Hollywood Fantasies of Miscegenation: Spectacular Narratives of Gender and Race, 1903–1967.* Princeton: Princeton University Press, 2005.

Cox, Fanshen. "Black White Supremacist." Blog entry, Mixed Chicks Chat Blog, August 16, 2007. http://mixedchickschat.typepad.com/mixed_chicks_chat/2007/08/black-white-sup.html.

Craft, William, and Ellen Craft. *Running a Thousand Miles for Freedom.* 1860; Athens: University of Georgia Press, 1999.

Crenshaw, Kimberlé. "Mapping the Margins: Intersectionality, Identity Politics, and Violence against Women of Color." *Stanford Law Review* 43 (1991): 1241–65.

DaCosta, Kimberly McClain. *Making Multiracials: State, Family, and Market in the Redrawing of the Color Line.* Stanford: Stanford University Press, 2007.

Daniel, G. Reginald. "Black and White Identity in the New Millennium." In Root, *The Multiracial Experience*, 121–39.

———. *More than Black?: Multiracial Identity and the New Racial Order.* Philadelphia: Temple University Press, 2002.

———. "Passers and Pluralists: Subverting the Racial Divide." In Root, *Racially Mixed People in America*, 91–107.

Daniel, G. Reginald, and Paul Spickard, eds. *Racial Thinking in the United States: Uncompleted Independence.* Notre Dame, Ind.: Notre Dame University Press, 2004.

Darlington, Patricia S. E., and Becky Michele Mulvaney. "Gender, Rhetoric, and Power: Toward a Model of Reciprocal Empowerment." *Women's Studies in Communication* 25 (2002): 139–72.

Davis, F. James. *Who Is Black? One Nation's Definition.* University Park: Pennsylvania State University Press, 1991.

Davis, Kenneth C. *Don't Know Much about History.* New York: HarperCollins, 2003.

Davis, S. "Synecdoche." In *Encyclopedia of Rhetoric and Composition*, edited by Theresa Enos, 712–13. New York: Garland Press, 1996.

Dawkins, Marcia Alesan. "In Search of a 'Singular I': A Structurational Analysis of Passing." *Ethnic Studies Review* 28, no. 2 (2005): 1–16.

———. "Mixed Messenger: Barack Obama and Post-racial Politics." *Spectator* 30, no. 2 (2010): 9–17. http://www.truthdig.com/report/item/mixed_race_beauty_gets_a_mainstream_makeover_20110307/.

———. "Mixed Race Beauty Gets a Mainstream Makeover." *Truthdig*, March 7, 2011.

———. "2010 Census: Stressed Out of the Box." *Huffington Post*, March 10, 2010.

DeCew, Judith Wagner. *In Pursuit of Privacy: Law, Ethics, and the Rise of Technology.* Ithaca: Cornell University Press, 1997.

Derrida, Jacques. *Dissemination.* Translated by Barbara Johnson. Chicago: University of Chicago Press, 1991.

Deuchar, Margaret. "Minority Language Survival in Northwest Wales: An Introduction." In *ISB4: Proceedings of the 4th International Symposium on Bilingualism*, edited by James Cohen, Kara T. McAlister, Kellie Rolstad, and Jeff MacSwan, 621–25. Somerville: Cascadilla Press, 2005.

Devil in a Blue Dress. DVD. Directed by Carl Franklin. Culver City, Calif.: Tri-Star Pictures, 1995.

Domínguez, Virginia R. *White by Definition: Social Classification in Creole Louisiana* New Brunswick, N.J.: Rutgers University Press, 1986.

Doniger, Mary. *The Woman Who Pretended to Be Who She Was: Myths of Self-Imitation*. Oxford: Oxford University Press, 2004.

Douglass, Frederick, and Harriet Ann Jacobs. *Narrative of the Life of Frederick Douglass, An American Slave, and Incidents in the Life of a Slave Girl*. Introduction by Kwame Anthony Appiah. New York: Random House, 2000.

Dreisinger, Baz. *Near Black: White-to-Black Passing in American Culture*. 1843; Amherst: University of Massachusetts Press, 2008.

Du Bois, W.E.B. *The Souls of Black Folk*. 1903; New York: Vintage Books, 1990.

Dumas, Alexander. *Georges*. Edited by Werner Sollors. Translated by Tina A. Kover. New York: Random House, 2008.

Durrow, Heidi W. *The Girl Who Fell from the Sky*. Chapel Hill, N.C.: Algonquin Books of Chapel Hill, 2010.

Durrow, Heidi W., and Fanshen Cox. "Passing." Unproduced screenplay draft, 2011.

Dworkin, Andrea. *Intercourse*. New York: Free Press, 1987.

Eckert, Susan. "The Birth of the Multiracial American." December 5, 2007. http://www.suite101.com/content/birth-of-the-multiracial -american-a37131.

Edwards, Justin D. *Gothic Passages: Racial Ambiguity and the American Gothic*. Iowa City: University of Iowa Press, 2003.

Ehlers, Nadine. *Racial Imperatives: Discipline, Performativity, and Struggles against Subjection*. Indianapolis: Indiana University Press, 2011.

Elam, Michele. *The Souls of Mixed Folk: Race, Politics, and Aesthetics in the New Millennium*. Stanford: Stanford University Press, 2011.

———. "2010 Census: Think Twice, Check Once." *Huffington Post*, March 8, 2010.

Ellinghaus, Katherine. "The Pocahontas Exception: Indigenous 'Absorption' and Racial Integrity in the United States, 1880s–1920s." In *Rethinking Colonial Histories: New and Alternative Approaches*, edited by Penelope Edmonds and Samuel Furphy, 123–36. Melbourne: RMIT, 2006.

Elliott, Mark. "Race, Color Blindness, and the Democratic Public: Albion W. Tourgée's Radical Principles in *Plessy v. Ferguson*." *Journal of Southern History* 67, no. 2 (2000): 287–330.

Enck-Wanzer, Darrel. "Trashing the System: Social Movement, Intersectional Rhetoric, and Collective Agency in the Young Lords Organization's Garbage Offensive." *Quarterly Journal of Speech* 92, no. 2 (2006): 174–201.

Engstrom, David Wells, and Lissette M. Piedra, eds. *Our Diverse Society: Race, Ethnicity and Class—Implications for 21st Century America.* Washington, D.C.: NASW Press, 2006.

Ernest, John. "Representing Chaos: William Craft's *Running a Thousand Miles for Freedom.*" *PMLA* 121, no. 2 (2006): 469–83.

Fauset, Jessie Redmon. *Plum Bun: A Novel without a Moral.* New York: Frederick A. Stokes, 1929.

———. *There Is Confusion.* New York: Beacon Press, 1924.

Feagin, Susan L. "The Pleasures of Tragedy." *American Philosophical Quarterly* 20, no. 1 (1983): 95–104.

Federal Trade Commission. "FTC Issues Final Rules on FACTA Identity Theft Definitions, Active Duty Alert Duration, and Appropriate Proof of Identity." http://www.ftc.gov/opa/2004/10/facataidtheft.shtm.

Fields, Barbara. "Ideology and Race in American History." In *Region, Race, and Reconstruction: Essays in Honor of C. Vann Woodward*, edited by J. Kousser and J. McPherson, 143–77. New York: Oxford University Press, 1982.

Finch, Emily. "What a Tangled Web We Weave: Identity Theft and the Internet." In *Dot.cons: Crime, Deviance, and Identity on the Internet*, edited by Yvonne Jewkes, 86–104. Cullompton, U.K.: Willan, 2002.

Fireside, Harvey. *Separate and Unequal: Homer Plessy and the Supreme Court Decision That Legalized Racism.* New York: Carroll & Graf, 2004.

Fish, Stanley. *Doing What Comes Naturally: Change, Rhetoric, and the Practice of Theory in Literary and Legal Studies.* Durham, N.C.: Duke University Press, 1989.

Fiske, John. *Media Matters: Race and Gender in U.S. Politics.* Minneapolis: University of Minnesota Press, 1994.

Flores, Lisa A., Drema G. Moon, and Thomas K. Nakayama. "Dynamic Rhetorics of Race: California's Racial Privacy Initiative and the Shifting Grounds of Racial Politics." *Communication and Critical/Cultural Studies* 3, no. 3 (2006): 181–201.

Foeman, Anita Kathy, and Teresa Nance. "From Miscegenation to Multiculturalism: Perceptions and Stages of Interracial Relationship Development." *Journal of Black Studies* 29, no. 4 (1999): 540–57.

———. "On Being Biracial in the United States." In *Readings in Intercultural Communication: Experiences and Contexts*, edited by Judith N. Martin, Thomas K. Nakayama, and Lisa A. Flores, 35–43. New York: McGraw-Hill, 2001.

Foreman, Gabrielle P. "'Reading Aright': White Slavery, Black Referents, and the Strategy of Histotextuality in *Iola Leroy.*" *Yale Journal of Criticism* 10, no. 2 (1997): 327–54.

Fosberg, Michael Sidney. *Incognito: An American Odyssey of Race and Self-Discovery.* Chicago: Incognito, 2011.

Foss, Karen A., and Kathy L. Domenici, "Haunting Argentina: Synecdoche in the Protests of the Mothers of the Plaza de Mayo." *Quarterly Journal of Speech* 87, no. 3 (2001): 237–58.

Foss, Sonja K., and Cindy L. Griffin. "Beyond Persuasion: A Proposal for an Invitational Rhetoric." Essay presented at the Speech Communication Association Convention, November 1993, Miami, Fla.

Foucault, Michel. *Power.* Edited by James D. Faubion. New York: New Press, 2001.

Frank, Justin A. *Obama on the Couch: Inside the Mind of the President.* New York: Simon & Schuster, 2011.

Fredal, James. "Why Shouldn't the Sophists Charge Fees?" *Rhetoric Society Quarterly* 38, no. 2 (2008): 148–70.

Fredrickson, George M. *White Supremacy: A Comparative Study in American and South African History.* New York: Oxford University Press, 1982.

Freedman, Florence B. *Two Tickets for Freedom: The True Story of Ellen and William Craft, Fugitive Slaves.* New York: Peter Bedrick Books, 1971.

Freeman, Sally, Stephen W. Littlejohn, and W. Barnett Pearce. "Communication and Moral Conflict." *Western States Speech Journal* 56 (1992): 311–29.

Fryer, Roland G., Lisa B. Kahn, Steven D. Levitt, and Jörg L. Spenkuch. "The Plight of Mixed Race Adolescents." National Bureau of Economic Research Working Paper Series, vol. W14192. http://papers.ssrn.com/sol3/papers.cfm?abstract_id=1179862.

Fulbeck, Kip. *Mixed: Portraits of Multiracial Kids.* San Francisco: Chronicle Books, 2010.

Funderburg, Lise. *Black, White, Other.* New York: William Morrow, 1994.

Gara, Larry. "The Professional Fugitive in the Abolition Moment." *Wisconsin Magazine of History* 48, no. 3 (1965): 196–204.

Garber, Marjorie. *Vested Interests: Cross-Dressing and Cultural Anxiety.* New York: Routledge, 1992.

Gardner, Leroy. *Black/White Race Mixing*. St. Paul: Paragon House, 2000.

Garner, Bryan A., ed. *Black's Law Dictionary*. Abridged 9th ed. St. Paul, Minn.: Thomson Reuters, 2010.

Garrison, William Lloyd. "The Crafts in New Bedford." *Liberator*, February 16, 1849. http://www.theliberatorfiles.com/crafts-in-new-bedford/.

Gaskins, Pearl Fuyo, ed. *What Are You? Voices of Mixed-Race Young People*. New York: Henry Holt, 1999.

Gates, Henry Louis, Jr. Foreword to Harper, *Iola Leroy*, vii–xxii.

———. *"Race," Writing, and Difference*. Chicago: University of Chicago Press, 1986.

Gelder, Rachel. "Passing and Failing: Reflections on the Limitations of Showing the Passer in *The Human Stain*." *Women and Performance Quarterly* 15, no. 1 (2005): 293–312.

Gentleman's Agreement. DVD. Directed by Elia Kazan. Los Angeles, Calif.: Twentieth Century Fox Film, 1947.

Gilman, Sander L. *Difference and Pathology: Stereotypes of Sexuality, Race and Madness*. Ithaca: Cornell University Press, 1985.

Gilroy, Paul. *Against Race: Imagining Political Culture beyond the Color Line*. Cambridge, Mass.: Harvard University Press, 2000.

Ginsberg, Elaine K., ed. *Passing and Fictions of Identity*. Durham, N.C.: Duke University Press, 1996.

Goldhill, Simon. "The Language of Tragedy: Rhetoric and Communication." In *The Cambridge Companion to Greek Tragedy*, edited by P. E. Easterling, 127–50. Cambridge: Cambridge University Press, 2008.

Goldstein, Eric. *The Price of Whiteness: Jews, Race, and American Identity*. Princeton: Princeton University Press, 2006.

Goodman, Amy. "WikiLeaks, Wimbledon and War." *Democracy Now*, July 6, 2011, http://www.democracynow.org/blog/2011/7/6/wikileaks_wimbledon_and_war.

Gordon, James W. "Did First Justice Harlan Have a Black Brother?" *Western New England Law Review* 15, no. 2 (1993): 159–238.

Gordon-Reed, Annette. *The Hemingses of Monticello: An American Family*. New York: W. W. Norton, 2008.

Gotanda, Neil. "A Critique of 'Our Constitution Is Color-blind.'" In *Critical Race Theory: The Key Writings that Formed the Movement*, edited by Kimberlé Crenshaw, Neil Gotanda, and Garry Peller, 257–75. New York: New Press, 1995.

Gottesdiener, Laura. "The Cross-Dressing Girls of Afghanistan." *Ms Magazine*, October 7, 2010. http://msmagazine.com/blog/blog/2010/10/07/the-cross-dressing-girls-of-afghanistan/.

Graham, Lawrence Otis. *Our Kind of People: Inside America's Black Upper Class*. New York: HarperCollins, 2000.

Graves, Joseph L. *The Emperor's New Clothes: Biological Theories of Race at the Millennium*. New Brunswick, N.J.: Rutgers University Press, 2001.

Grier, David Alan. *Barack Like Me: The Chocolate-Covered Truth*. New York: Simon & Schuster, 2009.

Gross, Ariela Julie. *What Blood Won't Tell: A History of Race on Trial in America*. Cambridge, Mass.: Harvard University Press, 2008.

Gross, Theodore L. *Albion W. Tourgée*. New York: Twayne, 1963.

Guthrie, William K. *The Sophists*. Cambridge: Cambridge University Press, 1971.

Gyory, Andrew. *Closing the Gate: Race, Politics, and Chinese Exclusion*. Chapel Hill: University of North Carolina Press, 1998.

Haggins, Bambi. *Laughing Mad: The Black Comic Persona in Post-Soul America*. New Brunswick, N.J.: Rutgers University Press, 2007.

Hall, Gwendolyn Midlo. "The Formation of Afro-Creole Culture." In *Creole New Orleans: Race and Americanization*, edited by Arnold Richard Hirsch and Joseph Logsdon, 58–90. Baton Rouge: Louisiana State University Press, 1992.

Hall, Stuart. "Gramsci's Relevance for the Study of Race and Ethnicity." In *Stuart Hall: Critical Dialogues in Cultural Studies*, edited by David Morley and Kusan-Hsing Chen, 411–41. London: Routledge, 1996.

Hariman, Robert. "Status, Marginality, and Rhetorical Theory." In *Contemporary Rhetorical Theory: A Reader,* edited by John Louis Lucaites, Celeste Michelle Condit, and Sally Caudill, 35–51. New York: Guilford Press, 1999.

Harper, Frances E. W. *Iola Leroy, or, Shadows Uplifted*. 2nd ed. Philadelphia: Garrigues Brothers, 1893.

———. *Iola Leroy, or, Shadows Uplifted*. Oxford: Oxford University Press, 1988.

Harper, Phillip Brian. "Passing for What? Racial Masquerade and the Demands of Upward Mobility." *Callaloo* 21 (1998): 381–97.

Harris, Cheryl I. "Whiteness as Property." *Harvard Law Review* 106, no. 8 (1993): 1706–91.

Harris-Perry, Melissa. "Black by Choice." *The Nation*, April 15, 2010. http://www. thenation.com/article/black-choice.

Hasian Jr., Marouf. "Critical Legal Theorizing, Rhetorical Intersectionalities and the Multiple Transgressions of the 'Tragic Mullata,' Anastasie Desarzant." *Women's Studies in Communication* 27 (2004): 119–48.

————. "Performative Law and the Maintenance of Interracial Social Boundaries: Assuaging Antebellum Fears of 'White Slavery' and the case of Sally Miller/ Salome Müller." *Text and Performance Quarterly* 23, no. 1 (2003): 55–86.

Haskins, Ekaterina V. *Logos and Power in Isocrates and Aristotle.* Columbia: University of South Carolina Press, 2004.

Hauser, Gerard A. *Introduction to Rhetorical Theory.* Long Grove, Ill.: Waveland Press, 2002.

Healy, Melissa. "White and Mixed-Race Youths Rank High in Alcohol, Substance Abuse." *Los Angeles Times*, November 7, 2011. http://www.latimes.com/health/boostershots/la-heb-drug-alcohol-adolescents-20111107,0,2331740.story.

Heglar, Charles J. *Rethinking the Slave Narrative.* Westport, Conn.: Greenwood Press, 2001.

Hickman, Christine B. "The Devil and the One Drop Rule: Racial Categories, African Americans, and the U.S. Census." *Michigan Law Review* 95, no. 5 (1997): 1161–1265.

Ho, Arnold K., Jim Sidanius, Daniel T. Levin, and Mahzarin R. Banaji. "Evidence for Hypodescent and Racial Hierarchy in the Categorization and Perception of Biracial Individuals." *Journal of Personality and Social Psychology* 100, no. 3 (2010): 1–15.

Hobbs, Allyson Vanessa. "The Fictions of Race, Custom, and Law: The Problem of Racial Passing in U.S. Social and Cultural History, 1840–1950." Ph.D. diss., University of Chicago, 2007.

Hodes, Martha Elizabeth, ed. *Sex, Love, Race: Crossing Boundaries in North American History.* New York: New York University Press, 1999.

Hoffman, Sandra K., and Tracy C. McGinley. *Identity Theft: A Reference Handbook.* Santa Barbara, Calif.: ABC-CLIO, 2010.

Holland, Glenn Stanfield. *Divine Irony.* Cranbury, N.J.: Associated University Presses, 2000.

Holleran, Scott. "Interview: Robert Benton on 'The Human Stain.'" Box Office Mojo. November 26, 2003. http://www.boxofficemojo.com/features/?id=1260&p=.htm.

Howard, Heather M. "The Negligent Enablement of Imposter Fraud: A Common-Sense Common Law Claim." *Duke Law Journal* 54 (2005): 1263–94.

Howe, Irving. *World of Our Fathers: The Journey of the Eastern European Jews to America and the Life They Found and Made.* New York: New York University Press, 2005.

Huggins, Nathan Irvin. *Revelations: American History, American Myths.* Oxford: Oxford University Press, 1995.

Hughes, Langston. *The Ways of White Folks.* New York: Knopf, 1933.

The Human Stain. DVD. Directed by Robert Benton. Santa Monica, Calif.: Miramax Films, 2003.

Hume, David. *Four Dissertations.* London: A. Millar, 1757.

Hungerford, Amy. "Philip Roth, *The Human Stain.*" Class lecture, Yale University, New Haven, Conn. Spring 2008. http://freevideo lectures.com/Course/2460/The-American-Novel-Since-1945/21.

Hunter, Margaret L. *Race, Gender and the Politics of Skin Tone.* New York: Routledge, 2005.

Hyde, Michael. *The Life-Giving Gift of Acknowledgment.* West Lafayette, Ill.: Purdue University Press, 2006.

Identity Theft and Assumption Deterrence Act of 1998, Pub. L. No. 105-318, 112 Stat. 3007 (1998).

Ifekwunigwe, Jayne O., ed. *"Mixed Race" Studies: A Reader.* London: Routledge, 2004.

Ijsseling, Samuel. *Rhetoric and Philosophy in Conflict.* The Hague: Martinus Nijhoff, 1976.

Illusions. DVD. Directed by Julie Dash. New York: Kino International, 1982.

Imitation of Life (1934). DVD. Directed by John M. Stahl. Universal City, Calif.: Universal Pictures (1959). DVD. Directed by Douglas Sirk. Universal City, Calif.: Universal International Pictures.

International Justice Mission. "Forced Labor Slavery," December 31, 2010. http://www.ijm.org/sites/default/files/resources/Factsheet-Forced-Labor-Slavery.pdf.

Iser, Wolfgang. "The Reality of Fiction: A Functionalist Approach to Literature." *New Literary History* 7, no. 1 (1975): 7–38.

Itzkovitz, Daniel. "Passing Like Me: Jewish Chameleonism and the Politics of Race." In *Passing and Interpretation in Sexuality, Race, and Religion,* edited by María Carla Sánchez and Linda Schlossberg, 38–63. New York: New York University Press, 2001.

Jackson, Cassandra. *Barriers between Us: Interracial Sex in Nineteenth-Century American Literature.* Bloomington: Indiana University Press, 2004.

Jackson, John L. *Real Black: Adventures in Racial Sincerity.* Chicago: University of Chicago Press, 2005.

Jackson, Kelly F. "Ethical Considerations in Social Work for Research with Multiracial Individuals." *Journal of Social Work Values and Ethics* 7, no. 1 (2010): 1–10.

Jarratt, Susan J. *Rereading the Sophists: Classical Rhetoric Refigured.* Carbondale: Southern Illinois University Press, 1991.

Jayson, Sharon. "Interracial Marriage, More Accepted, Still Growing." *USA Today,* November 7, 2011. http://yourlife.usatoday

.com/sex-relationships/marriage/story/2011-11-07/Interracial
-marriage-More-accepted-still-growing/51115322/1.

Johnson, James Weldon. *Autobiography of an Ex-Coloured Man.*
New York: Vintage Books, 1912.

Johnson, Kevin R., ed. *Mixed Race America and the Law: A Reader.*
New York: New York University Press, 2003.

Johnson, Mat. *Incognegro.* New York: Vertigo/DC Comics, 2008.

———. *Pym.* New York: Spiegel & Grau, 2011.

Jones, Lisa. *Bulletproof Diva: Tales of Race, Sex, and Hair,* New York:
Random House, 1994.

Kanuha, Valli Kalei. "The Social Process of 'Passing' to Manage
Stigma: Acts of Internalized Oppression, or Acts of Resistance?"
Journal of Sociology and Social Welfare 26, no. 4 (1999): 27–46.

Kaplan, Jeffrey. *Encyclopedia of White Power: A Sourcebook on the
Radical Racist Right.* Lanham, Md.: Altamira Press, 2000.

Kennedy, George A. *A New History of Classical Rhetoric.* Princeton:
Princeton University Press, 1994.

Kennedy, Randall. "Racial Passing." *Ohio State Law Journal* 62
(2001): 1145–73. http://moritzlaw.osu.edu/lawjournal/issues/
volume62/number3/kennedy.pdf.

Keresztesi, Rita. *Strangers at Home.* Lincoln: University of Nebraska
Press, 2005.

Khanna, Nikki, and Cathryn Johnson. "Passing as Black: Racial Identity Work among Biracial Americans." *Social Psychology Quarterly* 73, no. 4 (2010): 380–97.

Kilson, Marion. *Claiming Place: Biracial Young Adults of the Post–
Civil Rights Era.* Westport, Conn.: Greenwood, 2000.

Kluger, Richard. *Simple Justice: The History of Brown v. Board of
Education and Black America's Struggle for Equality.* New York:
Vintage Books, 1975.

Korgen, Kathleen Odell. *From Black to Biracial: Transforming Racial
Identity among Americans.* Westport, Conn.: Praeger, 1998.

Krebs, Nina Boyd. *Edgewalkers: Defusing Cultural Boundaries on the
New Global Frontier.* Far Hills, N.J.: New Horizon Press, 2000.

Kristof, Nicholas D., and Sheryl WuDunn. *Half the Sky: Turning
Oppression into Opportunity for Women Worldwide.* New York:
Random House, 2009.

Kroger, Brooke. *Passing: When People Can't Be Who They Are.* New
York: Public Affairs, 2003.

Kuo, Ryan. "What's Next for Angry Birds?" *Wall Street Journal,*
March 1, 2011.

Kuryla, Peter. "Barack Obama and the American Island of the Colour
Blind." *Patterns of Prejudice* 45, nos. 1–2 (2011): 119–32.

Lake, Randall A. "Argumentation and Self: The Enactment of Identity in *Dances With Wolves*." *Argumentation and Advocacy* 34, no. 2 (1997): 66–90.

Lane, Anthony. Review of *The Human Stain*. 2003. *New Yorker*, November 10, 2003. http://www.newyorker.com/arts/reviews/film/the_human_stain_benton.

Larsen, Nella. *Passing*. New York: Penguin Classics, 1929.

Leary, Kimberlyn. "Passing, Posing, and Keeping It Real." *Constellations* 6 (1999): 85–96. doi: 10.1111/1467-8675.00122.

Leff, Michael, and Ebony A. Utley. "Instrumental and Constitutive Rhetoric in Martin Luther King Jr.'s 'Letter From a Birmingham Jail.' " *Rhetoric and Public Affairs* 7, no. 1 (2004): 37–52.

Legal Information Center. "Fourteenth Amendment Equal Protection Clause." http://public.getlegal.com/legal-info-center/14th-amendment-equal-protection-clause.

Lewis, Elliott. *Fade: My Journeys in Multiracial America*. New York: Carroll & Graf, 2006.

Lindisfarne, Nancy. "Gender, Shame, and Culture: An Anthropological Perspective." In *Shame: Interpersonal Behavior, Psychopathology, and Culture*, edited by Paul Gilbert and Bernice Andrews, 246–60. Oxford: Oxford University Press, 1998.

Lipsitz, George. *The Possessive Investment in Whiteness: How White People Benefit from Identity Politics*. Philadelphia: Temple University Press, 1998.

Littleton, C. Scott. *Gods, Goddesses, and Mythology*. Vol. 4. White Plains, N.Y.: Marshall Cavendish, 2005.

Locke, John. *The Second Treatise of Civil Government*. Rockville, Md.: Wildside Press, 2008.

Logsdon, Joseph, and Caryn Cosse Bell. "The Americanization of Black New Orleans, 1850–1900." In *Creole New Orleans: Race and Americanization*, edited by Arnold R. Hirsch and Joseph Logsdon, 201–320. Baton Rouge: Louisiana State University Press, 1992.

Lopez, Ian Haney. *White by Law: The Legal Construction of Race*. New York: New York University Press, 1996.

Lost Boundaries. DVD. Directed by Alfred L. Werker. Burbank, Calif.: Warner Home Video, 1949.

Maguire, Joseph P. "Protagoras—or Plato?" *Phronesis* 18, no. 2 (1973): 115–38.

Mailloux, Steven. *Rhetorical Power*. Ithaca: Cornell University Press, 1989.

Mapes, Marty. Review of *The Human Stain*. Movie Habit.Com. http://www.moviehabit.com/reviews/hum_ji03.shtml.

Martin, Joan M. "Placage and the Louisiana Gens de Couleur Libre: How Race and Sex Defined the Lifestyles of Free Women of Color." In *Creole: The History and Legacy of Louisiana's Free People of Color*, edited by Sybil Kein, 57–70. Baton Rouge: Louisiana State University Press, 2000.

Mayer, Henry. *All on Fire: William Lloyd Garrison and the Abolition of Slavery*. New York: St. Martin's Press, 1998.

McBride, James. *The Color of Water: A Black Man's Tribute to His White Mother*. New York: Riverhead Books, 1997.

McCaskill, Barbara. "'Trust No Man!' But What about a Woman? Ellen Craft and a Genealogical Model for Teaching Douglass' *Narrative*." In *Approaches to Teaching the Narrative of the Life of Frederick Douglass*, edited by James C. Hall, 95–101. New York: MLA, 1999.

———. "'Yours Very Truly': Ellen Craft—The Fugitive Slave as Text and Artifact." *African American Review* 28, no. 4 (1994): 509–29.

McDonald, Andrew. *The Turner Diaries*. New York: Barricade Books, 1996.

McMillan, Uri. "Ellen Craft's Radical Techniques of Subversion." *E-misférica* 5, no. 2 (2008). http://hemi.nyu.edu/hemi/en/e-misferica-52/mcmillan.

McRoy, Ruth G., and Edith Freeman. "Racial-Identity Issues among Mixed Race Children." *Social Work in Education* 8, no. 3 (1986): 164–74.

Medley, Keith Weldon. *We as Freedmen: Plessy v. Ferguson*. Gretna, La.: Pelican, 2003.

Melnick, Jeffrey. *A Right to Sing the Blues: African Americans, Jews, and American Popular Song*. Cambridge, Mass.: Harvard University Press, 1999.

Mencke, John G. *Mulattoes and Race Mixture: American Attitudes and Images, 1865–1918*. Ann Arbor: UMI Research Press, 1979.

Merton, Robert K. "Intermarriage and the Social Structure: Fact and Theory." *Psychiatry* 4 (1941): 361–74.

Michaels, Walter Benn. "The No-Drop Rule." *Critical Inquiry* 20, no. 4 (1994): 758–69.

Miller, Loren. *The Petitioners: The Story of the Supreme Court of the United States and the Negro*. New York: Random House, 1966.

Mirón, Louis F., and Jonathan Xavier Inda. "Race as a Kind of Speech Act." *Cultural Studies* 5 (2000): 83–105.

Mock, Shirley Boteler. *Dreaming with the Ancestors: Black Seminole Women in Texas and Mexico*. Norman: University of Oklahoma Press, 2010.

Montagu, Ashley. *The Concept of Race*. New York: Free Press, 1965.

Moran, Rachel F. *Interracial Intimacy: The Regulation of Race and Romance*. Chicago: University of Chicago Press, 2001.

———. "Love With a Proper Stranger: What Anti-Miscegenation Laws Can Tell Us about the Meaning of Race, Sex, and Marriage." *Hofstra Law Review* 32 (2004): 1663–79.

Morris, Charles E., III. "Pink Herring and the Fourth Persona: J. Edgar Hoover's Sex Crime Panic." *Quarterly Journal of Speech* 88, no. 2 (2002): 228–44.

Moser, Bob. "From the Belly of the Beast." *Southern Poverty Law Center*. http://www.splcenter.org/get-informed/intelligence-report/browse -all-issues/2002/winter/from-the-belly-of-the-beast?page=0,2.

Moynihan, Sinead. *Passing into the Present: Contemporary American Fiction of Racial and Gender Passing*. Manchester, U.K.: Manchester University Press, 2010.

Mullen, Harryette. "Optic White: Blackness and the Production of Whiteness." *Diacritics* 24, nos. 2–3 (1994): 71–89.

Nakamura, Lisa. *Cybertypes: Race, Ethnicity, and Identity on the Internet*. New York: Routledge, 2002.

Nakayama, Thomas K., and Robert L. Krizek. "Whiteness: A Strategic Rhetoric." *Quarterly Journal of Speech* 81, no. 3 (1995): 291–309.

Nash, Gary. *Forbidden Love: The Secret History of Mixed Race Identity*. New York: Henry Holt, 1999.

Nelson, Camille. "Racial Paradox and Eclipse: Obama as a Balm for What Ails Us." *Denver University Law Review* 86 (2009): 743–83.

Nerad, Julie Cary. "Slippery Language and False Dilemmas: The Passing Novels of Child, Howells, and Harper." *American Literature* 75, no. 4 (2003): 813–40.

Nerlich, Bridgette, and David D. Clarke. "Synecdoche as Cognitive and Communication Strategy." In *Historical Semantics and Cognition*, edited by Andreas Blank and Peter Koch, 197–214. Berlin: de Gruyter, 1999.

Nissel, Angela. *Mixed: My Life in Black and White*. New York: Villard Books, 2006.

Norris, Christoper. *Derrida*. Cambridge, Mass.: Harvard University Press, 1987.

Nunley. Vorris L. "From the Harbor to Da Academic Hood: Hush Harbors and an African American Rhetorical Tradition." In *African American Rhetorics: Interdisciplinary Perspectives*, edited by Ronald Jackson and Elaine Richardson, 221–41. Carbondale: Southern Illinois University Press, 2004.

Obama, Barack H. *The Audacity of Hope: Thoughts on Reclaiming the American Dream*. New York: Random House, 2006.

———. *Dreams from My Father: A Story of Race and Inheritance*. New York: Three Rivers Press, 2004.

Oberst, Paul. "The Strange Career of *Plessy v. Ferguson*." 15 *Arizona Law Review* 389 (1973): 433–41.

O'Brien, Soledad, with Rose Marie Arce. *The Next Big Story: My Journey through the Land of Possibilities*. New York: Penguin, 2010.

Olsen, Otto H. *The Carpetbagger's Crusade: A Life of Albion Winegar Tourgée*. Baltimore, Md.: Johns Hopkins Press, 1965.

———. *The Thin Disguise: Plessy v. Ferguson, a Documentary Presentation*. New York: Humanities Press, 1967.

Olson, Gary A. "Jacques Derrida on Rhetoric and Composition: A Conversation." *Journal of Advanced Composition* 10, no. 1 (1990): 1–21.

Omi, Michael, and Howard Winant. *Racial Formation in the United States*. New York: Routledge, 1994.

O'Neill, John. "Rhetoric, Science, and Philosophy." *Philosophy of the Social Sciences* 28, no. 2 (1998): 205–25.

O'Toole, James M. *Passing: Race, Religion, and the Healy Family, 1820–1920*. Amherst: University of Massachusetts Press, 1996.

Pabst, Naomi. "Blackness/Mixedness: Contestations over Crossing Signs." *Cultural Critique* 54, no. 1 (2003): 178–212.

Palin, Sarah. "The Charge of Racism: It's Time to Bury the Divisive Politics of the Past." Comment on Facebook, July 13, 2010 (8:58 p.m.). http://www.facebook.com/note.php?note_id=408166998434.

Pariser, Eli. *The Filter Bubble: What the Internet Is Hiding from You*. New York: Penguin, 2011.

Park, Robert E. "Human Migration and the Marginal Man." *American Journal of Sociology* 33, no. 6 (1928): 881–93.

Parker, David, and Miri Song, eds. *Rethinking "Mixed Race."* London: Pluto Press, 2001.

Pascoe, Peggy. "Miscegenation Law, Court Cases, and Ideologies of 'Race' in Twentieth-Century America." *Journal of American History* 83, no. 1 (1996): 44–69.

———. *What Comes Naturally: Miscegenation Law and the Making of Race in America*. Oxford: Oxford University Press, 2009.

Paulin, Diana R. "Acting Out Miscegenation." In *African American Performance and Theater History: A Critical Reader*, edited by Harry Elam and David Krasner, 251–70. Oxford: Oxford University Press, 2001.

———. "Performing Miscegenation: Rescuing *The White Slave* from the Threat of Interracial Desire." *Journal of Dramatic Theory and Criticism* 13, no. 1 (1998): 71–86.

Paumgarten, Nick. "Central Casting: The Race Card." *New Yorker,* December 10, 2003.

Pearce, W. Barnett, and Stephen W. Littlejohn. *Moral Conflict.* Thousand Oaks, Calif.: Sage, 1997.

Pesta, Abigail. "Diary of an Escaped Sex Slave." *Marie Claire,* October 9, 2009. http://www.marieclaire.com/world-reports/news/inter national/diary-escaped-sex-slave.

Pinderhughes, Elaine. "Bi-racial Identity—Asset or Handicap?" In *Racial and Ethnic Identity: Psychological Development and Creative Expression,* edited by Herbert W. Harris, Howard C. Blue, and Ezra E. H. Griffith, 73–94. New York: Routledge, 1995.

Pinky. DVD. Directed by Elia Kazan. Los Angeles, Calif.: Twentieth Century Fox, 1949.

Piper, Adrian. "Passing for White, Passing for Black." *Transition* 58 (1992): 4–32.

Plato. *The Complete Works of Plato.* Edited by John M. Cooper. Translated by Nicholas P. White. Indianapolis: Hackett, 1997.

———. *Plato's Republic.* Translated by Benjamin Jowett. New York: Vintage Books, 1970.

———. *Plato's Republic.* Translated by I. A. Richards. Cambridge: Cambridge University Press, 1966.

———. *The Republic of Plato.* Translated by Allan Bloom. New York: ·Basic Books, 1968.

———. *The Republic of Plato.* Translated by Francis MacDonald Cornford. Oxford: Oxford University Press, 1941.

Plessy v. Ferguson, 163 U.S. 537 (1896).

Poe, Edgar Allan. *The Narrative of Arthur Gordon Pym of Nantucket.* New York: Harper & Brothers, 1838.

Pollack, Mica. *Colormute: Race Talk Dilemmas in an American School.* Princeton: Princeton University Press, 2005.

Posnock, Ross. "Purity and Danger: On Philip Roth." *Raritan* 21, no. 2 (2001): 85–101.

Poster, Mark. "The Secret Self: The Case of Identity Theft." *Cultural Studies* 21, no. 1 (2007): 118–40.

Poston, W. S. Carlos. "The Biracial Identity Development Model: A Needed Addition." *Journal of Counseling and Development* 69, no. 2 (1990): 152–55.

Poulakos, John. *Sophistical Rhetoric in Classical Greece.* Columbia: University of South Carolina Press, 1995.

———. "Toward a Sophistic Definition of Rhetoric." *Philosophy and Rhetoric* 16, no. 1 (1983): 35–48.

Powell, A. D. *Passing for Who You Really Are.* Palm Coast, Fla.: Backintyme Press, 2005.

Przybyszewski, Linda. *The Republic According to John Marshall Harlan*. Chapel Hill: University of North Carolina Press, 1999.

Rabinowitz, Peter J. " 'Betraying the Sender': The Rhetoric and Ethics of Fragile Texts." *Narrative* 2, no. 3 (1994): 201–13.

Ransohoff, Kate. *Money: Contradictions and Conundrums*. Boston: KRQ Publishing, 2011.

Ray, Carina. "Why Do You Call Yourself Black and African?" Blog entry, The Zeleza Post: Informed News and Commentary on the Pan African World, July 4, 2009. http://www.zeleza.com/blogging/african-affairs/why-do-you-call-yourself-black-and-african.

Resnick, Brian. "The Ever-Changing American 'Race.' " *Atlantic*, July 21, 2011. http://www.theatlantic.com/national/archive/2011/07/the-ever-changing-american-race/242017/.

Roberts, Mary Louise. "True Womanhood Revisited." *Journal of Women's History* 14, no. 1 (2002): 150–55.

Robinson, Amy. "Forms of Appearance of Value: Homer Plessy and the Politics of Privacy." In *Performance and Cultural Politics*, edited by Elin Diamond, 237–61. New York: Routledge, 1996.

———. "It Takes One to Know One: Passing and Communities of Common Interest." *Critical Inquiry* 20, no. 4 (1994): 715–36.

———. "To Pass//In Drag: Strategies of Entrance into the Visible." Ph.D. diss., University of Pennsylvania, 1993.

Robinson, Eugene. *Disintegration: The Splintering of Black America*. New York: Random House, 2010.

Rockquemore, Kelly Ann, and Tracy Laszloffy. *Raising Biracial Children*. Lanham, Md.: Altamira Press, 2005.

Rogin, Michael. *Blackface, White Noise: Jewish Immigrants in the Hollywood Melting Pot*. Berkeley: University of California Press, 1996.

———. "Blackface, White Noise: The Jewish Jazz Singer Finds His Voice." *Critical Inquiry* 18, no. 3 (1992): 417–53.

Root, Maria P. P. "A Bill of Rights for Racially Mixed People." In Root, *The Multiracial Experience*, 3–14.

———. *The Multiracial Experience: Racial Borders as the New Frontier*. Thousand Oaks, Calif.: Sage, 1996.

———. *Racially Mixed People in America*. Thousand Oaks, Calif.: Sage, 1992.

Rosenblatt, Paul C., Terri A. Karis, and Richard D. Powell. *Multiracial Couples: Black and White Voices*. Thousand Oaks, Calif.: Sage, 1995.

Roth, Philip. *The Human Stain*. New York: Knopf, 2000.

Rovio Entertainment Limited. "Angry Birds." http://www.rovio.com/en/our-work/games/view/1/angry-birds/reviews/.

Rowe, Jill E. "Mixing It Up: Early African American Settlements in Northwestern Ohio." *Journal of Black Studies* 39, no. 6 (2009): 924–36.

Rozin, Paul, and Edward B. Royzman. "Negativity Bias, Negativity Dominance, and Contagion." *Personality and Social Psychology Review* 5, no. 4 (2001): 296–320.

Rubin, Gayle. " 'Thinking Sex': Notes for a Radical Theory of the Politics of Sexuality." In *Pleasure and Danger: Exploring Female Sexuality*, edited by Carole S. Vance, 267–319. London: Routledge, 1984.

Rubin-Dorsky, Jeffrey. "Philip Roth and American Jewish Identity: The Question of Authenticity." *American Literary History* 13, no. 1 (2001): 79–107.

Ryder, Ulli K. " 'As Shelters against the Cold': Women Poets of the Black Arts and Chicano Movements, 1965–1978." Ph.D. diss., University of Southern California, 2008.

———. "Gender Neutral or Wishful Thinking." *The Feminist Wire,* May 30, 2011. http://thefeministwire.com/2011/05/gender-neutral-or-wishful-thinking/

———. "The Sheen Defense: Charlie Sheen and Multiracial Identity." Blog entry, Open Salon, March 12, 2011. http://open.salon.com/blog/ulli_k_ryder/2011/03/12/the_sheen_defense_charlie_sheen_and_multiracial_identity.

Said, Edward W. *The World, the Text, and the Critic.* Cambridge, Mass.: Harvard University Press, 1983.

Saks, Eva. "Representing Miscegenation Law." In *Interracialism: Black-White Intermarriage in American History, Literature, and Law*, edited by Werner Sollors, 61–80. New York: Oxford University Press, 2000.

Samuels, Ellen. "A Complication of Complaints: Untangling Disability, Race, and Gender in William and Ellen Craft's *Running a Thousand Miles for Freedom*." *MELUS* 31, no. 3 (2006): 15–49.

Samuels, Gina Miranda. "Beyond the Rainbow: Multiraciality in the 21st Century." In *Our Diverse Society: Race and Ethnicity—Implications for 21st-Century American Society*, edited by David Wells Engstrom and Lissette M. Piedra, 37–66. Washington, D.C.: NASW Press, 2006.

Sánchez-Casal, Susan, and Amie A. Macdonald. *Identity in Education.* New York: Palgrave Macmillan, 2009.

Sand, Shlomo. *The Invention of the Jewish People.* London: Verso, 2010.

Sandborn, Geoffrey. "Mother's Milk: Frances Harper and the Circulation of Blood." *English Literary History* 72, no. 3 (2005): 691–715.

Sapphire. DVD. Directed by Basil Dearden. Universal City, Calif.: Universal Pictures, 1959.

Saunders, Kurt M., and Bruce Zucker. "Counteracting Identity Fraud in the Information Age: The Identity Theft and Assumption Deterrence Act." *Cornell Journal of Law and Public Policy* 8 (1999): 661–75.

Schopenhauer, Arthur. *The World as Will and Idea*. Vol. 2. Translated by E. F. Payne. Mineola, N.Y.: Dover, 1966.

Scott, James C. *Domination and the Arts of Resistance: Hidden Transcripts*. New Haven: Yale University Press, 1990.

———. *Weapons of the Weak*. New Haven: Yale University Press, 1985.

Scott, Robert L. "Epistemic Rhetoric and Criticism: Where Barry Brummett Goes Wrong." *Quarterly Journal of Speech* 76 (1990): 300–303.

———. "The Necessary Pluralism of Any Future History of Rhetoric." *Journal of Rhetorical Theory* 12 (1991): 195–209.

———. "Non-discipline as a Remedy for Rhetoric? A Reply to Victor Vitanza." *Rhetoric Review* 6, no. 2 (1988): 233–37.

———. "On Viewing Rhetoric as Epistemic." *Central States Speech Journal* 18, no. 1 (1967): 9–17.

———. "On Viewing Rhetoric as Epistemic: Ten Years Later." *Central States Speech Journal* 27 (1976): 258–66.

———. "Rhetoric Is Epistemic: What Difference Does That Make?" In *Defining the New Rhetorics*, edited by Theresa Enos and Stuart C. Brown, 120–36. Newbury Park, Calif.: Sage, 1993.

Scott v. Sanford, 60 U.S. 393 (1856).

Scruggs, Charles. "Jean Toomer and Kenneth Burke and the Persistence of the Past." *American Literary History* 13, no. 1 (2001): 41–66.

Sedgwick, Eve Kosofsky, and Adam Frank. Introduction to *Shame and Its Sisters: A Silvan Tomkins Reader*, edited by Eve Kosofsky Sedgwick and Adam Frank, 1–28. Durham, N.C.: Duke University Press, 1995.

Senna, Danzy. *Caucasia*. New York: Riverhead Books, 1998.

———. "Passing and the Problematic of Multiracial Pride (or, Why One Mixed Girl Still Answers to Black)." In *Black Cultural Traffic: Crossroads in Global Performance and Popular Culture*, edited by Harry J. Elam Jr. and Kennell A. Jackson, 83–87. Ann Arbor: University of Michigan Press, 2005.

———. *Symptomatic: A Novel*. New York: Riverhead Books, 2004.

———. *Where Did You Sleep Last Night? A Personal History*. New York: Macmillan, 2009.

———. *You Are Free: Stories*. New York: Riverhead Books, 2011.

Sexton, Jared. *Amalgamation Schemes: Antiblackness and the Critique of Multiracialism.* Minneapolis: University of Minnesota Press, 2008.

Seybold, Patrick, II. "Settlement in George Hotz Case." PlayStation Blog. Last modified April 11, 2011. http://blog.us.playstation.com/2011/04/11/settlement-in-george-hotzcase/?utm_source=twitter&utm_medium=social&utm_campaign=george_hotz_041111.

Sharfstein, Daniel. *The Invisible Line: Three American Families and the Secret Journey from Black to White.* New York: Penguin, 2011.

Show-Boat. Directed by George Sidney. Burbank, Calif.: Warner Brothers, 1951.

Siebers, Tobin Anthony. "Disability as Masquerade." *Literature and Medicine* 23 (2004): 1–22.

———. "Disability in Theory: From Social Constructionism to the New Realism of the Body." In *The Disability Studies Reader,* 2nd ed., edited by Lennard J. Davis, 173–84. New York: Routledge, 2006.

Slosarik, Katherine. "Identity Theft: An Overview of the Problem." *Criminal Justice Studies* 15, no. 4 (2002): 329–43.

Smith, Valerie. *Not Just Race, Not Just Gender.* London: Routledge, 1998.

Snow, David, and Leon Anderson. "Identity Work among the Homeless: The Verbal Construction and Avowal of Personal Identities." *American Journal of Sociology* 92, no. 6 (1987): 1336–71.

Sollors, Werner. *Neither Black Nor White yet Both: Thematic Explorations of Interracial Literature.* Cambridge, Mass.: Harvard University Press, 1997.

Song, Miri. *Choosing Ethnic Identity.* Malden, Mass.: Blackwell, 2003.

"Sorry Wenty Pal, You're Not Black and You'll Never Be Black." Internet Movie Database. Accessed March 22, 2011. http://www.imdb.com/name/nm0589505/board/flat/177479029 (url discontinued).

Spelman, Elizabeth B. *Inessential Woman: Problems of Exclusion in Feminist Thought.* Boston: Beacon Press, 1988.

Spencer, Jon Michael, and Richard E. Van der Ross. *The New Colored People.* New York: New York University Press, 1997.

Spencer, Rainier. "Beyond Pathology and Cheerleading." In *The Politics of Multiracialism: Challenging Racial Thinking,* edited by Heather M. Dalmage, 101–24. Albany: SUNY Press, 2004.

———*Reproducing Race: The Paradox of Generation Mix.* Boulder: Lynne Rienner, 2010.

———. *Spurious Issues: Race and Multiracial Identity Politics in the United States*. Boulder: Westview Press, 1999.

Spickard, Paul R. *Mixed Blood*. Madison: University of Wisconsin Press, 1989.

Sprague, Rosamond. *The Older Sophists*. Columbia: University of South Carolina Press, 1972.

Squires, Catherine R., and Daniel C. Brouwer. "In/Discernible Bodies: The Politics of Passing in Dominant and Marginal Media." *Critical Studies in Media Communication* 19, no. 3 (2002): 283–310.

Stanton, G. R. "Sophists and Philosophers: Problems of Classification." *American Journal of Philology* 94, no. 4 (1973): 350–64.

Sterling, Dorothy. *Black Foremothers: Three Lives*. 2nd ed. Old Westbury, N.Y.: Feminist Press, 1988.

Stetson, Earlene. "The Mulatto Motif in Black Fiction." Ph.D. diss., SUNY Buffalo, 1976.

Still, William. *The Underground Railroad*. 1872. Repr., New York: Arno Press, 1987.

Stonequist, Everett V. *The Marginal Man: A Study in Personality and Culture Conflict*. New York: Charles Scribner's Sons, 1937.

Sundquist, Eric. "Mark Twain and Homer Plessy." *Representations* 21 (1998): 102–28.

Sutton, Jane. "Rereading Sophistical Arguments: A Political Intervention." *Argumentation* 5, no. 2 (1991): 141–57.

Suzuki-Crumly, Julie, and Lauri L. Hyers. "The Relationship among Ethnic Identity, Psychological Well-Being, and Intergroup Competence: An Investigation of Two Biracial Groups." *Cultural Diversity and Ethnic Minority Psychology* 10, no. 2 (2004): 137–50.

Swearingen, C. Jan. *Rhetoric and Irony: Western Literacy and Western Lies*. Oxford: Oxford University Press, 1991.

Swietek, Frank. "Robert Benton on *The Human Stain*." Oneguysopinion.com. Accessed April 15, 2011. http://www.oneguysopinion.com/interview.asp?ID=232.

Sycamore, Matt (aka Mattilda) Bernstein, ed. *Nobody Passes: Rejecting the Rules of Gender and Conformity*, Emoryville, Calif.: Seal Press, 2006.

Taylor, Charles. "Life and Life Only." *Salon.com*, April 24, 2000. http://www1.salon.com/books/feature/2000/04/24/roth/index.html.

Thomas, Brook. "*Plessy v. Ferguson* and the Literary Imagination." *Cardozo Studies in Law and Literature* 91 (1997): 45–65.

Thompson, Shirley Elizabeth. *Exiles at Home: The Struggle to Become American in Creole New Orleans*. Cambridge, Mass.: Harvard University Press, 2009.

Thornton, Michael C. "Policing the Borderlands: White-and-Black-American Newspaper Perceptions of Multiracial Heritage and the Idea of Race, 1996–2006." *Journal of Social Issues* 65, no. 1 (2009): 105–27.

Toomer, Jean. *Cane.* New York: Boni & Liveright, 1923.

Tourgée, Albion W. Brief for Plaintiff in Error [Homer Plessy]. In *Landmark Briefs and Arguments of the Supreme Court of the United States: Constitutional Law*, edited by Philip B. Kurland and Gerhard Casper, vol. 13, 27–63. Washington, D.C.: University Publications of America, 1975.

———. *Pactolus Prime.* New York: Cassel, 1890.

Travers, Peter. Review of *The Human Stain. Rolling Stone.* September 25, 2003. http://www.rollingstone.com/movies/reviews/the-human-stain-20030925.

Trilling, Lionel. *Sincerity and Authenticity.* Cambridge, Mass.: Harvard University Press, 1972.

Twine, Frances Winddance. "Heterosexual Alliances: The Romantic Management of Racial Identity." In Root, *The Multiracial Experience*, 291–304.

U.S. Census Bureau. 2010 Census Data. http://2010.census.gov/2010census/data/.

U.S. Department of State. *Trafficking in Persons Report 2011.* June 27, 2011. http://www.state.gov/g/tip/rls/tiprpt/2011/.

U.S. Federal Trade Commission. "About Identity Theft." Federal Trade Commission, Fighting Back against Identity Theft. http://www.ftc.gov/bcp/edu/microsites/idtheft/consumers/about-identity-theft.html.

Van Dijk, Teun A. *Racism and the Press.* London: Routledge, 1991.

Varange, Ulick. *Imperium: The Philosophy of History and Politics.* Sausalito, Calif.: Noontide Press, 1948.

Vatz, Richard E. "The Mythical Status of Situational Rhetoric: Implications for Rhetorical Critics' Relevance in the Public Arena." *Review of Communication* 9, no. 1 (2009): 1–5.

Versenyl, Laszlo. "Protagoras' Man-Measure Fragment." *American Journal of Philology* 83 (1962): 178–84.

Vickers, Brian. *In Defence of Rhetoric.* Oxford: Clarendon, 1988.

Vico, Giambattista. *The Autobiography of Giambattista Vico.* Ithaca: Cornell University Press, 1944.

Vivian, Bradford. "Sophistic Rhetoric and Rhetorical Nomads." In *Professing Rhetoric: Selected Papers from the 2000 Rhetoric Society of America Conference*, edited by Frederick J. Antczak, Cinda Coggins, and Geoffrey D. Klinger, 193–98. Mahwah, N.J.: Lawrence Erlbaum, 2002.

Voss, Gretchen. "Hate Thy Neighbor." *Boston Magazine*. January 2002. http://www.bostonmagazine.com/articles/hate_thy_neighbor/.

Wald, Gayle. *Crossing the Line: Racial Passing in Twentieth-Century U.S. Literature and Culture*. Durham, N.C.: Duke University Press, 2000.

Walker, Rebecca. *Black, White, and Jewish: Autobiography of a Shifting Racial Self*. New York: Riverhead Books, 2002.

Wallace, Kendra R. *Relative/Outsider: The Art and Politics of Identity among Mixed Heritage Students*. Westport, Conn.: Greenwood, 2001.

Wallenstein, Peter. "Reconstruction, Segregation, and Miscegenation: Interracial Marriage and the Law in the Lower South, 1865–1900." *American Nineteenth Century History* 6, no. 1 (2005): 57–76.

Wardle, Francis. "Push Back: Academics Are the Enemies of the Multiracial Movement." CSBCHome.org Blog Archive for the Center for the Study of Biracial Children, April 2, 2009. http://www.csbchome.org/.

Wardrop, Daneen. "Ellen Craft and the Case of Salome Muller in *Running a Thousand Miles for Freedom*." *Women's Studies* 33, no. 7 (2004): 961–84.

Wehrly, Bea, Kelley R. Kenney, and Mark E. Kenney. *Counseling Multiracial Families*. Thousand Oaks, Calif.: Sage, 1999.

Weinauer, Ellen M. "'A Most Respectable Looking Gentleman': Passing, Possession, and Transgression in *Running a Thousand Miles for Freedom*." In *Passing and the Fictions of Identity*, edited by E. K. Ginsberg. Durham, N.C.: Duke University Press, 1996.

Welke, Barbara. *Recasting American Liberty: Gender, Race, Law, and the Railroad Revolution, 1865–1920*. Cambridge: Cambridge University Press, 2001.

White, Jack E., Tamala M. Edwards, Elaine Lafferty, Sylvester Monroe, and Victoria Rainert, "Race: I'm Just Who I Am." *Time*, May 5, 1997. http://www.time.com/time/magazine/article/0,9171,986278,00.html.

White, Walter. *Flight*. New York: Knopf, 1926.

———. *A Man Called White: The Autobiography of Walter White*. Athens: University of Georgia Press, 1948.

Wiegman, Robyn. *American Anatomies: Theorizing Race and Gender*. Durham, N.C.: Duke University Press, 1995.

"William Wells Brown Describes the Crafts' Escape." *Liberator*, January 12, 1849. Documenting the American South, University Library, University of North Carolina. http://docsouth.unc.edu/neh/craft/support1.html.

Williams, Kim M. *Mark One or More: Civil Rights in the Multiracial Era.* Ann Arbor: University of Michigan Press, 2006.

Williams, Patricia J. *The Alchemy of Race and Rights.* Cambridge, Mass.: Harvard University Press, 1991.

———. "Not-Black by Default." *Nation,* April 22, 2010. http://www.thenation.com/print/article/not-black-default.

Williamson, Joel. *New People: Miscegenation and Mulattoes in the United States.* Baton Rouge: Louisiana State University Press, 1995.

Wilmington, Michael. "Movie Review: 'The Human Stain.'" *Chicago Tribune,* October 30, 2003. http://www.chicagotribune.com/entertainment/movies/mmx-031029movies-review-mw-humanstain,0,7250714.story.

Woodward, C. Vann. *American Counterpoint: Slavery and Racism in the North-South Dialogue.* Boston: Little, Brown, 1964.

———. *The Strange Career of Jim Crow.* Oxford: Oxford University Press, 1955.

Wright, Lawrence. "One Drop of Blood." *New Yorker,* July 24, 1994. http://www.afn.org/~dks/race/wright.html.

Wright, Richard L. "The Word at Work: Ideological and Epistemological Dynamics of African American Rhetoric." In *Understanding African American Rhetoric: Classical Origins to Contemporary Innovations,* edited by Ronald L. Jackson II and Elaine B. Richardson, 85–98. New York: Routledge, 2003.

Wynter, Leon E. *American Skin: Pop Culture, Big Business, and the End of White America.* New York: Crown, 2002.

Yap, Stevie C., Isis H. Settles, and Jennifer S. Pratt-Hyatt. "Mediators of the Relationship between Racial Identity and Life Satisfaction in a Community Sample of African American Women and Men." *Cultural Diversity and Ethnic Minority Psychology* 17, no. 1 (2011): 89–97.

Yerby, Frank. *The Foxes of Harrow.* New York: Dial Press, 1946.

Yoshino, Kenji. *Covering: The Hidden Assault on Our Civil Rights.* New York: Random House, 2007.

———. *A Thousand Times More Fair: What Shakespeare's Plays Teach Us about Justice.* New York: HarperCollins, 2011.

Zack, Naomi, ed. *American Mixed Race: The Culture of Microdiversity.* Lanham, Md.: Rowman & Littlefield, 1995.

———. *Race and Mixed Race.* Philadelphia: Temple University Press, 1993.

Index

Public Broadcasting System (PBS), 76
Pym (Mat Johnson, 2011), 213n55

quadroons, 195n18

Rabinowitz, Peter J., 176n54
race: as a personal psychological
phenomenon, 137; as a symbolic
social construction, 60, 137, 147;
biological theories of, 62, 64, 103,
141, 146–48, 167n24; constructivist terminology on, 4; DNA testing
and, 214n57; effect of multiracial
identity on, 137–40, 222n76; hypodescent classifications, 179n80;
186n28; judicial challenges to,
59–60, 196n39; jury selection
and, 214n1–2; Welsh as not quite
"white," 107, 208n10
Race Awareness Project, 168n1–2
race preferences, 200n82
Rachmaninoff, Sergei, 122–23
racial ambiguity, 212n54
racial groups, 167n24; state assignment of, 59
racial mimicry, 180n84, 211n46
racial privacy: *see* privacy
Racial Privacy Initiative, 73, 157
racial profiling, 146
racial stereotypes, 181n94
"rahowa" (racial holy war), 145–46
railroads, 33–36, 184n13
Rainert, Victoria, 219n54
Ransohoff, Kate, 224n1
rape, 50–51; of slave women, legal-
ization of, 188n38; *see also partus
sequitur ventrem*
raven: *see* "Crow and the Raven,
The"
REAL ID Act (2005), 69–70, 199n68
Reconstruction era, 1, 80, 92, 101–2,
167, 183, 183n106, 184n13–14,
206n57
Resnick, Brian, 219n60
rhetoric, 3, 4, 8; as an epistemic
phenomenon, 11–12, 173n31;
as deception, 10–12; constitutive, 191n63; discourse of among

Sophists, 9–10, 172n21; effect of
subaltern speech, 10, 12, 173n30;
eloquence as, 28–29, 81, 91–92,
95–96, 103–4; employed as "passing" by members of a subordinate
group, 10, 12, 171n15, 171n17;
hush harbor, 99; intersectional,
182n104–105; instrumental,
191n63; need for objective content
in, 10, 12, 171n14; Plato's depiction of rhetoric as passing, 10–12,
176n48; Plato's pejorative adjectives for, 11, 171n11; position
"between" Plato and the Sophists,
176n50; racial stereotypes and,
181n94; role of identification in
persuasion, 177n59; "true irony"
and, 48
rhetorical passing, 10, 176n54,
183n106, 220n66
Riches, The, 199n71
Roberts, Mary Louise, 205n36
Roberts, Sam, 223n87
Robins, Clem, 169n4, 213n55
Robinson, Amy, 173n35, 174n35–36,
176n53–54, 177n57, 181n96
181n98, 193n7, 196n30, 197n44,
197n47, 197n51, 203n105,
208n15; triangulated dramatic
theatrical model of passing, 17–19
Robinson, Eugene, 203n6, 214n57
Rockquemore, Kelly Ann, 164n10
Rodriguez, Gregory, 222n77
Rogin, Michael, 207n2, 211n41
Root, Maria P.P., 163n10, 167n28,
168n30, 170n4
Rosenblatt, Paul C. , 163n10
Ross, Andrew S., 202n102
Roth, Philip, 105–6, 150, 208n14,
209n23; see also *Human Stain,
The*
Rothenstein, Kevin, 215n26
Rovio Mobile, 75
Rowe, Jill E., 219n55
Royzman, Edward, 186n28
Rozin, Paul, 186n28
Rubin, Gayle, 206n55
Rubin-Dorsky, Jeffrey, 208n14